A DAY IN THE LIFE
OF AN ASTRONAUT, MARS, AND THE DISTANT STARS

ALSO BY MIKE BARFIELD
AND JESS BRADLEY

A Day in the Life of a Poo, a Gnu, and You

A DAY IN THE LIFE
OF AN ASTRONAUT, MARS, AND THE DISTANT STARS

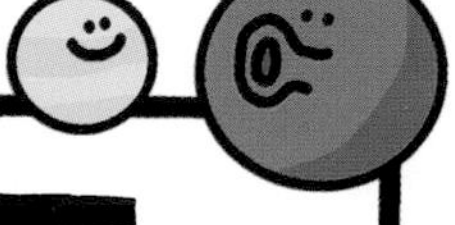

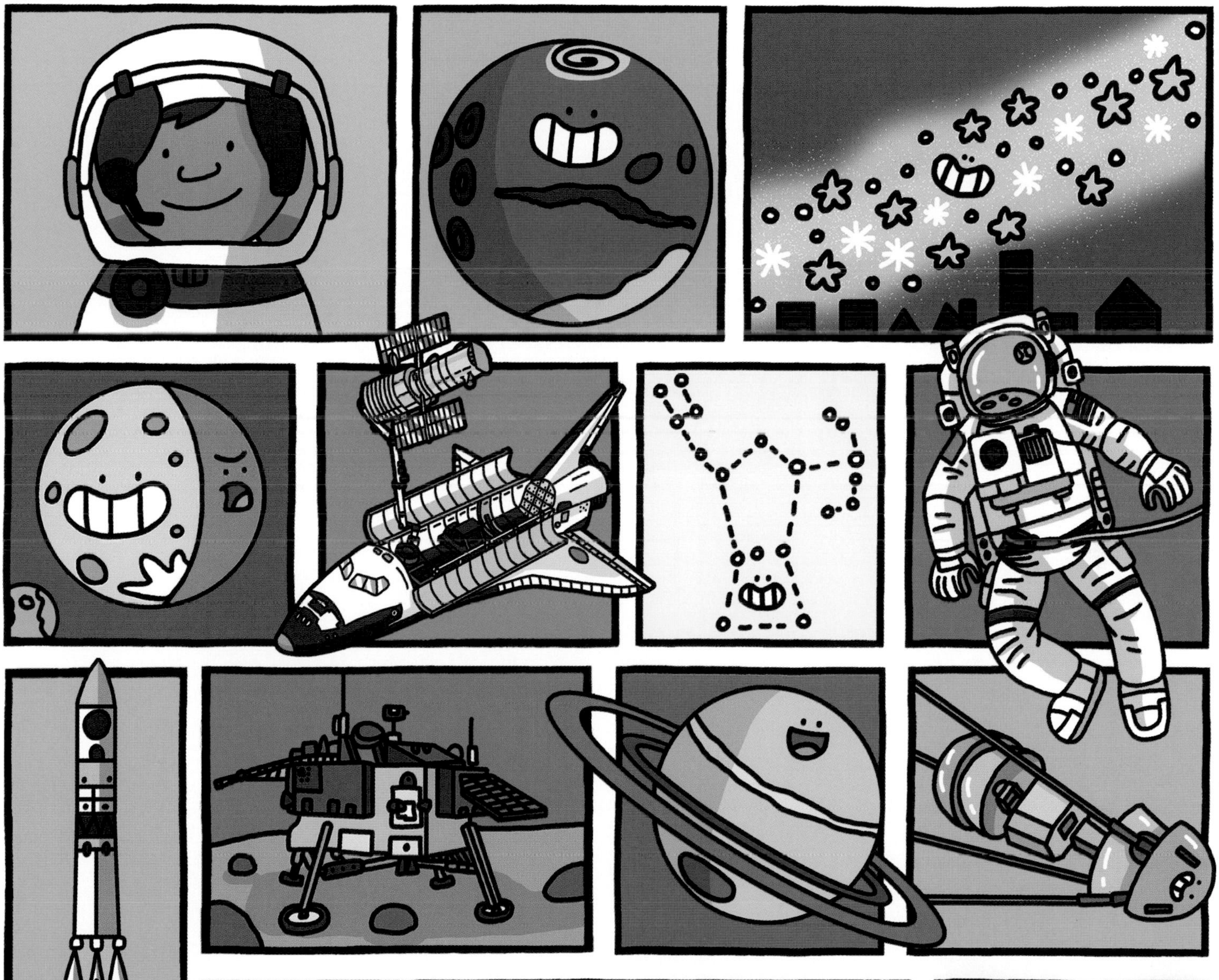

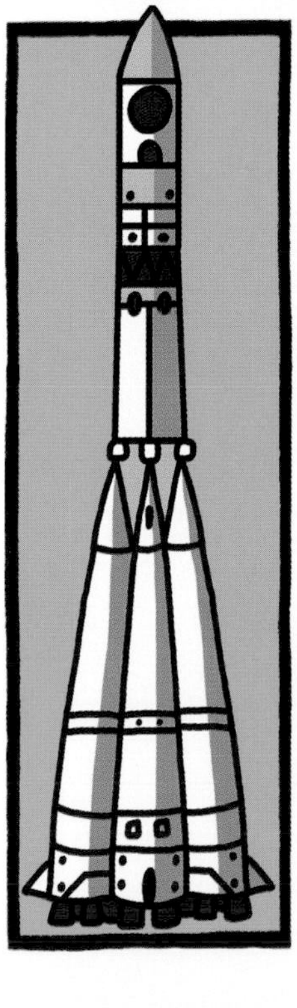

WRITTEN BY MIKE BARFIELD
ILLUSTRATED BY JESS BRADLEY

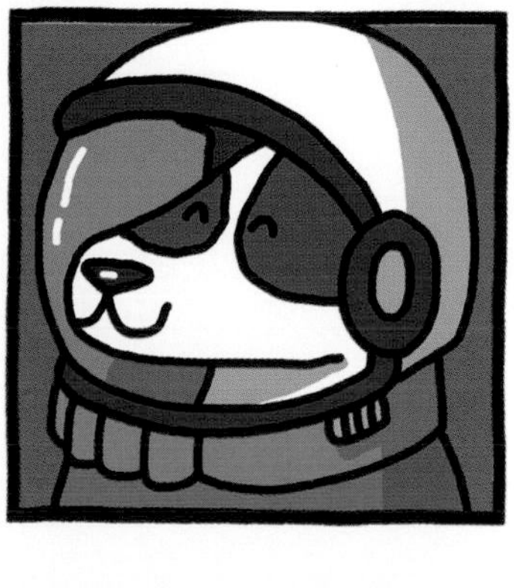

ALADDIN
NEW YORK LONDON TORONTO SYDNEY NEW DELHI

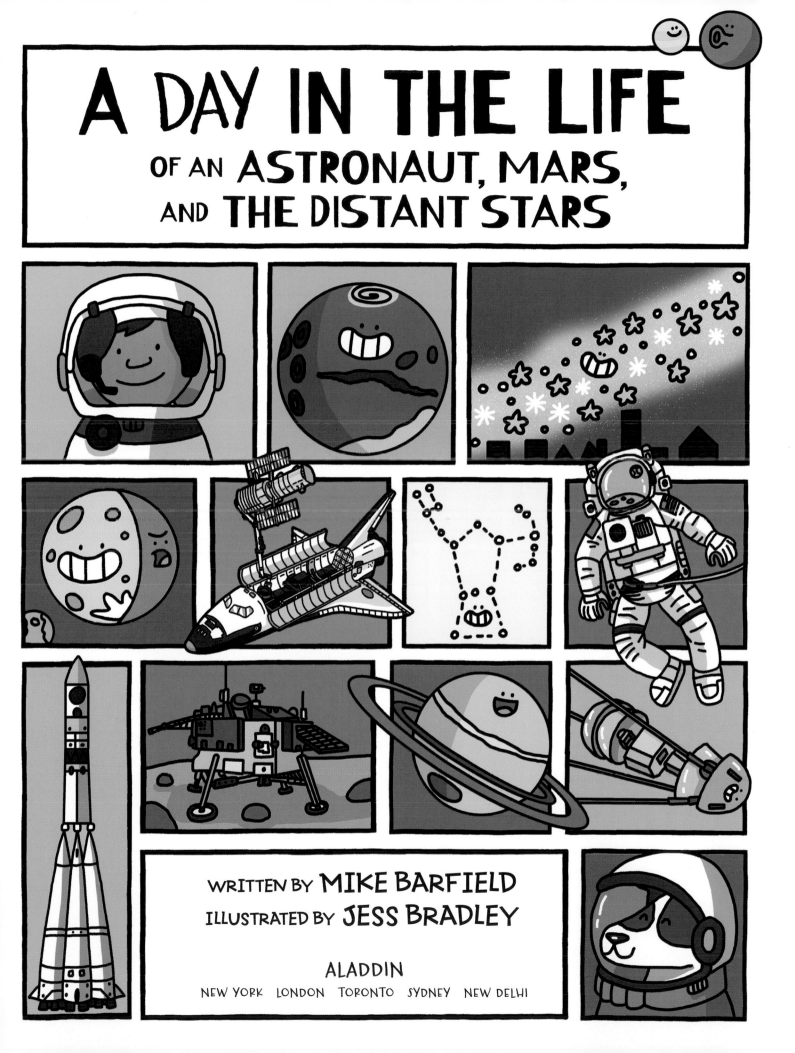

EDITED BY GARY PANTON
DESIGNED BY JACK CLUCAS
COVER DESIGN BY ANGIE ALLISON

CONSULTANCY BY STUART ATKINSON
ADDITIONAL ILLUSTRATIONS BY HELEN POOLE
WITH SPECIAL THANKS TO HELEN CUMBERBATCH

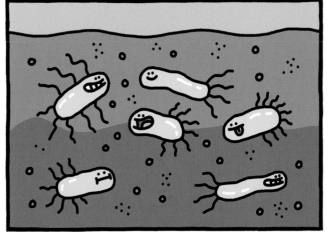

ALADDIN
An imprint of Simon & Schuster Children's Publishing Division
1230 Avenue of the Americas, New York, New York 10020
First Aladdin hardcover edition April 2023
Copyright © 2023 by Buster Books, an imprint of Michael O'Mara Books Limited
Originally published in Great Britain in 2023 by Buster Books,
an imprint of Michael O'Mara Books Limited
All rights reserved, including the right of reproduction
in whole or in part in any form.
ALADDIN and related logo are registered trademarks of Simon & Schuster, Inc.
For information about special discounts for bulk purchases,
please contact Simon & Schuster Special Sales
at 1-866-506-1949 or business@simonandschuster.com.
The Simon & Schuster Speakers Bureau can bring authors to your live event.
For more information or to book an event contact the Simon & Schuster Speakers
Bureau at 1-866-248-3049 or visit our website at www.simonspeakers.com.
The text of this book was set in Carrotflower.
Manufactured in China 1222 SCP
2 4 6 8 10 9 7 5 3 1
Library of Congress Control Number 2022943505
ISBN 9781534489219 (hc)
ISBN 9781534489226 (ebook)

FOR JAKE AND ALICE,
MY BRIGHT SHINING STARS
—M. B.

FOR JACOB. I AGREE, IT WOULD BE VERY BAD
IF A BLACK HOLE CAME TO OUR HOUSE
—J. B.

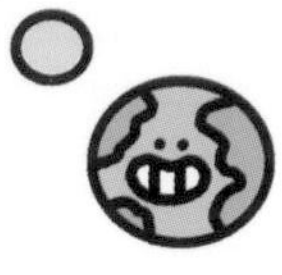

CONTENTS

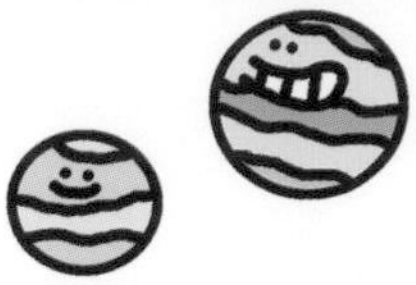

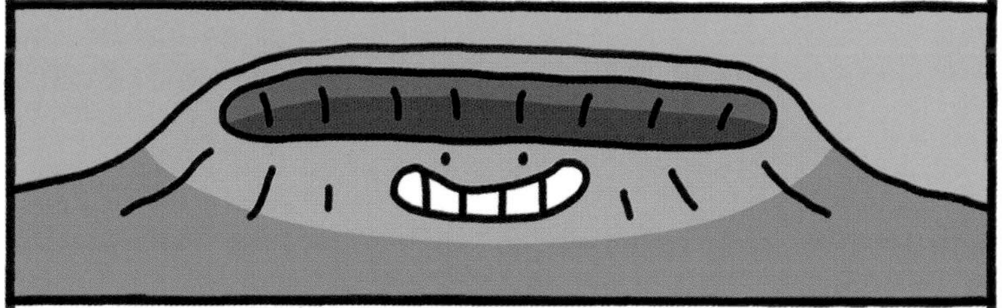

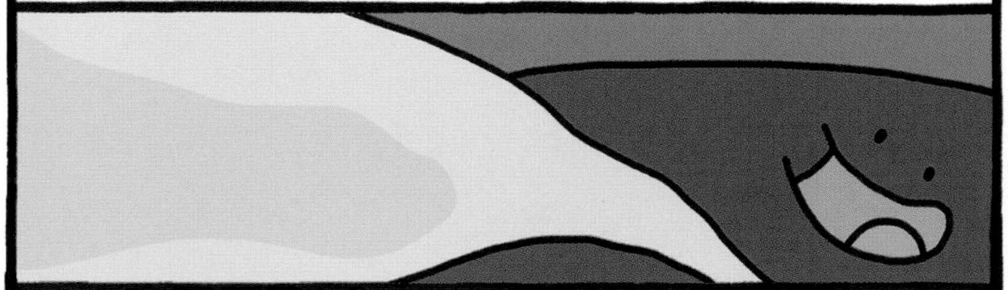

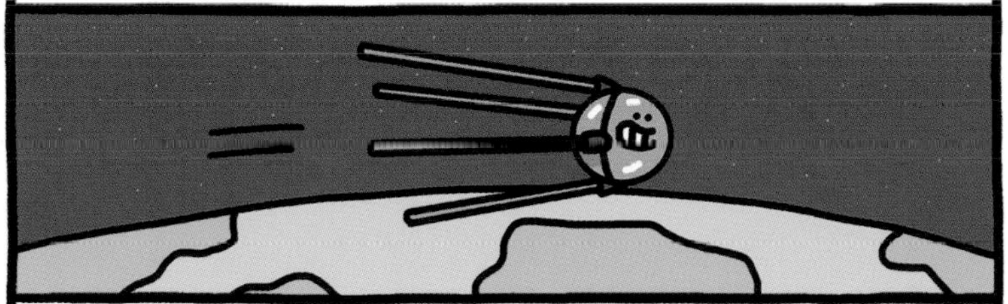

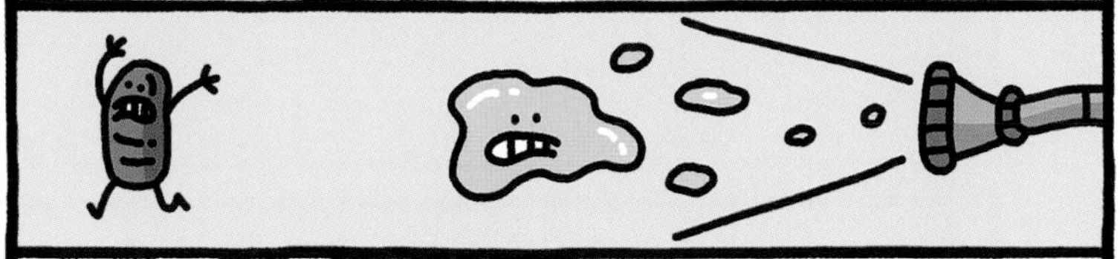

INTRODUCTION

Welcome to *A Day in the Life of an Astronaut, Mars, and the Distant Stars*—a laugh-out-loud guide to space that is completely out of this world!

The book is split into three sections: **The Solar System**, **Outer Space**, and **Space Travel**. Just like space itself, there's lots to discover, and you can land anywhere to start exploring.

There are **Day in the Life** comics where the wonders of space show you what they get up to, **Bigger Picture** pages packed with added info, and **Secret Diaries** where the heroes of the cosmos spill the beans. Because the universe is so vast, there are also space-tastic, two-page **Even Bigger Pictures**.

You'll also find a galaxy-sized **Glossary** at the back of the book, to help you with any alien words you encounter on your travels.

It's time to launch yourself into space. You haven't got all day!

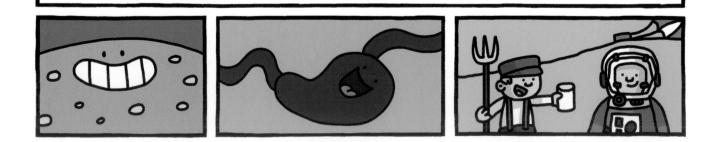

DISTANCES AND SIZES SHOWN IN THIS BOOK ARE NOT DRAWN TO SCALE.

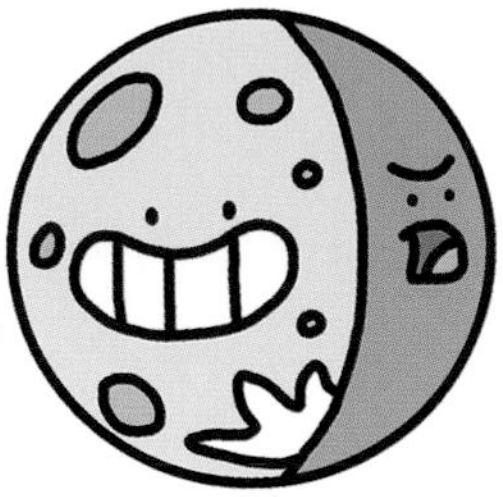

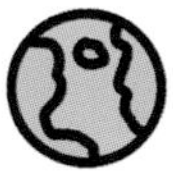

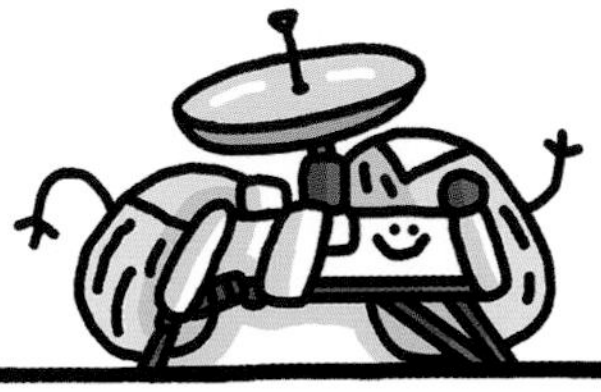

THE SOLAR SYSTEM

You could be forgiven for thinking that everything revolves around our nearest star, the Sun. In Earth's Solar System, most things do! From mini Mercury to giant Jupiter, all eight planets orbit the Sun, as does Earth itself.

This section shines a light on each of those planets, along with the Moon, meteorites, and much, much more.

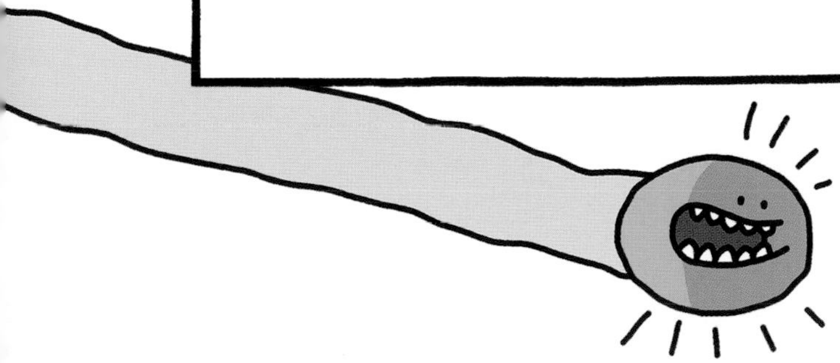

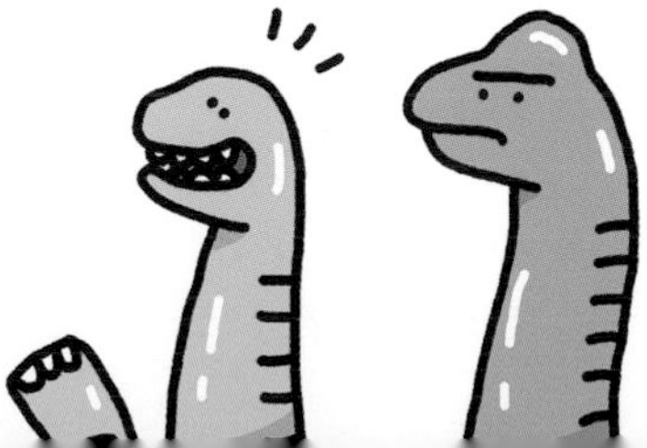

THE EVEN BIGGER PICTURE

Welcome to the Solar System. It's a great place to live. In fact, it's the only place where we know for sure that life exists. At the center is the Sun, our closest star, whose gravity keeps eight planets and all manner of other objects orbiting around it. As neighborhoods go it's far from peaceful, but somehow it's all stayed together for over 4.6 billion years. It's time to meet the neighbors.

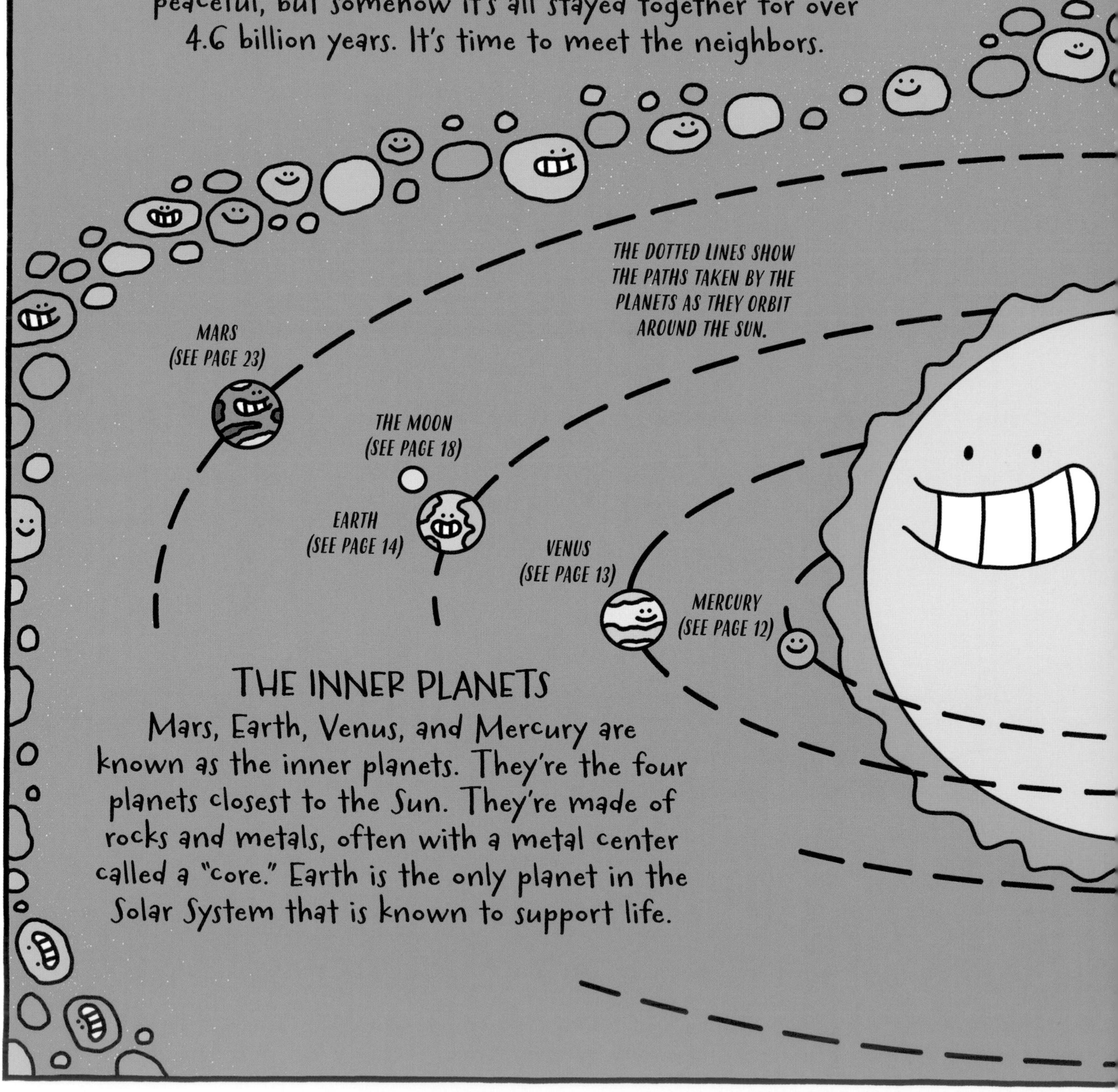

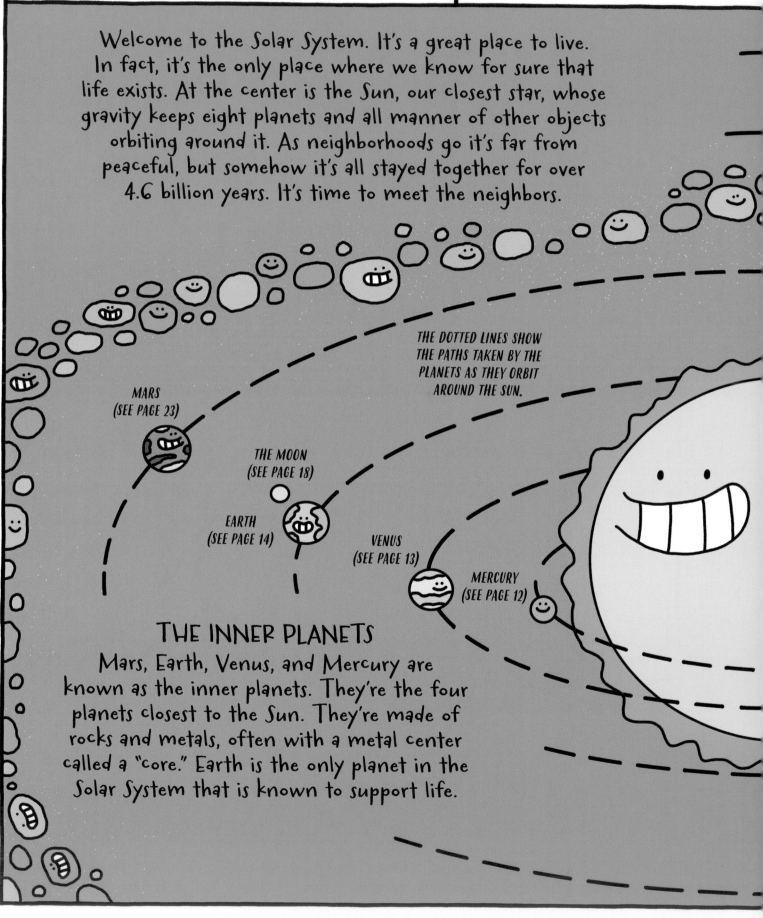

THE DOTTED LINES SHOW THE PATHS TAKEN BY THE PLANETS AS THEY ORBIT AROUND THE SUN.
MARS (SEE PAGE 23)
THE MOON (SEE PAGE 18)
EARTH (SEE PAGE 14)
VENUS (SEE PAGE 13)
MERCURY (SEE PAGE 12)

THE INNER PLANETS

Mars, Earth, Venus, and Mercury are known as the inner planets. They're the four planets closest to the Sun. They're made of rocks and metals, often with a metal center called a "core." Earth is the only planet in the Solar System that is known to support life.

MEET THE NEIGHBORS

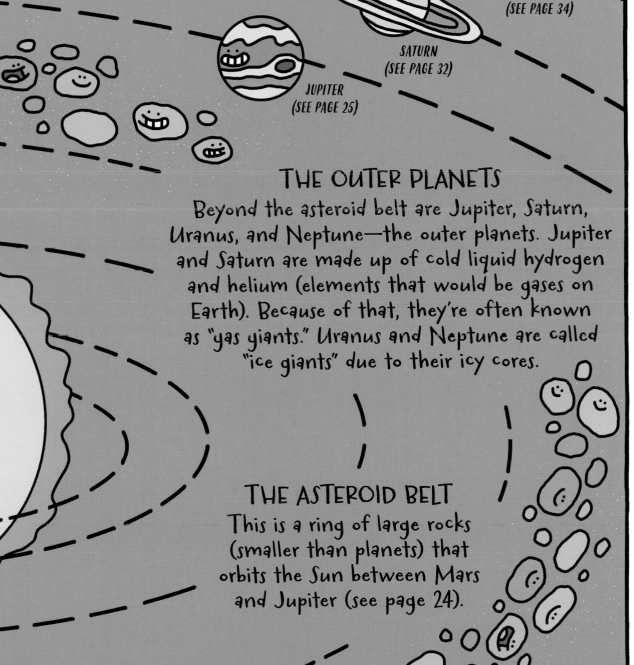

NEPTUNE
(SEE PAGE 35)

URANUS
(SEE PAGE 34)

SATURN
(SEE PAGE 32)

JUPITER
(SEE PAGE 25)

THE OUTER PLANETS

Beyond the asteroid belt are Jupiter, Saturn, Uranus, and Neptune—the outer planets. Jupiter and Saturn are made up of cold liquid hydrogen and helium (elements that would be gases on Earth). Because of that, they're often known as "gas giants." Uranus and Neptune are called "ice giants" due to their icy cores.

THE ASTEROID BELT

This is a ring of large rocks (smaller than planets) that orbits the Sun between Mars and Jupiter (see page 24).

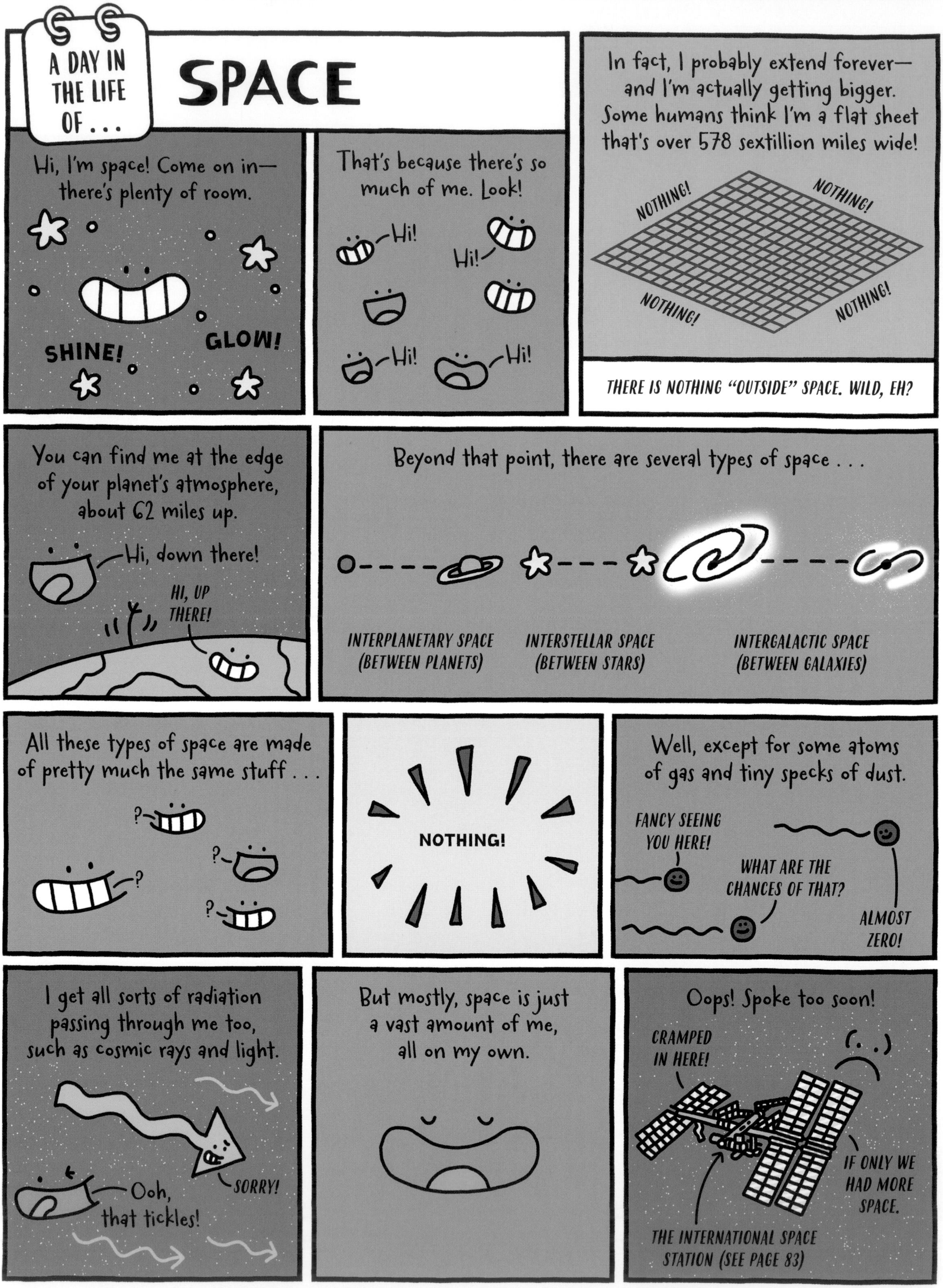
A DAY IN THE LIFE OF . . .
SPACE
Hi, I'm space! Come on in—there's plenty of room.
SHINE!
GLOW!
That's because there's so much of me. Look!
Hi!
Hi!
Hi!
Hi!
In fact, I probably extend forever—and I'm actually getting bigger. Some humans think I'm a flat sheet that's over 578 sextillion miles wide!
NOTHING!
NOTHING!
NOTHING!
NOTHING!
THERE IS NOTHING "OUTSIDE" SPACE. WILD, EH?
You can find me at the edge of your planet's atmosphere, about 62 miles up.
Hi, down there!
HI, UP THERE!
Beyond that point, there are several types of space . . .
INTERPLANETARY SPACE (BETWEEN PLANETS)
INTERSTELLAR SPACE (BETWEEN STARS)
INTERGALACTIC SPACE (BETWEEN GALAXIES)
All these types of space are made of pretty much the same stuff . . .
?
?
?
?
NOTHING!
Well, except for some atoms of gas and tiny specks of dust.
FANCY SEEING YOU HERE!
WHAT ARE THE CHANCES OF THAT?
ALMOST ZERO!
I get all sorts of radiation passing through me too, such as cosmic rays and light.
Ooh, that tickles!
SORRY!
But mostly, space is just a vast amount of me, all on my own.
Oops! Spoke too soon!
CRAMPED IN HERE!
IF ONLY WE HAD MORE SPACE.
THE INTERNATIONAL SPACE STATION (SEE PAGE 83)

THE BIGGER PICTURE

WHAT AN ATMOSPHERE!

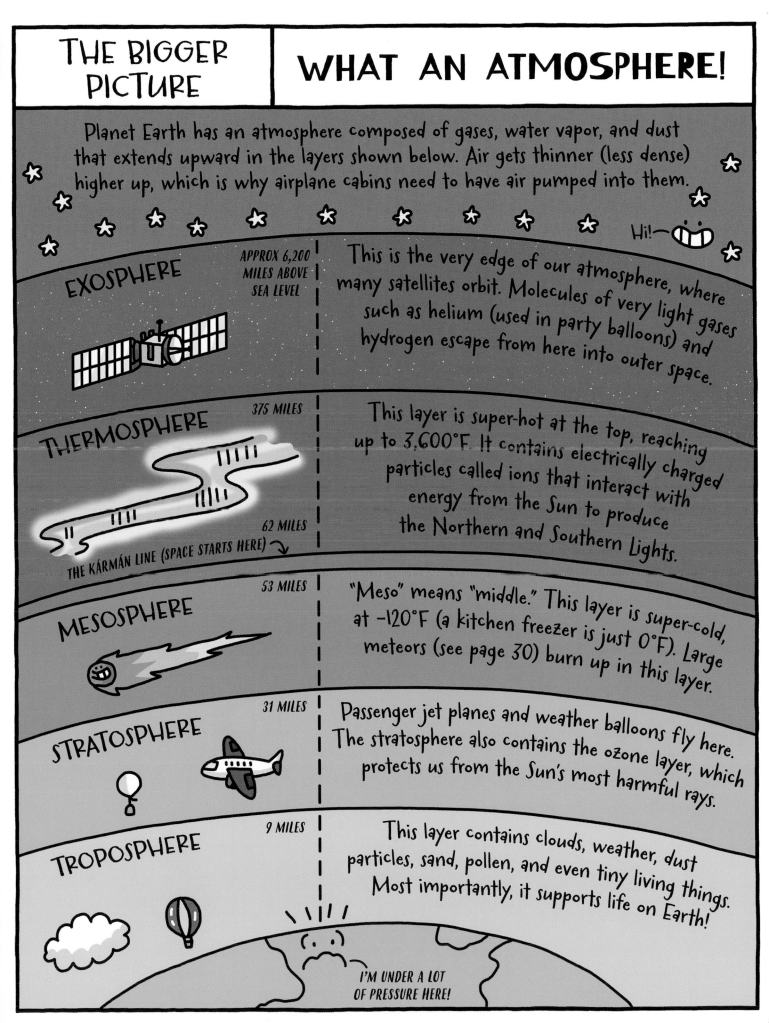

Planet Earth has an atmosphere composed of gases, water vapor, and dust that extends upward in the layers shown below. Air gets thinner (less dense) higher up, which is why airplane cabins need to have air pumped into them.

Hi!

EXOSPHERE

APPROX 6,200 MILES ABOVE SEA LEVEL

This is the very edge of our atmosphere, where many satellites orbit. Molecules of very light gases such as helium (used in party balloons) and hydrogen escape from here into outer space.

THERMOSPHERE

375 MILES

This layer is super-hot at the top, reaching up to 3,600°F. It contains electrically charged particles called ions that interact with energy from the Sun to produce the Northern and Southern Lights.

62 MILES

THE KÁRMÁN LINE (SPACE STARTS HERE)

MESOSPHERE

53 MILES

"Meso" means "middle." This layer is super-cold, at −120°F (a kitchen freezer is just 0°F). Large meteors (see page 30) burn up in this layer.

STRATOSPHERE

31 MILES

Passenger jet planes and weather balloons fly here. The stratosphere also contains the ozone layer, which protects us from the Sun's most harmful rays.

TROPOSPHERE

9 MILES

This layer contains clouds, weather, dust particles, sand, pollen, and even tiny living things. Most importantly, it supports life on Earth!

I'M UNDER A LOT OF PRESSURE HERE!

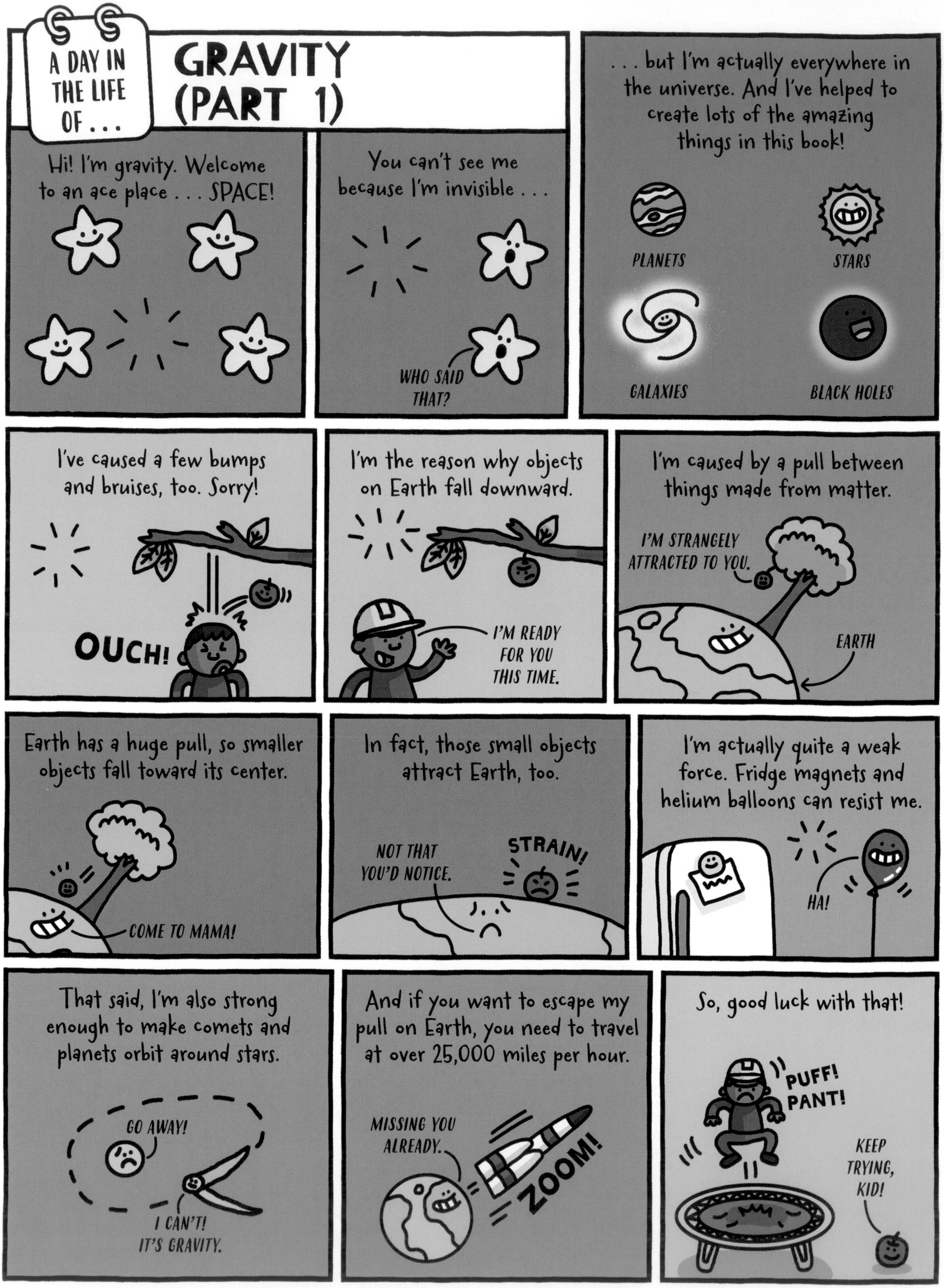
A DAY IN THE LIFE OF . . .
GRAVITY (PART 1)
Hi! I'm gravity. Welcome to an ace place . . . SPACE!
You can't see me because I'm invisible . . .
WHO SAID THAT?
. . . but I'm actually everywhere in the universe. And I've helped to create lots of the amazing things in this book!
PLANETS
STARS
GALAXIES
BLACK HOLES
I've caused a few bumps and bruises, too. Sorry!
OUCH!
I'm the reason why objects on Earth fall downward.
I'M READY FOR YOU THIS TIME.
I'm caused by a pull between things made from matter.
I'M STRANGELY ATTRACTED TO YOU.
EARTH
Earth has a huge pull, so smaller objects fall toward its center.
COME TO MAMA!
In fact, those small objects attract Earth, too.
NOT THAT YOU'D NOTICE.
STRAIN!
I'm actually quite a weak force. Fridge magnets and helium balloons can resist me.
HA!
That said, I'm also strong enough to make comets and planets orbit around stars.
GO AWAY!
I CAN'T! IT'S GRAVITY.
And if you want to escape my pull on Earth, you need to travel at over 25,000 miles per hour.
MISSING YOU ALREADY.
ZOOM!
So, good luck with that!
PUFF! PANT!
KEEP TRYING, KID!

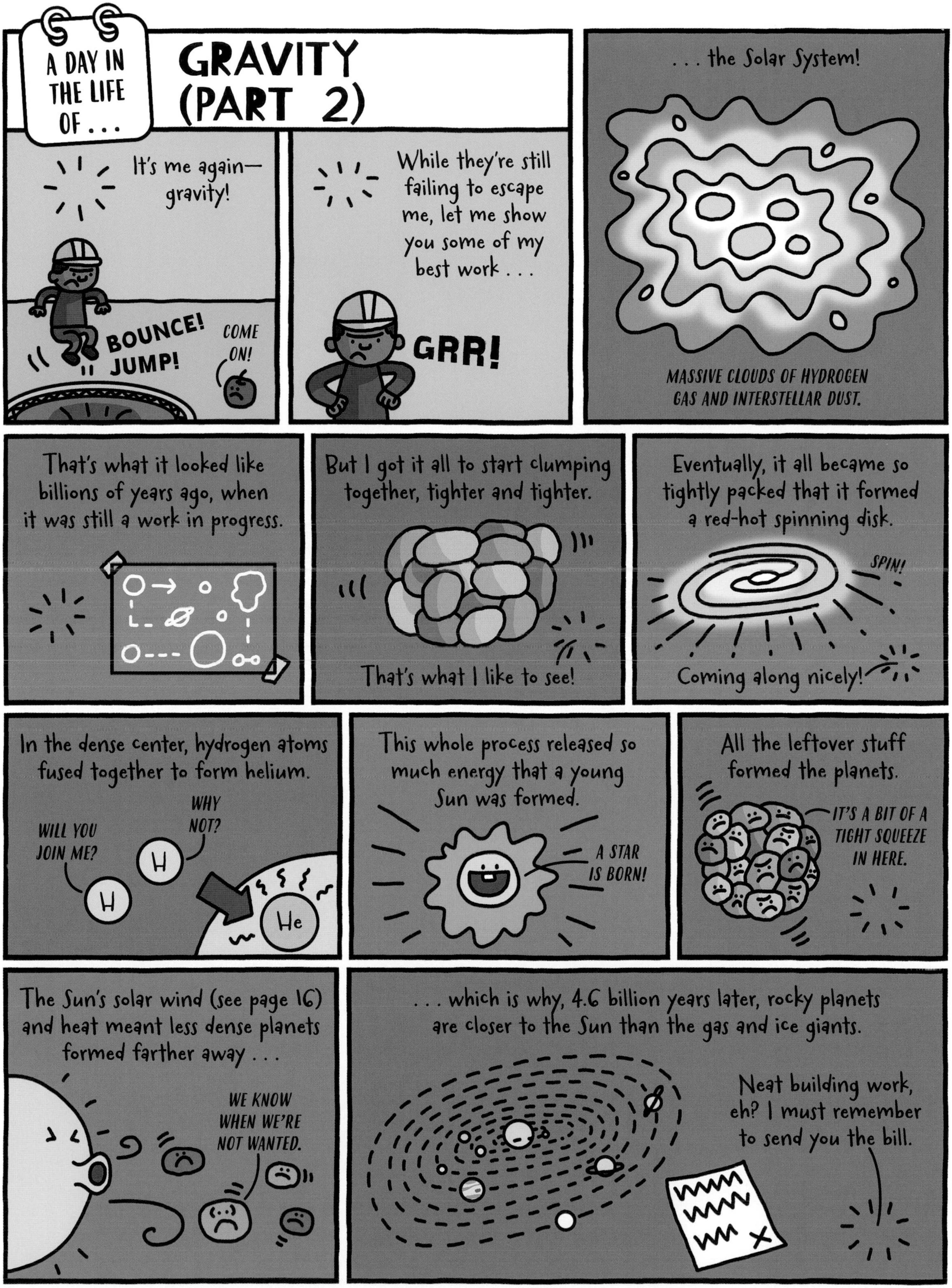
A DAY IN THE LIFE OF . . .
GRAVITY (PART 2)
It's me again—gravity!
BOUNCE! JUMP!
COME ON!
While they're still failing to escape me, let me show you some of my best work . . .
GRR!
. . . the Solar System!
MASSIVE CLOUDS OF HYDROGEN GAS AND INTERSTELLAR DUST.
That's what it looked like billions of years ago, when it was still a work in progress.
But I got it all to start clumping together, tighter and tighter.
That's what I like to see!
Eventually, it all became so tightly packed that it formed a red-hot spinning disk.
SPIN!
Coming along nicely!
In the dense center, hydrogen atoms fused together to form helium.
WILL YOU JOIN ME?
WHY NOT?
H
H
He
This whole process released so much energy that a young Sun was formed.
A STAR IS BORN!
All the leftover stuff formed the planets.
IT'S A BIT OF A TIGHT SQUEEZE IN HERE.
The Sun's solar wind (see page 16) and heat meant less dense planets formed farther away . . .
WE KNOW WHEN WE'RE NOT WANTED.
. . . which is why, 4.6 billion years later, rocky planets are closer to the Sun than the gas and ice giants.
Neat building work, eh? I must remember to send you the bill.

THE EVEN
BIGGER PICTURE

The Sun is stunning! At 2,000 octillion kilograms (you'd write that as a two followed by 30 zeros!), it makes up 99.86 percent of the entire mass of the Solar System. In fact, the Sun could easily fit a million Earths inside it. The Sun makes life on Earth possible. As you'll find out below, it is essentially a giant nuclear reactor spinning in space. Here are some far-out facts about Earth's nearest star.

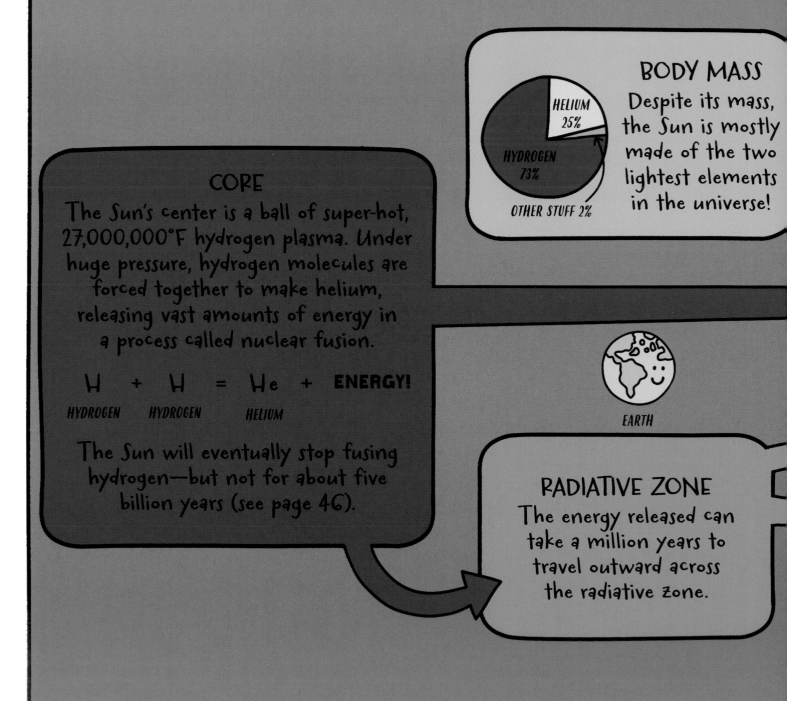

BODY MASS
Despite its mass, the Sun is mostly made of the two lightest elements in the universe!

HELIUM 25%

HYDROGEN 73%

OTHER STUFF 2%

CORE
The Sun's center is a ball of super-hot, 27,000,000°F hydrogen plasma. Under huge pressure, hydrogen molecules are forced together to make helium, releasing vast amounts of energy in a process called nuclear fusion.

$$H + H = He + \textbf{ENERGY!}$$

HYDROGEN   HYDROGEN   HELIUM

The Sun will eventually stop fusing hydrogen—but not for about five billion years (see page 46).

EARTH

RADIATIVE ZONE
The energy released can take a million years to travel outward across the radiative zone.

OUR STAR PERFORMER

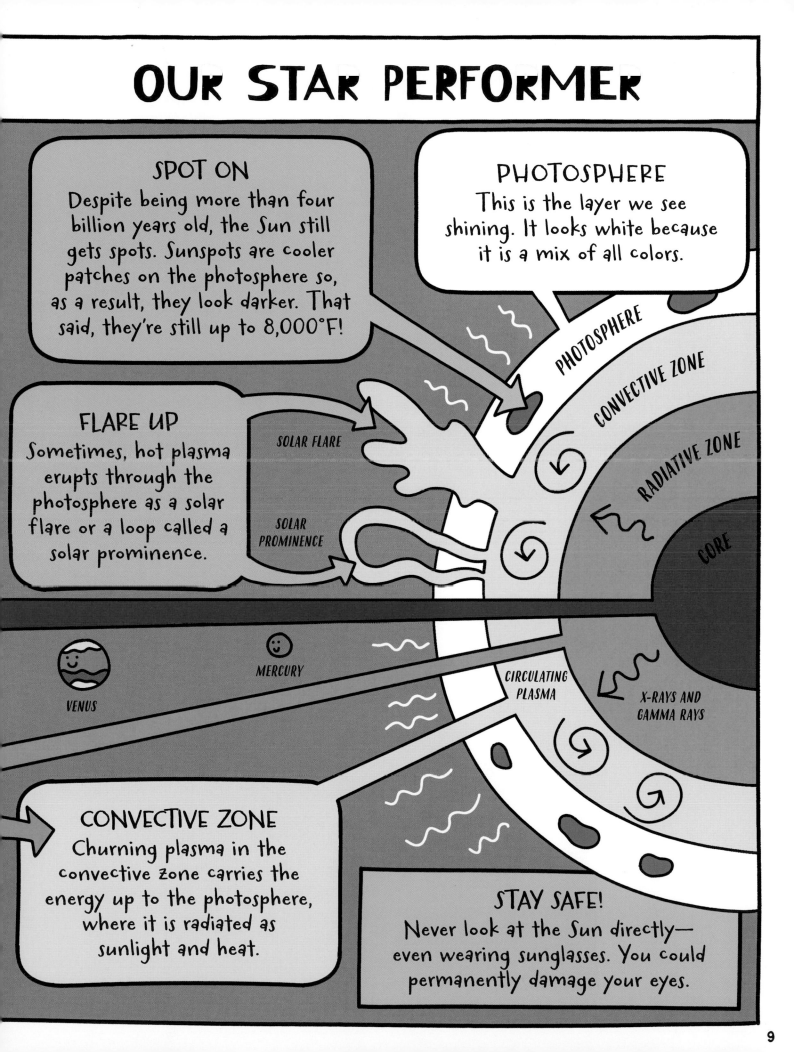

SPOT ON
Despite being more than four billion years old, the Sun still gets spots. Sunspots are cooler patches on the photosphere so, as a result, they look darker. That said, they're still up to 8,000°F!

PHOTOSPHERE
This is the layer we see shining. It looks white because it is a mix of all colors.

FLARE UP
Sometimes, hot plasma erupts through the photosphere as a solar flare or a loop called a solar prominence.

PHOTOSPHERE

CONVECTIVE ZONE

RADIATIVE ZONE

CORE

SOLAR FLARE

SOLAR PROMINENCE

VENUS

MERCURY

CIRCULATING PLASMA

X-RAYS AND GAMMA RAYS

CONVECTIVE ZONE
Churning plasma in the convective zone carries the energy up to the photosphere, where it is radiated as sunlight and heat.

STAY SAFE!
Never look at the Sun directly— even wearing sunglasses. You could permanently damage your eyes.

The secret diary of a
LITTLE BIT OF SUNSHINE

Extracts from the diary of "Ray," a small part of the Sun's light

ME!

TIME: 0.0001 SECONDS

Zap! It's hot here in the Sun's photosphere (that's the circular disk you humans can see in the sky). Around 10,000°F, in fact! All of us billions of newly formed photons are so keen to get away that we travel at 186,282 miles per second. That's the speed of light in a vacuum. There's nothing faster in the universe!

TIME: 1 SECOND

I'm just one particle of light in a big burst of photons constantly spreading out from the Sun. We all move at light speed on straight paths, but wiggle differently as we do it. The length of our wiggling "waves" determines what color of light we are. Blue has shorter waves, red has longer waves, and green's waves are somewhere in the middle. Combining all the different colors of visible light creates white sunlight. Clever, right?

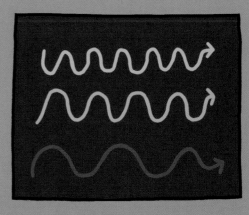

TIME: 2 SECONDS

Also traveling with us are some light waves you won't be able to see: infrared and ultraviolet. Infrared is what makes sunlight feel warm, while ultraviolet can burn your skin. We'll be with you soon, so you'd better put some sunblock on.

VENUS
MERCURY
EARTH

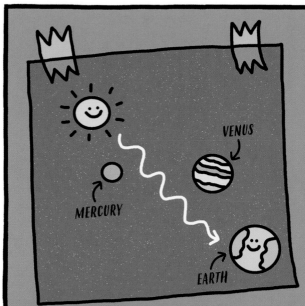

TIME: 8 MINUTES, 18 SECONDS

Almost there! It took just over three minutes for us to pass Mercury and about six minutes to pass Venus. Now we have hit your ozone layer, which soaks up some of those dangerous ultraviolet waves. Get ready to see the light!

BOING!

TIME: 8 MINUTES, 19 SECONDS

I traveled 93 million miles to see you (that's one Astronomical Unit, or AU), only to be bounced back into space by your mirrored shades! Oh well, at least it means you're smart enough not to look directly at the Sun. It's off back to space for me, now. There's a whole universe ahead of me.

TIME: 4 HOURS, 12 MINUTES

Still going! Just passed Neptune, with the Sun a very dim, distant object behind me. Amazingly, when I look back at the Sun from here, I see what it looked like just over four hours ago when I left. I'm looking into the past!

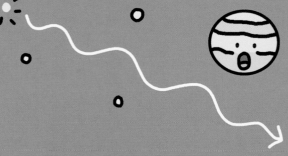

TIME: ONE YEAR

I've now been traveling at the speed of light for exactly one year. That's a distance of 6 trillion miles. Scientists call this distance one "light-year," which saves them from having to write out all those zeros. It also means I'm about to leave the Solar System behind. See ya!

BYE!

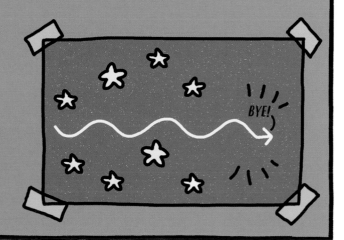

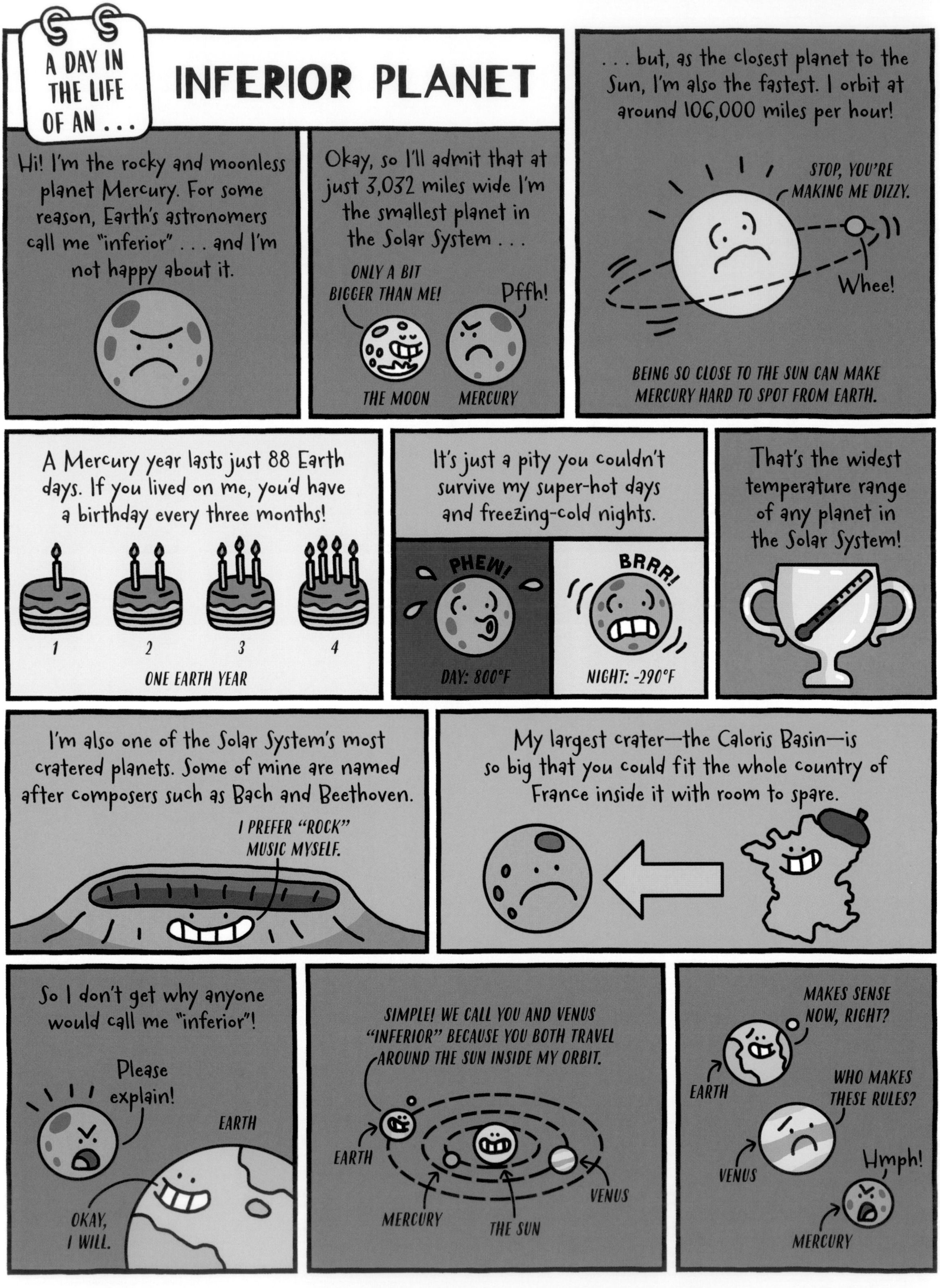

A DAY IN THE LIFE OF AN . . .
INFERIOR PLANET
Hi! I'm the rocky and moonless planet Mercury. For some reason, Earth's astronomers call me "inferior" . . . and I'm not happy about it.
Okay, so I'll admit that at just 3,032 miles wide I'm the smallest planet in the Solar System . . .
ONLY A BIT BIGGER THAN ME!
Pffh!
THE MOON
MERCURY
. . . but, as the closest planet to the Sun, I'm also the fastest. I orbit at around 106,000 miles per hour!
STOP, YOU'RE MAKING ME DIZZY.
Whee!
BEING SO CLOSE TO THE SUN CAN MAKE MERCURY HARD TO SPOT FROM EARTH.
A Mercury year lasts just 88 Earth days. If you lived on me, you'd have a birthday every three months!
1
2
3
4
ONE EARTH YEAR
It's just a pity you couldn't survive my super-hot days and freezing-cold nights.
PHEW!
DAY: 800°F
BRRR!
NIGHT: -290°F
That's the widest temperature range of any planet in the Solar System!
I'm also one of the Solar System's most cratered planets. Some of mine are named after composers such as Bach and Beethoven.
I PREFER "ROCK" MUSIC MYSELF.
My largest crater—the Caloris Basin—is so big that you could fit the whole country of France inside it with room to spare.
So I don't get why anyone would call me "inferior"!
Please explain!
EARTH
OKAY, I WILL.
SIMPLE! WE CALL YOU AND VENUS "INFERIOR" BECAUSE YOU BOTH TRAVEL AROUND THE SUN INSIDE MY ORBIT.
EARTH
MERCURY
THE SUN
VENUS
MAKES SENSE NOW, RIGHT?
EARTH
WHO MAKES THESE RULES?
VENUS
Hmph!
MERCURY

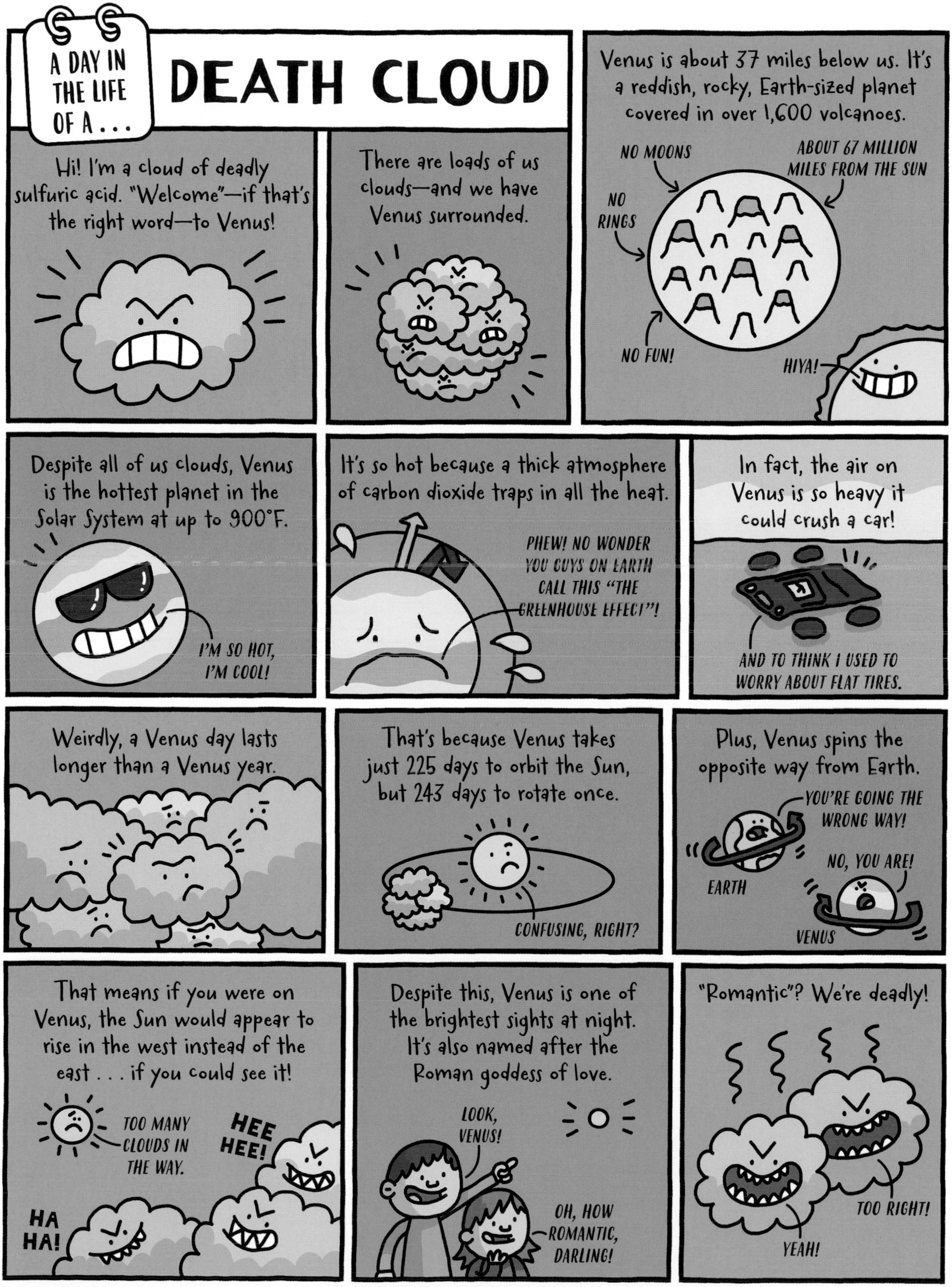
A DAY IN THE LIFE OF A . . .
DEATH CLOUD
Hi! I'm a cloud of deadly sulfuric acid. "Welcome"—if that's the right word—to Venus!
There are loads of us clouds—and we have Venus surrounded.
Venus is about 37 miles below us. It's a reddish, rocky, Earth-sized planet covered in over 1,600 volcanoes.
NO MOONS
ABOUT 67 MILLION MILES FROM THE SUN
NO RINGS
NO FUN!
HIYA!
Despite all of us clouds, Venus is the hottest planet in the Solar System at up to 900°F.
I'M SO HOT, I'M COOL!
It's so hot because a thick atmosphere of carbon dioxide traps in all the heat.
PHEW! NO WONDER YOU GUYS ON EARTH CALL THIS "THE GREENHOUSE EFFECT"!
In fact, the air on Venus is so heavy it could crush a car!
AND TO THINK I USED TO WORRY ABOUT FLAT TIRES.
Weirdly, a Venus day lasts longer than a Venus year.
That's because Venus takes just 225 days to orbit the Sun, but 243 days to rotate once.
CONFUSING, RIGHT?
Plus, Venus spins the opposite way from Earth.
YOU'RE GOING THE WRONG WAY!
NO, YOU ARE!
EARTH
VENUS
That means if you were on Venus, the Sun would appear to rise in the west instead of the east . . . if you could see it!
TOO MANY CLOUDS IN THE WAY.
HEE HEE!
HA HA!
Despite this, Venus is one of the brightest sights at night. It's also named after the Roman goddess of love.
LOOK, VENUS!
OH, HOW ROMANTIC, DARLING!
"Romantic"? We're deadly!
TOO RIGHT!
YEAH!

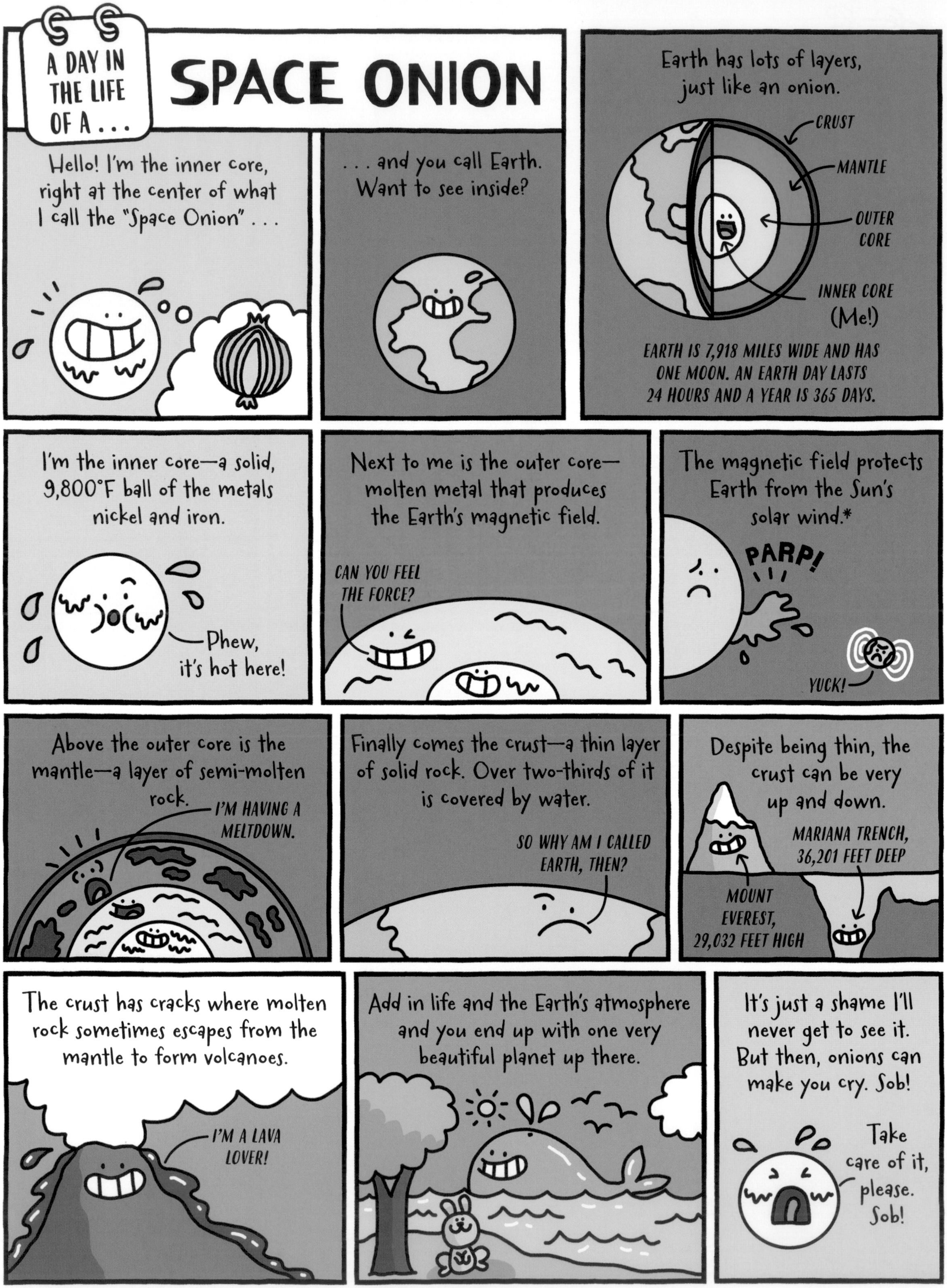

A DAY IN THE LIFE OF A . . .
SPACE ONION
Hello! I'm the inner core, right at the center of what I call the "Space Onion" . . .
. . . and you call Earth. Want to see inside?
Earth has lots of layers, just like an onion.
CRUST
MANTLE
OUTER CORE
INNER CORE (Me!)
EARTH IS 7,918 MILES WIDE AND HAS ONE MOON. AN EARTH DAY LASTS 24 HOURS AND A YEAR IS 365 DAYS.
I'm the inner core—a solid, 9,800°F ball of the metals nickel and iron.
Phew, it's hot here!
Next to me is the outer core—molten metal that produces the Earth's magnetic field.
CAN YOU FEEL THE FORCE?
The magnetic field protects Earth from the Sun's solar wind.*
PARP!
YUCK!
Above the outer core is the mantle—a layer of semi-molten rock.
I'M HAVING A MELTDOWN.
Finally comes the crust—a thin layer of solid rock. Over two-thirds of it is covered by water.
SO WHY AM I CALLED EARTH, THEN?
Despite being thin, the crust can be very up and down.
MARIANA TRENCH, 36,201 FEET DEEP
MOUNT EVEREST, 29,032 FEET HIGH
The crust has cracks where molten rock sometimes escapes from the mantle to form volcanoes.
I'M A LAVA LOVER!
Add in life and the Earth's atmosphere and you end up with one very beautiful planet up there.
It's just a shame I'll never get to see it. But then, onions can make you cry. Sob!
Take care of it, please. Sob!

*SEE PAGES 16 AND 17.

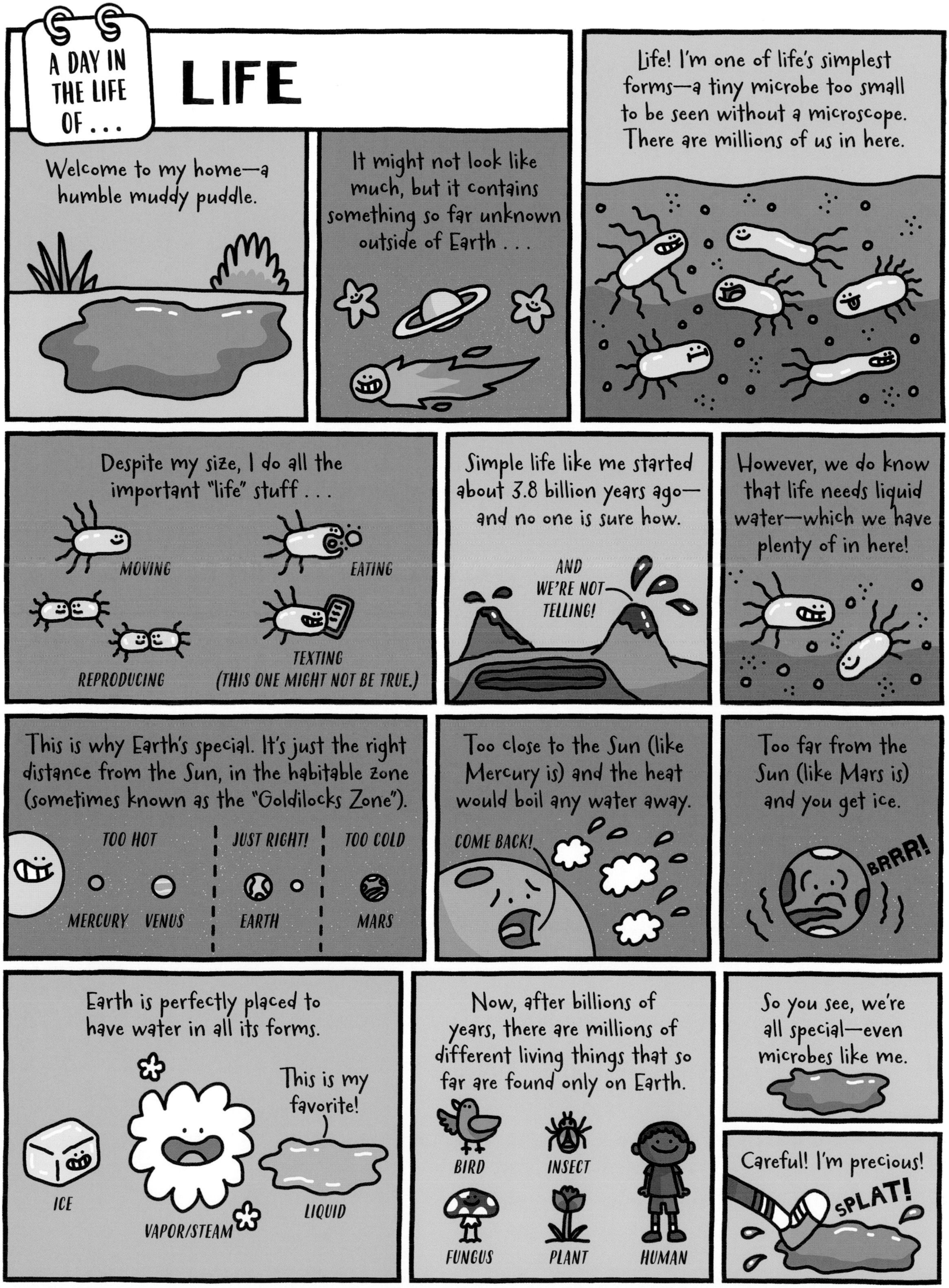

A DAY IN THE LIFE OF . . .
LIFE
Welcome to my home—a humble muddy puddle.
It might not look like much, but it contains something so far unknown outside of Earth . . .
Life! I'm one of life's simplest forms—a tiny microbe too small to be seen without a microscope. There are millions of us in here.
Despite my size, I do all the important "life" stuff . . .
MOVING
EATING
REPRODUCING
TEXTING (THIS ONE MIGHT NOT BE TRUE.)
Simple life like me started about 3.8 billion years ago—and no one is sure how.
AND WE'RE NOT TELLING!
However, we do know that life needs liquid water—which we have plenty of in here!
This is why Earth's special. It's just the right distance from the Sun, in the habitable zone (sometimes known as the "Goldilocks Zone").
TOO HOT
JUST RIGHT!
TOO COLD
MERCURY
VENUS
EARTH
MARS
Too close to the Sun (like Mercury is) and the heat would boil any water away.
COME BACK!
Too far from the Sun (like Mars is) and you get ice.
BRRR!
Earth is perfectly placed to have water in all its forms.
This is my favorite!
ICE
VAPOR/STEAM
LIQUID
Now, after billions of years, there are millions of different living things that so far are found only on Earth.
BIRD
INSECT
HUMAN
FUNGUS
PLANT
So you see, we're all special—even microbes like me.
Careful! I'm precious!
SPLAT!

The secret diary of a
SHIMMER
Extracts from the diary of "Gus," part of a gust of solar wind

ME IN THE SUN'S CORONA

MONDAY MORNING
Wow! What a start to the week! Me and millions of other electrically charged particles were all kicked out of the Sun's corona while innocently enjoying the 3,500,000°F heat. Now we all seem to be speeding in the direction of some distant blue planet, at about 310 miles per second. I wonder what we'll do when we get there . . .

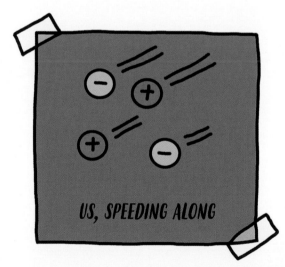
US, SPEEDING ALONG

MONDAY AFTERNOON
Quick update. Apparently, all us supercharged particles—some positive, some negative—make up a giant gust of "solar wind." Sounds a bit rude to me. I think I prefer the term "solar weather." Anyway, looks like we're still on course for that little blue planet.

MONDAY EVENING
Just heard that some gusts went off in completely different directions. One gust even met a comet and gave it a big, long tail, pointing away from the Sun. I hope our gust gets to do something just as spectacular.

COMET

SOLAR WIND

TUESDAY

Well, today was very dull. Lots of traveling through empty space at high speed. That little blue planet is looking bigger all the time, though. I think we might hit it tomorrow.

WEDNESDAY MORNING

Wow (again)! That little blue planet had a trick in store for us—an invisible particle shield! I thought it was MAGIC but it turned out to be MAG-net-IC! The planet acts like a giant magnet, deflecting most of us around and behind it. By sheer luck, me and some others slipped through. Maybe now we'll get our chance to shine.

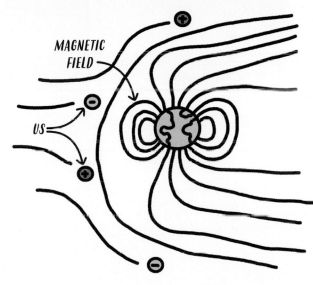

MAGNETIC FIELD

US

OUR AURORA IN THE SKY. ISN'T IT BEAUTIFUL?

WEDNESDAY NIGHT

Triple wow! We didn't just get to shine, but also shimmer and glow! Us rogue particles bumped into lots of nitrogen and oxygen atoms in the atmosphere over the planet's North and South Poles. Those particles took our energy and turned it into an amazing colored light display called an "aurora." It was well worth traveling 93 million miles to be part of it. Bye!

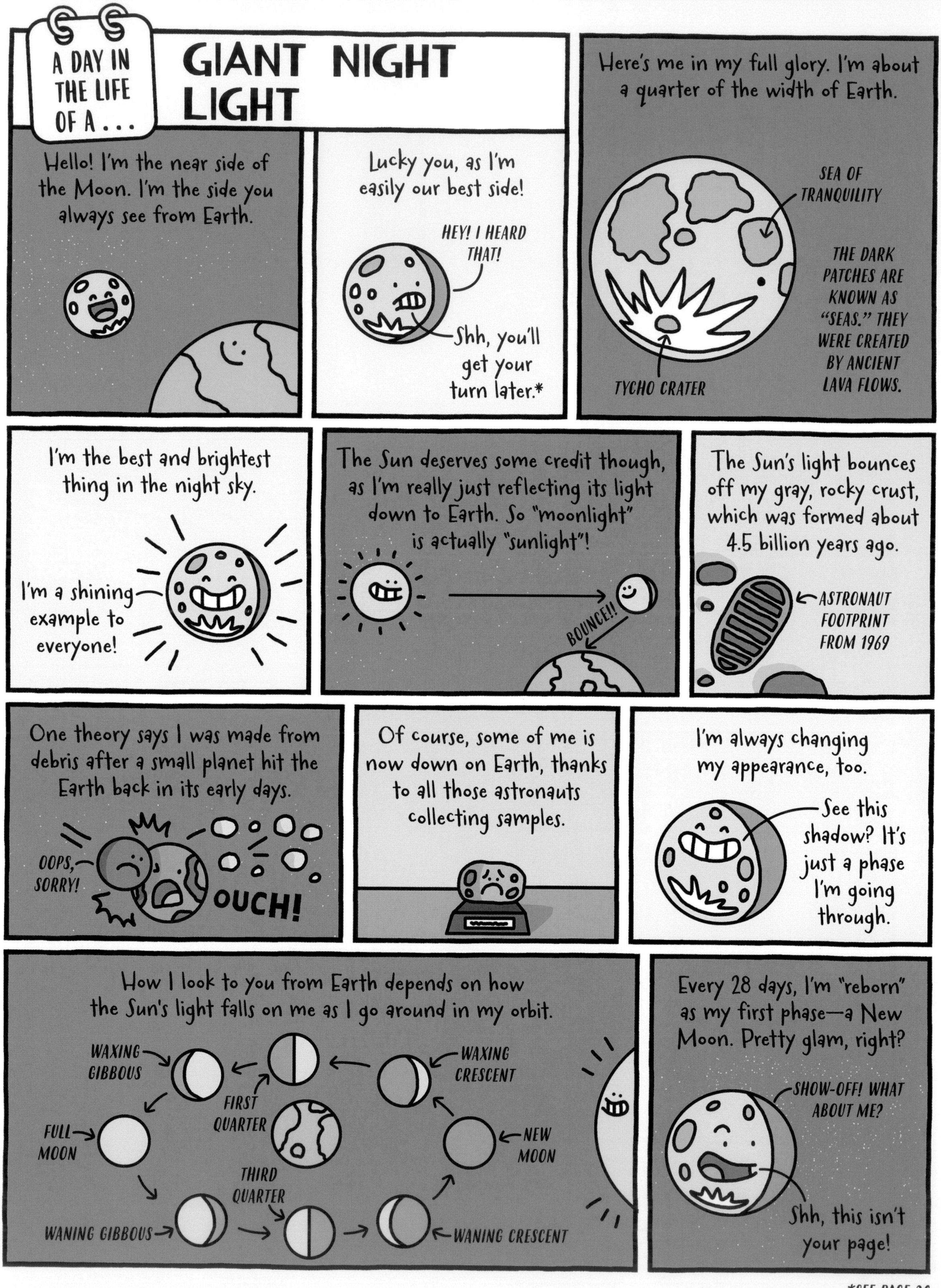
A DAY IN THE LIFE OF A . . .
GIANT NIGHT LIGHT
Hello! I'm the near side of the Moon. I'm the side you always see from Earth.
Lucky you, as I'm easily our best side!
HEY! I HEARD THAT!
Shh, you'll get your turn later.*
Here's me in my full glory. I'm about a quarter of the width of Earth.
SEA OF TRANQUILITY
THE DARK PATCHES ARE KNOWN AS "SEAS." THEY WERE CREATED BY ANCIENT LAVA FLOWS.
TYCHO CRATER
I'm the best and brightest thing in the night sky.
I'm a shining example to everyone!
The Sun deserves some credit though, as I'm really just reflecting its light down to Earth. So "moonlight" is actually "sunlight"!
BOUNCE!!
The Sun's light bounces off my gray, rocky crust, which was formed about 4.5 billion years ago.
ASTRONAUT FOOTPRINT FROM 1969
One theory says I was made from debris after a small planet hit the Earth back in its early days.
OOPS, SORRY!
OUCH!
Of course, some of me is now down on Earth, thanks to all those astronauts collecting samples.
I'm always changing my appearance, too.
See this shadow? It's just a phase I'm going through.
How I look to you from Earth depends on how the Sun's light falls on me as I go around in my orbit.
WAXING GIBBOUS
WAXING CRESCENT
FIRST QUARTER
FULL MOON
NEW MOON
THIRD QUARTER
WANING GIBBOUS
WANING CRESCENT
Every 28 days, I'm "reborn" as my first phase—a New Moon. Pretty glam, right?
SHOW-OFF! WHAT ABOUT ME?
Shh, this isn't your page!

*SEE PAGE 20.

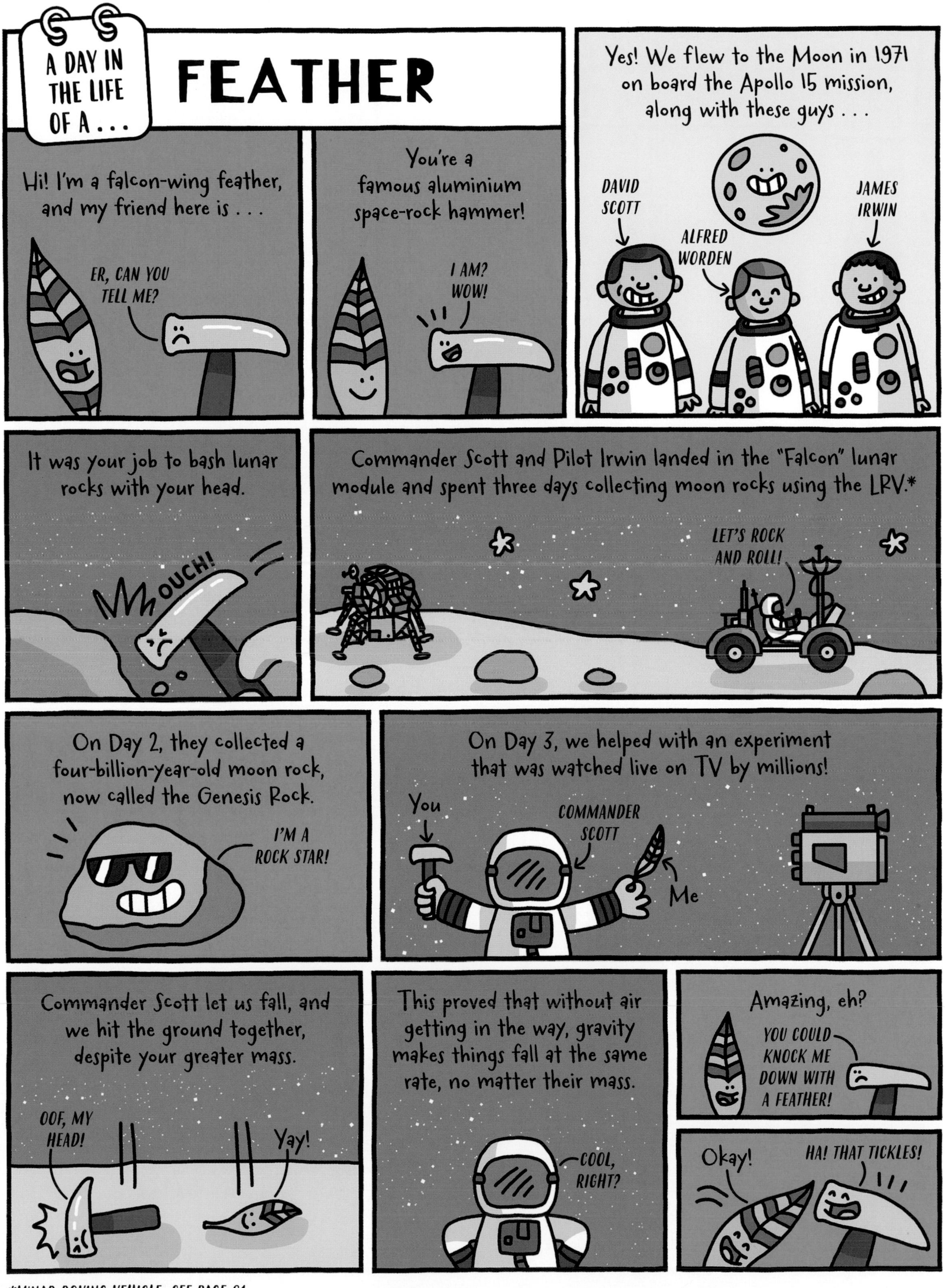
A DAY IN THE LIFE OF A . . .
FEATHER
Hi! I'm a falcon-wing feather, and my friend here is . . .
ER, CAN YOU TELL ME?
You're a famous aluminium space-rock hammer!
I AM? WOW!
Yes! We flew to the Moon in 1971 on board the Apollo 15 mission, along with these guys . . .
DAVID SCOTT
ALFRED WORDEN
JAMES IRWIN
It was your job to bash lunar rocks with your head.
OUCH!
Commander Scott and Pilot Irwin landed in the "Falcon" lunar module and spent three days collecting moon rocks using the LRV.*
LET'S ROCK AND ROLL!
On Day 2, they collected a four-billion-year-old moon rock, now called the Genesis Rock.
I'M A ROCK STAR!
On Day 3, we helped with an experiment that was watched live on TV by millions!
You
COMMANDER SCOTT
Me
Commander Scott let us fall, and we hit the ground together, despite your greater mass.
OOF, MY HEAD!
Yay!
This proved that without air getting in the way, gravity makes things fall at the same rate, no matter their mass.
COOL, RIGHT?
Amazing, eh?
YOU COULD KNOCK ME DOWN WITH A FEATHER!
Okay!
HA! THAT TICKLES!

*LUNAR ROVING VEHICLE. SEE PAGE 81.

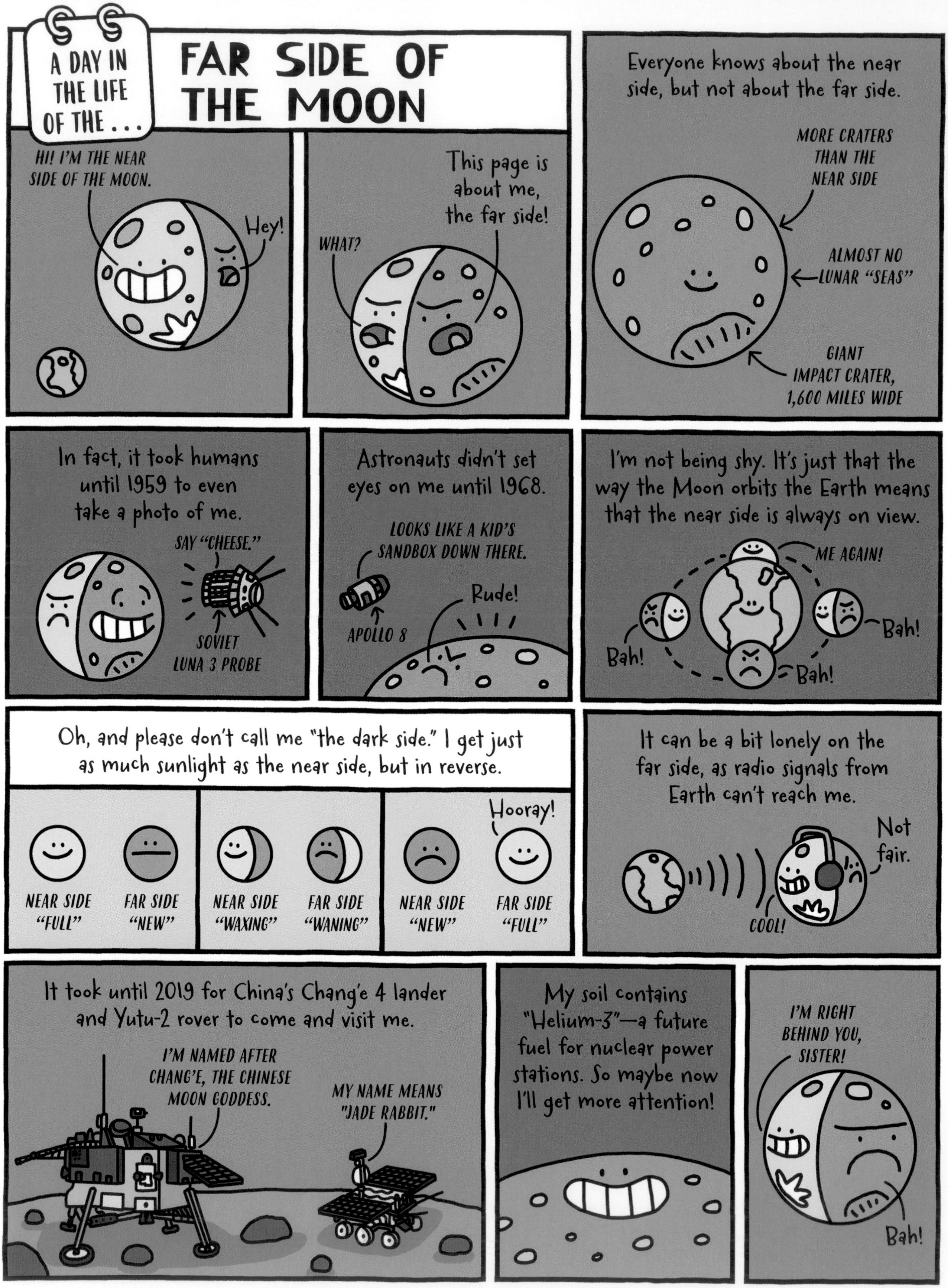
A DAY IN THE LIFE OF THE . . .
FAR SIDE OF THE MOON
HI! I'M THE NEAR SIDE OF THE MOON.
Hey!
This page is about me, the far side!
WHAT?
Everyone knows about the near side, but not about the far side.
MORE CRATERS THAN THE NEAR SIDE
ALMOST NO LUNAR "SEAS"
GIANT IMPACT CRATER, 1,600 MILES WIDE
In fact, it took humans until 1959 to even take a photo of me.
SAY "CHEESE."
SOVIET LUNA 3 PROBE
Astronauts didn't set eyes on me until 1968.
LOOKS LIKE A KID'S SANDBOX DOWN THERE.
APOLLO 8
Rude!
I'm not being shy. It's just that the way the Moon orbits the Earth means that the near side is always on view.
ME AGAIN!
Bah!
Bah!
Bah!
Oh, and please don't call me "the dark side." I get just as much sunlight as the near side, but in reverse.
NEAR SIDE "FULL"
FAR SIDE "NEW"
NEAR SIDE "WAXING"
FAR SIDE "WANING"
NEAR SIDE "NEW"
Hooray!
FAR SIDE "FULL"
It can be a bit lonely on the far side, as radio signals from Earth can't reach me.
Not fair.
COOL!
It took until 2019 for China's Chang'e 4 lander and Yutu-2 rover to come and visit me.
I'M NAMED AFTER CHANG'E, THE CHINESE MOON GODDESS.
MY NAME MEANS "JADE RABBIT."
My soil contains "Helium-3"—a future fuel for nuclear power stations. So maybe now I'll get more attention!
I'M RIGHT BEHIND YOU, SISTER!
Bah!

DARK SECRETS

Imagine the shock it must have been to ancient civilizations when the Sun was blocked out and the land went dark. Today, we know that this is a solar eclipse. It's caused by the Moon getting in the way of the Sun's disk of light, as seen from the Earth.

THE MOON CROSSES AND BLOCKS THE SUN

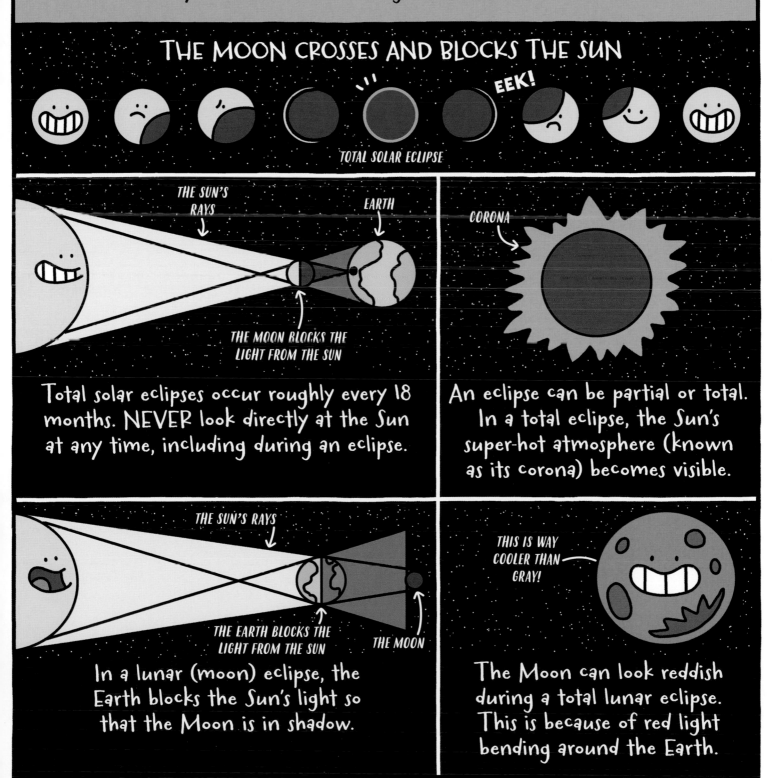

EEK!

TOTAL SOLAR ECLIPSE

THE SUN'S RAYS

EARTH

THE MOON BLOCKS THE LIGHT FROM THE SUN

Total solar eclipses occur roughly every 18 months. NEVER look directly at the Sun at any time, including during an eclipse.

CORONA

An eclipse can be partial or total. In a total eclipse, the Sun's super-hot atmosphere (known as its corona) becomes visible.

THE SUN'S RAYS

THE EARTH BLOCKS THE LIGHT FROM THE SUN

THE MOON

In a lunar (moon) eclipse, the Earth blocks the Sun's light so that the Moon is in shadow.

THIS IS WAY COOLER THAN GRAY!

The Moon can look reddish during a total lunar eclipse. This is because of red light bending around the Earth.

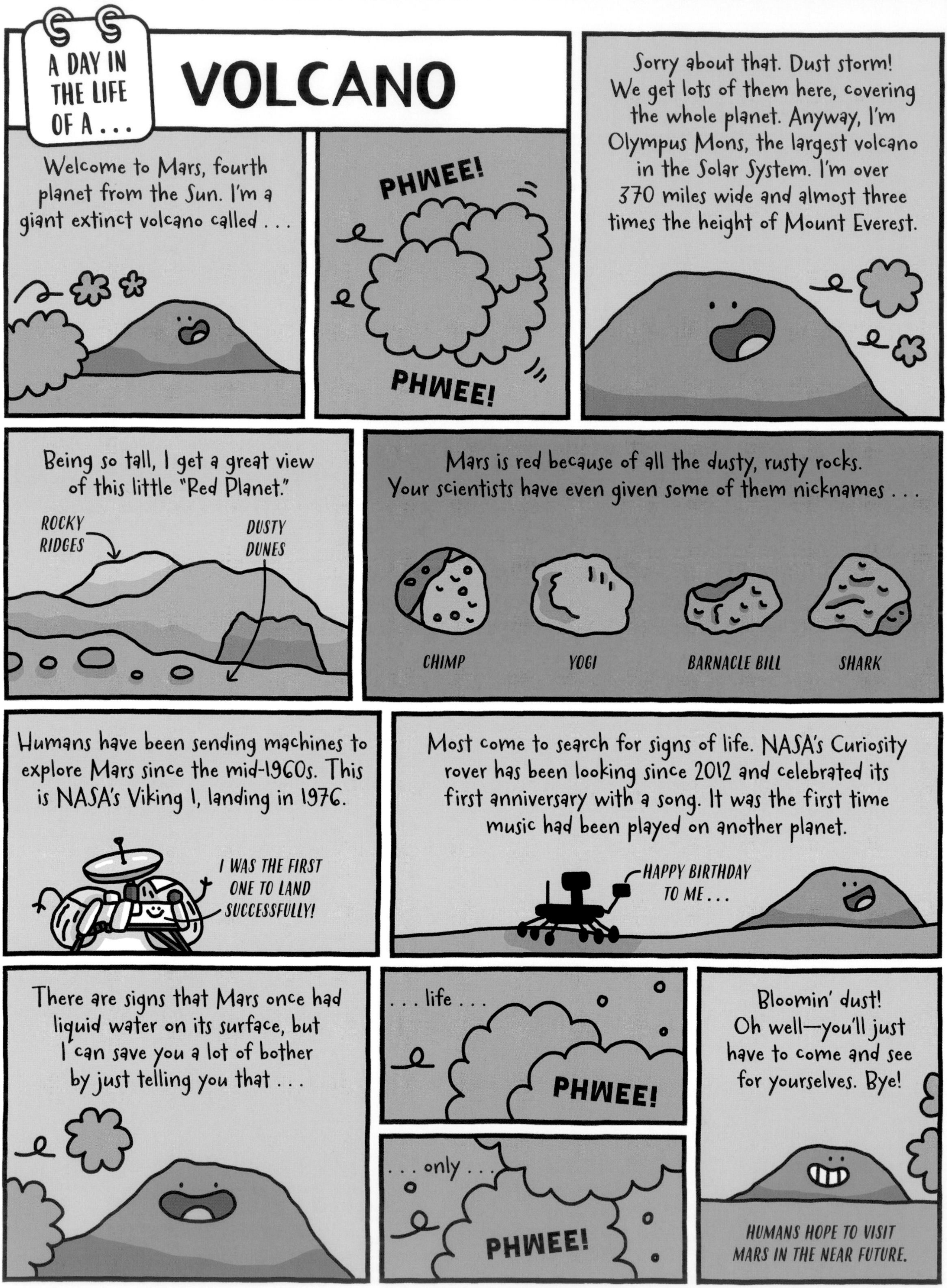
A DAY IN THE LIFE OF A . . .
VOLCANO
Welcome to Mars, fourth planet from the Sun. I'm a giant extinct volcano called . . .
PHWEE!
PHWEE!
Sorry about that. Dust storm! We get lots of them here, covering the whole planet. Anyway, I'm Olympus Mons, the largest volcano in the Solar System. I'm over 370 miles wide and almost three times the height of Mount Everest.
Being so tall, I get a great view of this little "Red Planet."
ROCKY RIDGES
DUSTY DUNES
Mars is red because of all the dusty, rusty rocks. Your scientists have even given some of them nicknames . . .
CHIMP
YOGI
BARNACLE BILL
SHARK
Humans have been sending machines to explore Mars since the mid-1960s. This is NASA's Viking 1, landing in 1976.
I WAS THE FIRST ONE TO LAND SUCCESSFULLY!
Most come to search for signs of life. NASA's Curiosity rover has been looking since 2012 and celebrated its first anniversary with a song. It was the first time music had been played on another planet.
HAPPY BIRTHDAY TO ME . . .
There are signs that Mars once had liquid water on its surface, but I can save you a lot of bother by just telling you that . . .
. . . life . . .
PHWEE!
. . . only . . .
PHWEE!
Bloomin' dust! Oh well—you'll just have to come and see for yourselves. Bye!
HUMANS HOPE TO VISIT MARS IN THE NEAR FUTURE.

THE BIGGER PICTURE

RED PLANET

Shining bloodred in the night sky, it's no wonder Mars was named after the ancient Roman god of war. Mars is about half the width of Earth, and its days are almost 40 minutes longer than Earth days. However, because Mars is so much farther from the Sun, a Martian year lasts 687 Earth days.

THIN AIR

Mars has a very thin atmosphere of unbreathable carbon dioxide, and about 40 percent of the gravity Earth has. This means future human visitors will weigh a whole lot less than they do back home.

THE BIG FREEZE

Like Earth, Mars has ice caps at its north and south poles. Temperatures there can go as low as –225°F.

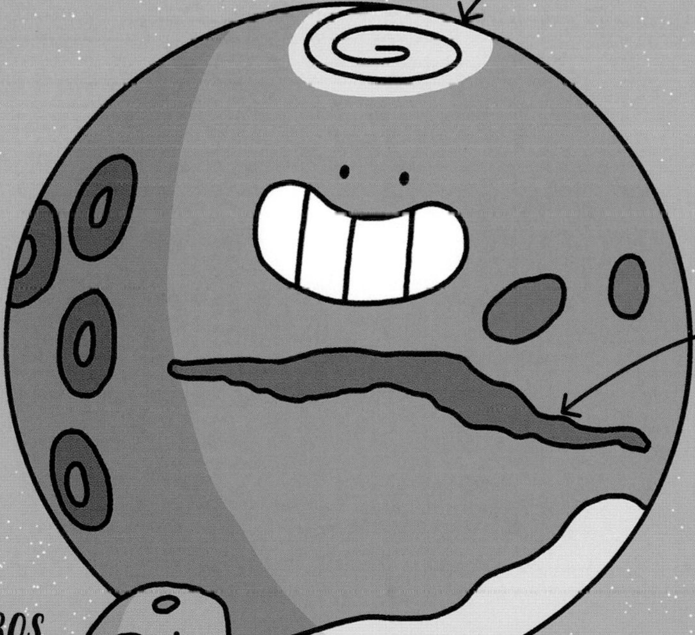

GROOVY!

Valles Marineris is a giant valley, five times longer and four times deeper than Earth's Grand Canyon.

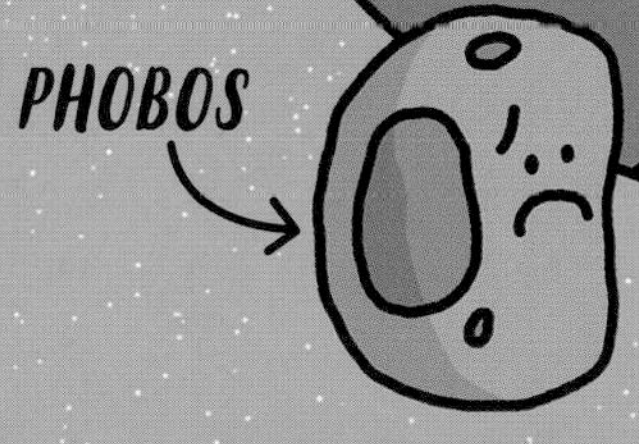
PHOBOS

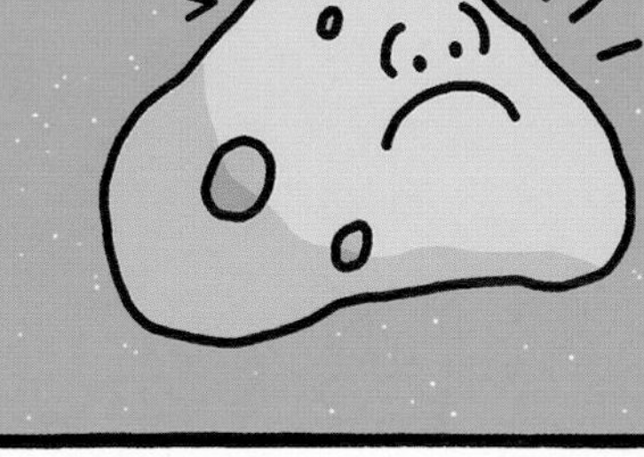
DEIMOS

A TERRIFYING PAIR

Mars has two potato-shaped moons called Phobos and Deimos (named after the Greek gods of fear and dread!). Phobos orbits very close to Mars and will one day crash into it and break up.

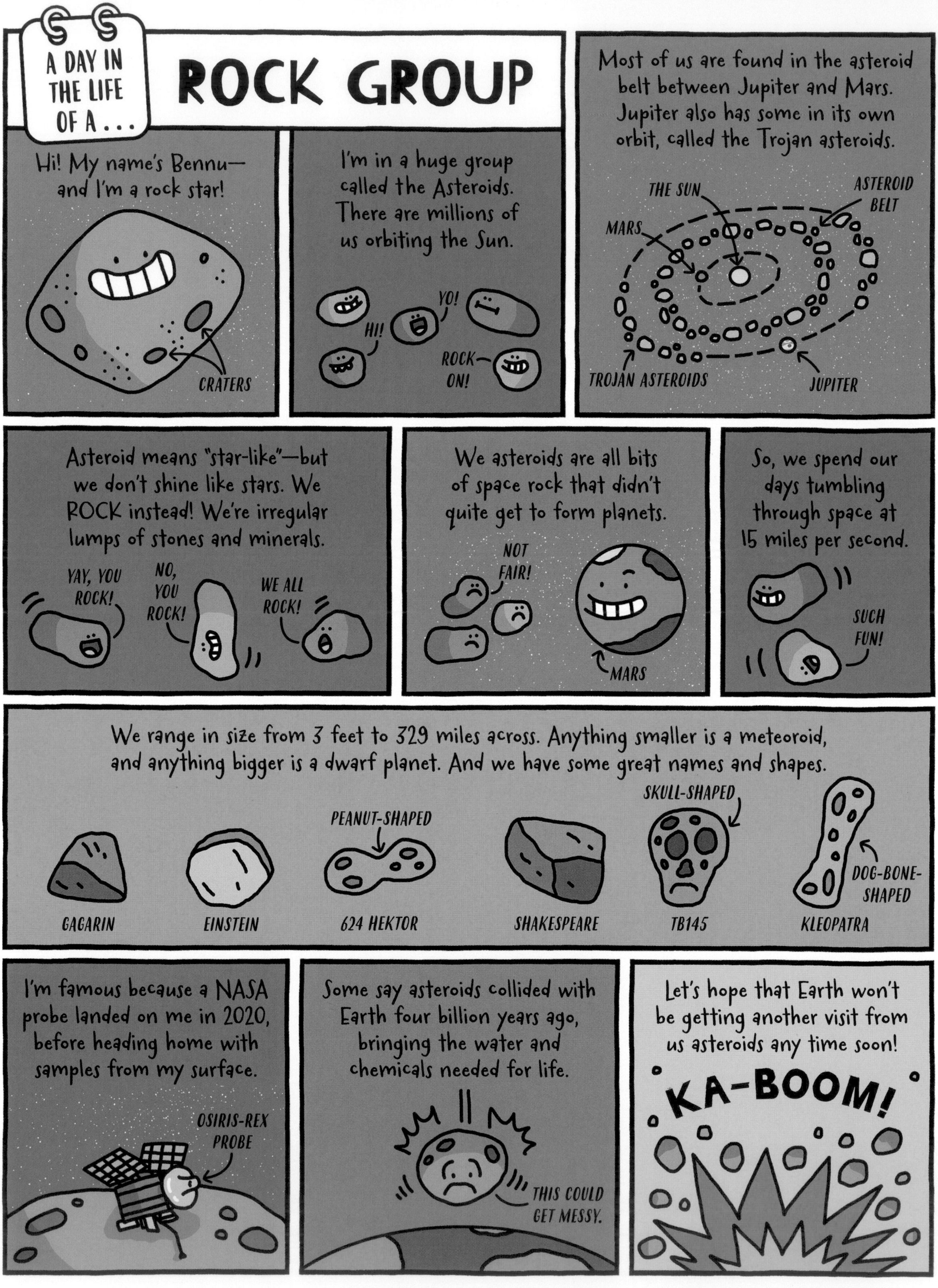

A DAY IN THE LIFE OF A . . .
ROCK GROUP
Hi! My name's Bennu—and I'm a rock star!
CRATERS
I'm in a huge group called the Asteroids. There are millions of us orbiting the Sun.
YO!
HI!
ROCK—ON!
Most of us are found in the asteroid belt between Jupiter and Mars. Jupiter also has some in its own orbit, called the Trojan asteroids.
THE SUN
ASTEROID BELT
MARS
TROJAN ASTEROIDS
JUPITER
Asteroid means "star-like"—but we don't shine like stars. We ROCK instead! We're irregular lumps of stones and minerals.
YAY, YOU ROCK!
NO, YOU ROCK!
WE ALL ROCK!
We asteroids are all bits of space rock that didn't quite get to form planets.
NOT FAIR!
MARS
So, we spend our days tumbling through space at 15 miles per second.
SUCH FUN!
We range in size from 3 feet to 329 miles across. Anything smaller is a meteoroid, and anything bigger is a dwarf planet. And we have some great names and shapes.
PEANUT-SHAPED
SKULL-SHAPED
DOG-BONE-SHAPED
GAGARIN
EINSTEIN
624 HEKTOR
SHAKESPEARE
TB145
KLEOPATRA
I'm famous because a NASA probe landed on me in 2020, before heading home with samples from my surface.
OSIRIS-REX PROBE
Some say asteroids collided with Earth four billion years ago, bringing the water and chemicals needed for life.
THIS COULD GET MESSY.
Let's hope that Earth won't be getting another visit from us asteroids any time soon!
KA-BOOM!

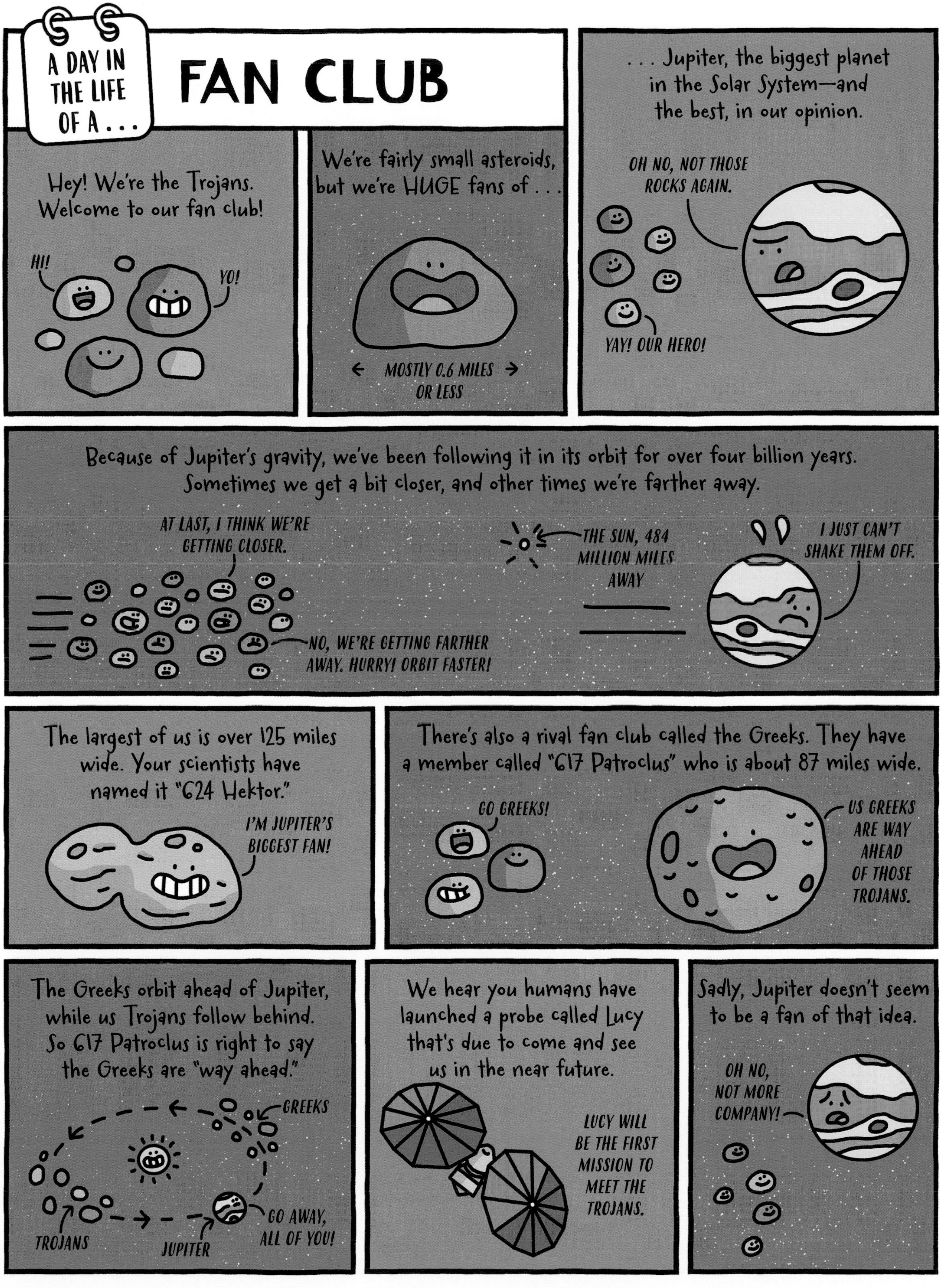

A DAY IN THE LIFE OF A . . .
FAN CLUB
Hey! We're the Trojans. Welcome to our fan club!
HI!
YO!
We're fairly small asteroids, but we're HUGE fans of . . .
MOSTLY 0.6 MILES OR LESS
. . . Jupiter, the biggest planet in the Solar System—and the best, in our opinion.
OH NO, NOT THOSE ROCKS AGAIN.
YAY! OUR HERO!
Because of Jupiter's gravity, we've been following it in its orbit for over four billion years. Sometimes we get a bit closer, and other times we're farther away.
AT LAST, I THINK WE'RE GETTING CLOSER.
NO, WE'RE GETTING FARTHER AWAY. HURRY! ORBIT FASTER!
THE SUN, 484 MILLION MILES AWAY
I JUST CAN'T SHAKE THEM OFF.
The largest of us is over 125 miles wide. Your scientists have named it "624 Hektor."
I'M JUPITER'S BIGGEST FAN!
There's also a rival fan club called the Greeks. They have a member called "617 Patroclus" who is about 87 miles wide.
GO GREEKS!
US GREEKS ARE WAY AHEAD OF THOSE TROJANS.
The Greeks orbit ahead of Jupiter, while us Trojans follow behind. So 617 Patroclus is right to say the Greeks are "way ahead."
GREEKS
TROJANS
JUPITER
GO AWAY, ALL OF YOU!
We hear you humans have launched a probe called Lucy that's due to come and see us in the near future.
LUCY WILL BE THE FIRST MISSION TO MEET THE TROJANS.
Sadly, Jupiter doesn't seem to be a fan of that idea.
OH NO, NOT MORE COMPANY!

The secret diary of a
PLANETARY STORM

The diary of "Norm," a giant storm on the surface of Jupiter (also known as its Great Red Spot)

THAT'S ME IN THE MIDDLE. HI!

DAY 1

It's great fun being a giant red spot. Every day I have a blast (literally!), even though a day on Jupiter only lasts ten Earth hours. Days here are so short because Jupiter spins really quickly, despite being the largest planet in the Solar System. I'm bigger than Earth, too (you could fit over a thousand Earths inside Jupiter itself). In fact, Jupiter is more than twice as heavy as all seven other planets combined, even though it's made mostly of hydrogen gas—the lightest element there is.

DAY 2

Another whirlwind day spent spinning my storm clouds super-fast over the planet. I travel between the brownish "belts" and the whiteish "zones" you can see from space. It takes me 14 Jupiter days to complete a full circuit. On we go!

HERE I AM!

DAY 3

Fancied a change, so today I went from brick red to a nice salmon pink. (Sometimes I go gray or white as well.) No one on Earth knows what causes my color—and I'm not going to tell them. This is a secret diary after all.

BRICK RED

SCARLET

SALMON PINK

GRAY

BEFORE

DAY 4

Hard to believe I've been raging for at least a couple of centuries now. That makes me the oldest storm in the Solar System! Earth people first, er, "spotted" me back in the 1830s, when I was more oval in shape. Nowadays, I'm a bit smaller and rounder—but I'm still great! Sometimes I wish I was warmer, though. It was −220°F on Jupiter today, because we're so far from the Sun. Brr!

NOW

DAY 14

Well, that's another lap of the planet completed. I'm pretty speedy compared to Jupiter itself, which takes 12 Earth years to orbit the Sun. Still, being so big, I bet we look nice and bright in the night sky above Earth. People can probably even see a few of our 79 moons if they use binoculars or a telescope. Anyway, must get back to my raging. Here's to the next 200 years!

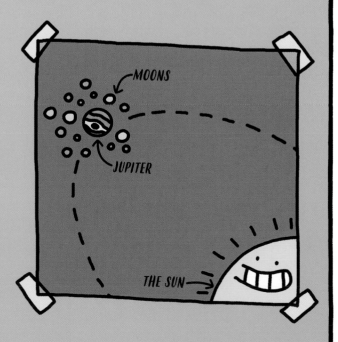
MOONS
JUPITER
THE SUN

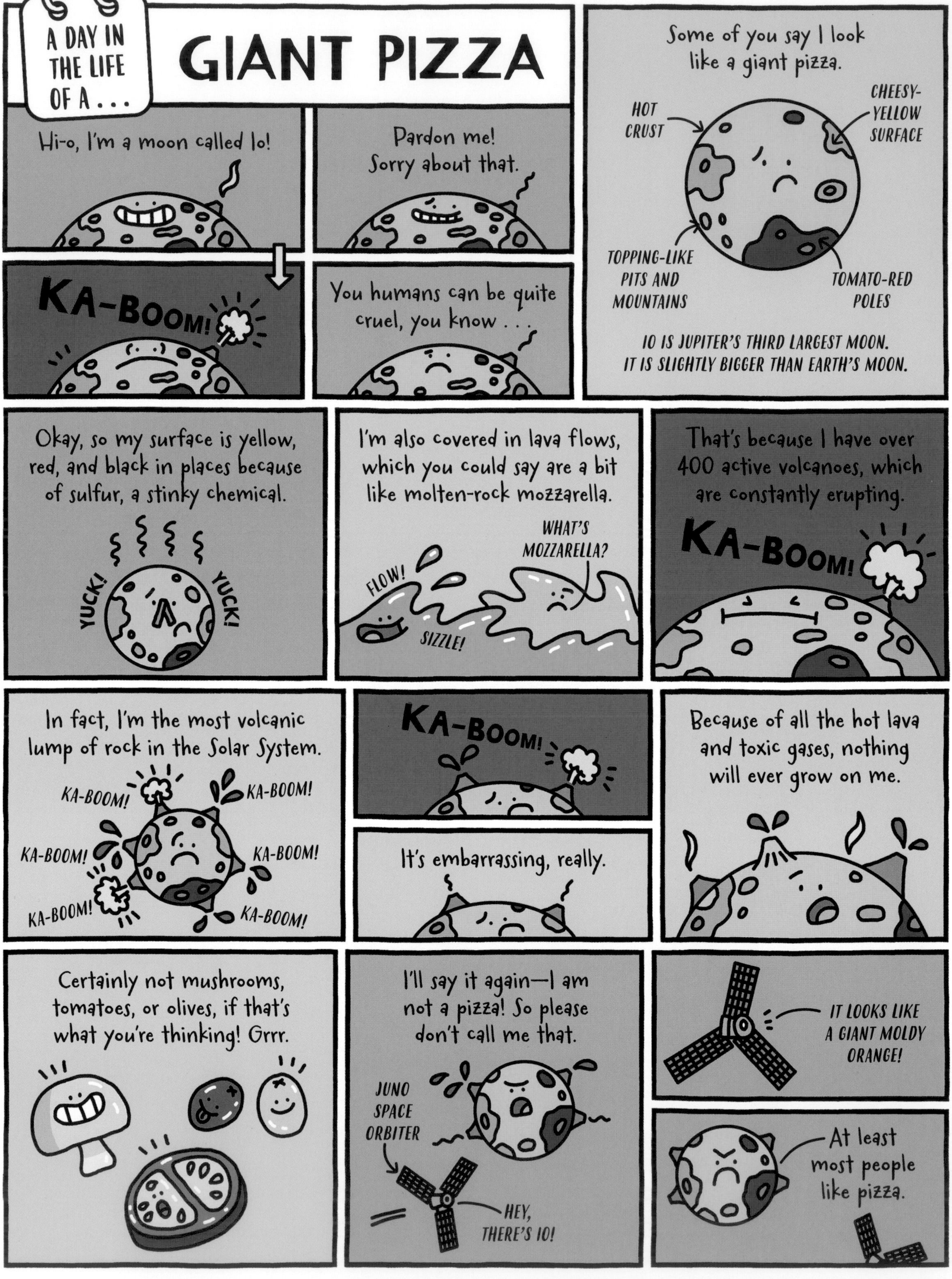
A DAY IN THE LIFE OF A . . .
GIANT PIZZA
Hi-o, I'm a moon called Io!
Pardon me! Sorry about that.
KA-BOOM!
You humans can be quite cruel, you know . . .
Some of you say I look like a giant pizza.
HOT CRUST
CHEESY-YELLOW SURFACE
TOPPING-LIKE PITS AND MOUNTAINS
TOMATO-RED POLES
IO IS JUPITER'S THIRD LARGEST MOON. IT IS SLIGHTLY BIGGER THAN EARTH'S MOON.
Okay, so my surface is yellow, red, and black in places because of sulfur, a stinky chemical.
YUCK! YUCK!
I'm also covered in lava flows, which you could say are a bit like molten-rock mozzarella.
FLOW!
WHAT'S MOZZARELLA?
SIZZLE!
That's because I have over 400 active volcanoes, which are constantly erupting.
KA-BOOM!
In fact, I'm the most volcanic lump of rock in the Solar System.
KA-BOOM!
KA-BOOM!
KA-BOOM!
KA-BOOM!
KA-BOOM!
KA-BOOM!
KA-BOOM!
It's embarrassing, really.
Because of all the hot lava and toxic gases, nothing will ever grow on me.
Certainly not mushrooms, tomatoes, or olives, if that's what you're thinking! Grrr.
I'll say it again—I am not a pizza! So please don't call me that.
JUNO SPACE ORBITER
HEY, THERE'S IO!
IT LOOKS LIKE A GIANT MOLDY ORANGE!
At least most people like pizza.

THE BIGGER PICTURE

MOON MADNESS

Jupiter is so huge that its gravity has trapped at least 79 moons in orbit around it. The four largest (Ganymede, Callisto, Io, and Europa) are called Galilean moons after Galileo Galilei, the Italian astronomer who discovered them in 1610. They're so big that you can spot them yourself at night with just a pair of binoculars!

ICE MAIDEN

A vast ocean, with more water than exists on Earth, is thought to lie beneath Europa's icy crust. Could it contain life?

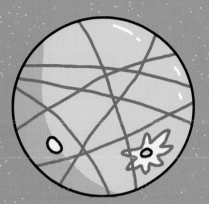

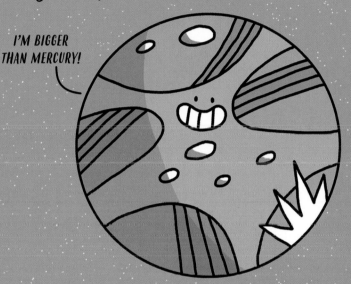

I'M BIGGER THAN MERCURY!

JAILED BY JUPITER

Ganymede is the largest moon in the Solar System. It's so big that it could be a planet itself, but because it orbits another planet (instead of the Sun), it's stuck with its moon status.

UNDER FIRE

Callisto has been bombarded by so many meteorites over the years that it's now the most cratered object in the Solar System.

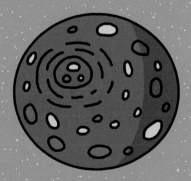

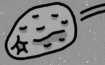

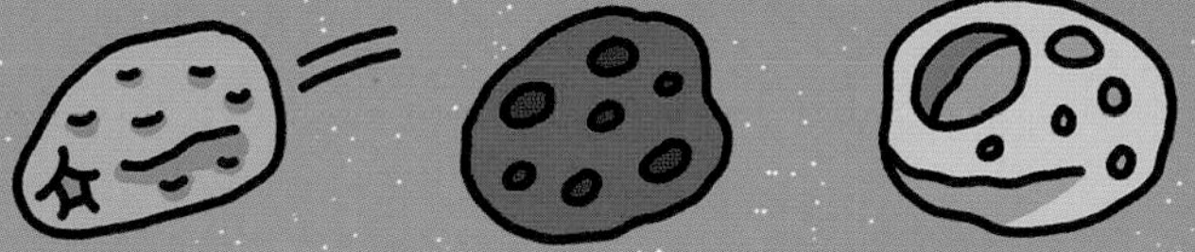

METIS IS JUPITER'S SPEEDIEST MOON.

AMALTHEA IS BRIGHT RED.

THEBE HAS A HUGE CRATER.

MINI-MOONS

Jupiter has so many moons that some of the tinier ones haven't even been named.

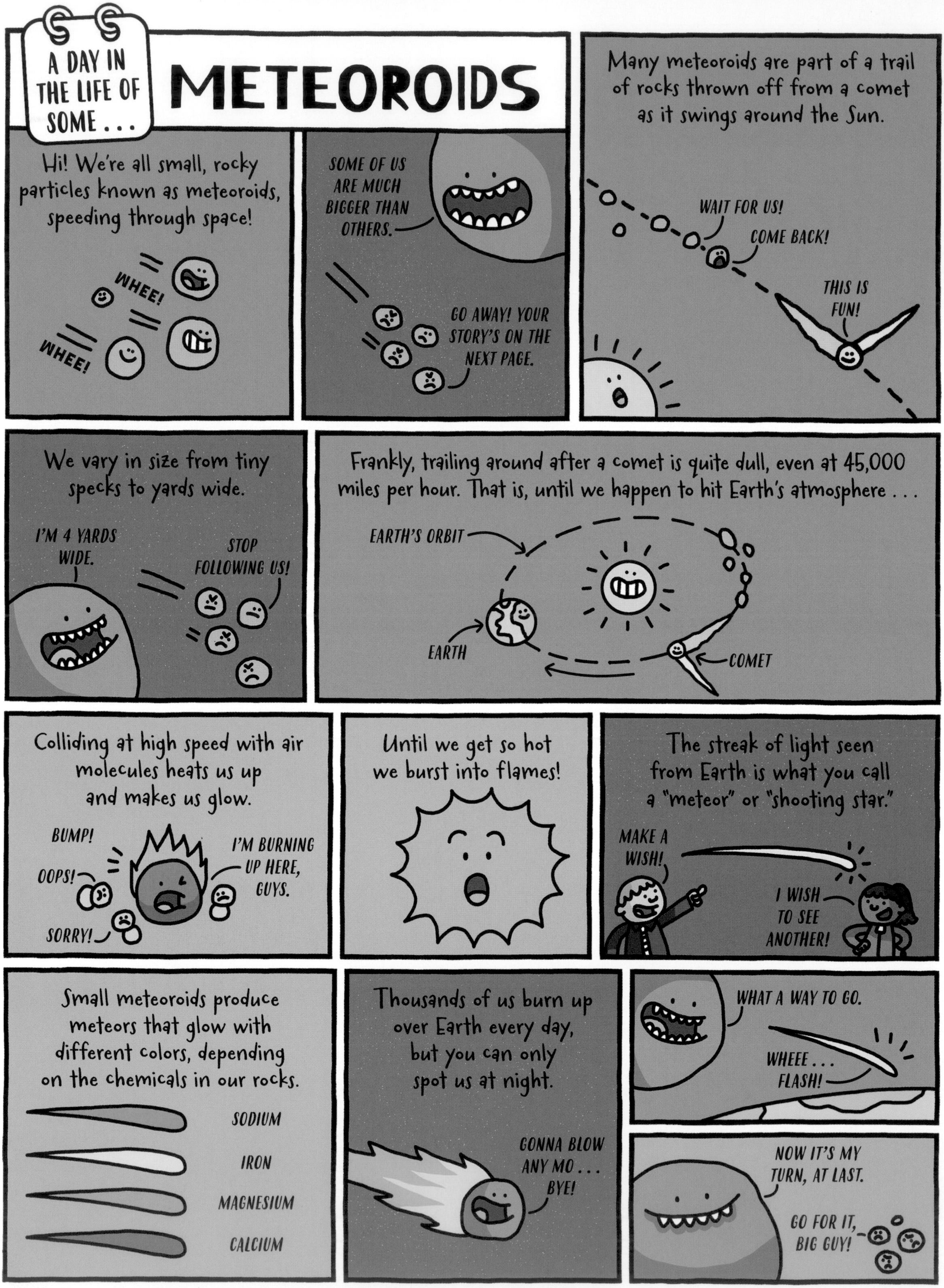
A DAY IN THE LIFE OF SOME . . .
METEOROIDS
Hi! We're all small, rocky particles known as meteoroids, speeding through space!
WHEE!
WHEE!
SOME OF US ARE MUCH BIGGER THAN OTHERS.
GO AWAY! YOUR STORY'S ON THE NEXT PAGE.
Many meteoroids are part of a trail of rocks thrown off from a comet as it swings around the Sun.
WAIT FOR US!
COME BACK!
THIS IS FUN!
We vary in size from tiny specks to yards wide.
I'M 4 YARDS WIDE.
STOP FOLLOWING US!
Frankly, trailing around after a comet is quite dull, even at 45,000 miles per hour. That is, until we happen to hit Earth's atmosphere . . .
EARTH'S ORBIT
EARTH
COMET
Colliding at high speed with air molecules heats us up and makes us glow.
BUMP!
OOPS!
SORRY!
I'M BURNING UP HERE, GUYS.
Until we get so hot we burst into flames!
The streak of light seen from Earth is what you call a "meteor" or "shooting star."
MAKE A WISH!
I WISH TO SEE ANOTHER!
Small meteoroids produce meteors that glow with different colors, depending on the chemicals in our rocks.
SODIUM
IRON
MAGNESIUM
CALCIUM
Thousands of us burn up over Earth every day, but you can only spot us at night.
GONNA BLOW ANY MO . . . BYE!
WHAT A WAY TO GO.
WHEEE . . . FLASH!
NOW IT'S MY TURN, AT LAST.
GO FOR IT, BIG GUY!

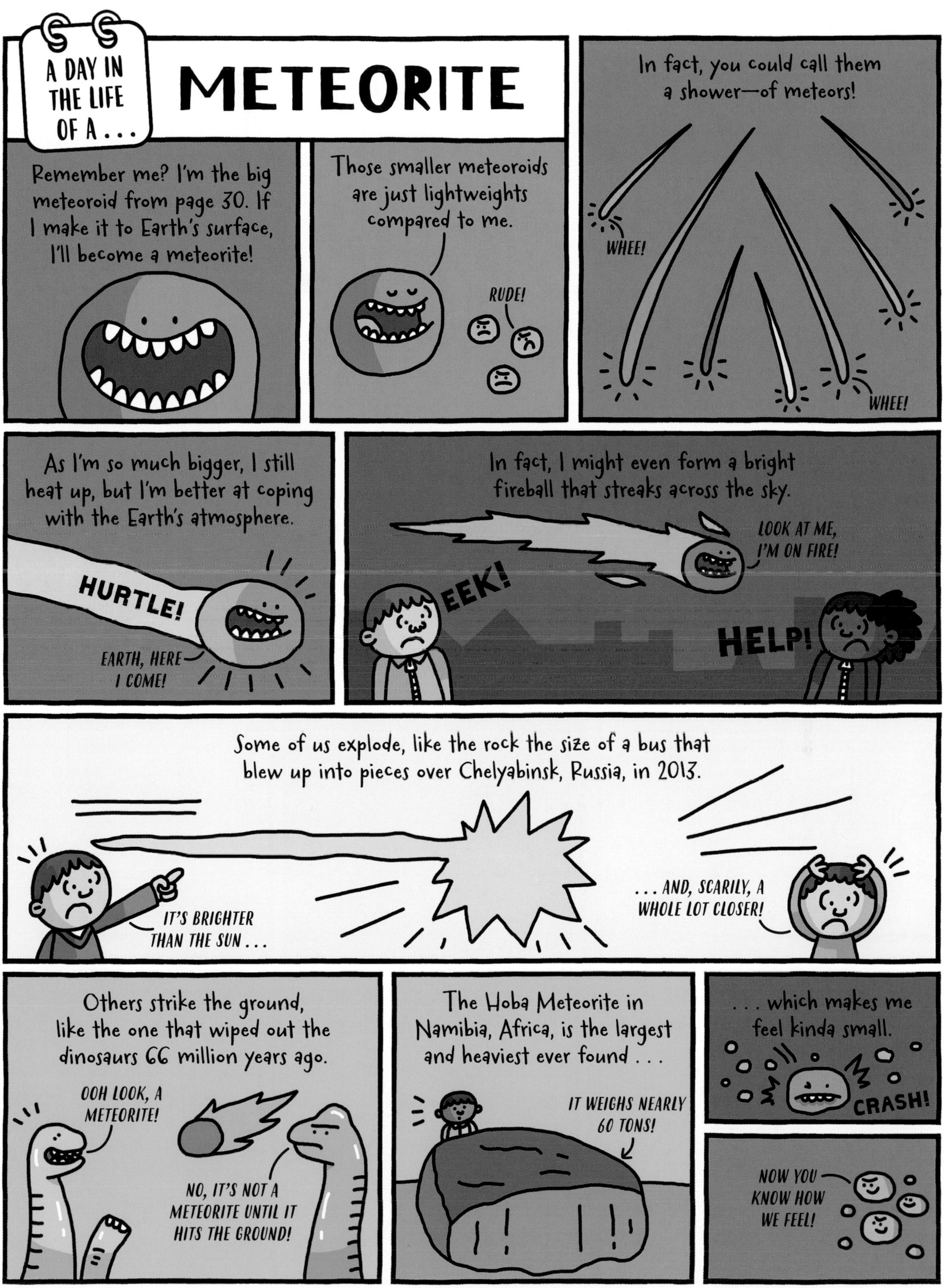
A DAY IN THE LIFE OF A . . .
METEORITE
Remember me? I'm the big meteoroid from page 30. If I make it to Earth's surface, I'll become a meteorite!
Those smaller meteoroids are just lightweights compared to me.
RUDE!
In fact, you could call them a shower—of meteors!
WHEE!
WHEE!
As I'm so much bigger, I still heat up, but I'm better at coping with the Earth's atmosphere.
HURTLE!
EARTH, HERE I COME!
In fact, I might even form a bright fireball that streaks across the sky.
LOOK AT ME, I'M ON FIRE!
EEK!
HELP!
Some of us explode, like the rock the size of a bus that blew up into pieces over Chelyabinsk, Russia, in 2013.
IT'S BRIGHTER THAN THE SUN . . .
. . . AND, SCARILY, A WHOLE LOT CLOSER!
Others strike the ground, like the one that wiped out the dinosaurs 66 million years ago.
OOH LOOK, A METEORITE!
NO, IT'S NOT A METEORITE UNTIL IT HITS THE GROUND!
The Hoba Meteorite in Namibia, Africa, is the largest and heaviest ever found . . .
IT WEIGHS NEARLY 60 TONS!
. . . which makes me feel kinda small.
CRASH!
NOW YOU KNOW HOW WE FEEL!

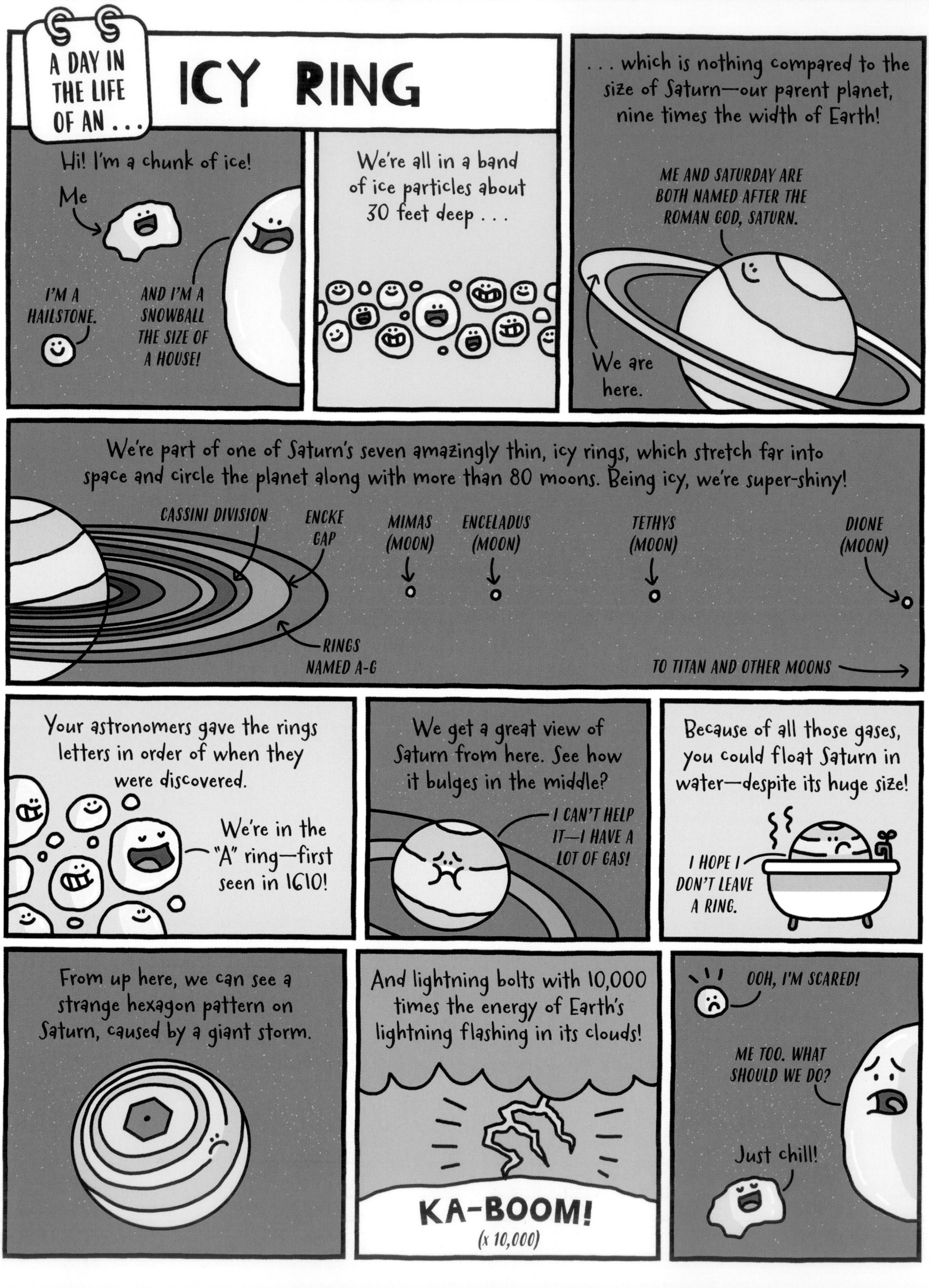

A DAY IN THE LIFE OF AN . . .
ICY RING
Hi! I'm a chunk of ice!
Me
I'M A HAILSTONE.
AND I'M A SNOWBALL THE SIZE OF A HOUSE!
We're all in a band of ice particles about 30 feet deep . . .
. . . which is nothing compared to the size of Saturn—our parent planet, nine times the width of Earth!
ME AND SATURDAY ARE BOTH NAMED AFTER THE ROMAN GOD, SATURN.
We are here.
We're part of one of Saturn's seven amazingly thin, icy rings, which stretch far into space and circle the planet along with more than 80 moons. Being icy, we're super-shiny!
CASSINI DIVISION
ENCKE GAP
MIMAS (MOON)
ENCELADUS (MOON)
TETHYS (MOON)
DIONE (MOON)
RINGS NAMED A–G
TO TITAN AND OTHER MOONS
Your astronomers gave the rings letters in order of when they were discovered.
We're in the "A" ring—first seen in 1610!
We get a great view of Saturn from here. See how it bulges in the middle?
I CAN'T HELP IT—I HAVE A LOT OF GAS!
Because of all those gases, you could float Saturn in water—despite its huge size!
I HOPE I DON'T LEAVE A RING.
From up here, we can see a strange hexagon pattern on Saturn, caused by a giant storm.
And lightning bolts with 10,000 times the energy of Earth's lightning flashing in its clouds!
KA-BOOM!
(x 10,000)
OOH, I'M SCARED!
ME TOO. WHAT SHOULD WE DO?
Just chill!

THE BIGGER PICTURE

MANY MOONS

Saturn has more than 80 known moons, as well as lots of smaller "moonlets." Many remain unnamed, while others are some of the most intriguing objects in the Solar System—such as the five shown here:

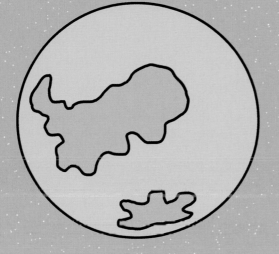

TITAN-IC!

Titan is Saturn's largest moon. It's even greater in size than the planet Mercury! It accounts for 96 percent of the mass of objects orbiting Saturn, and may have a saltwater ocean hidden under its surface. Could it contain life?

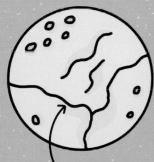

THE CRACKS IN ENCELADUS'S SOUTH POLAR REGION ARE NICKNAMED "TIGER STRIPES."

SHINE ON

Enceladus is the shiniest object in the Solar System, due to its covering of ice. It's thought that it may also have a hidden ocean.

HERSCHEL CRATER

DEATH STAR-A-LIKE?

Mimas's large crater makes it look like the Death Star from Star Wars, but the crater wasn't discovered until three years after the film came out.

THROW A WOBBLER

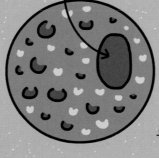

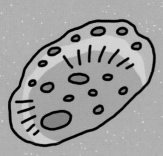

Hyperion is a heavily cratered moon shaped like a bath sponge. It's known for its odd wobbling movement as it orbits Saturn.

PAN-TASTIC

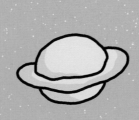

Pan is a small "shepherd moon" whose orbit helps the ice in the "A" ring to keep its shape.

THE BIGGER PICTURE

A DIFFERENT SPIN

Uranus is a giant icy ball, and the only planet in the Solar System that spins on its side. It's visible to the naked eye—but only just!

WHY SO BLUE?

Uranus's atmosphere is mostly hydrogen and helium, plus a small amount of methane. The methane is what gives the planet its blue-green color.

GIVE US A RING

Uranus's 13 dark rings are so faint that they weren't spotted until 1977—nearly 200 years after the planet's discovery in 1781.

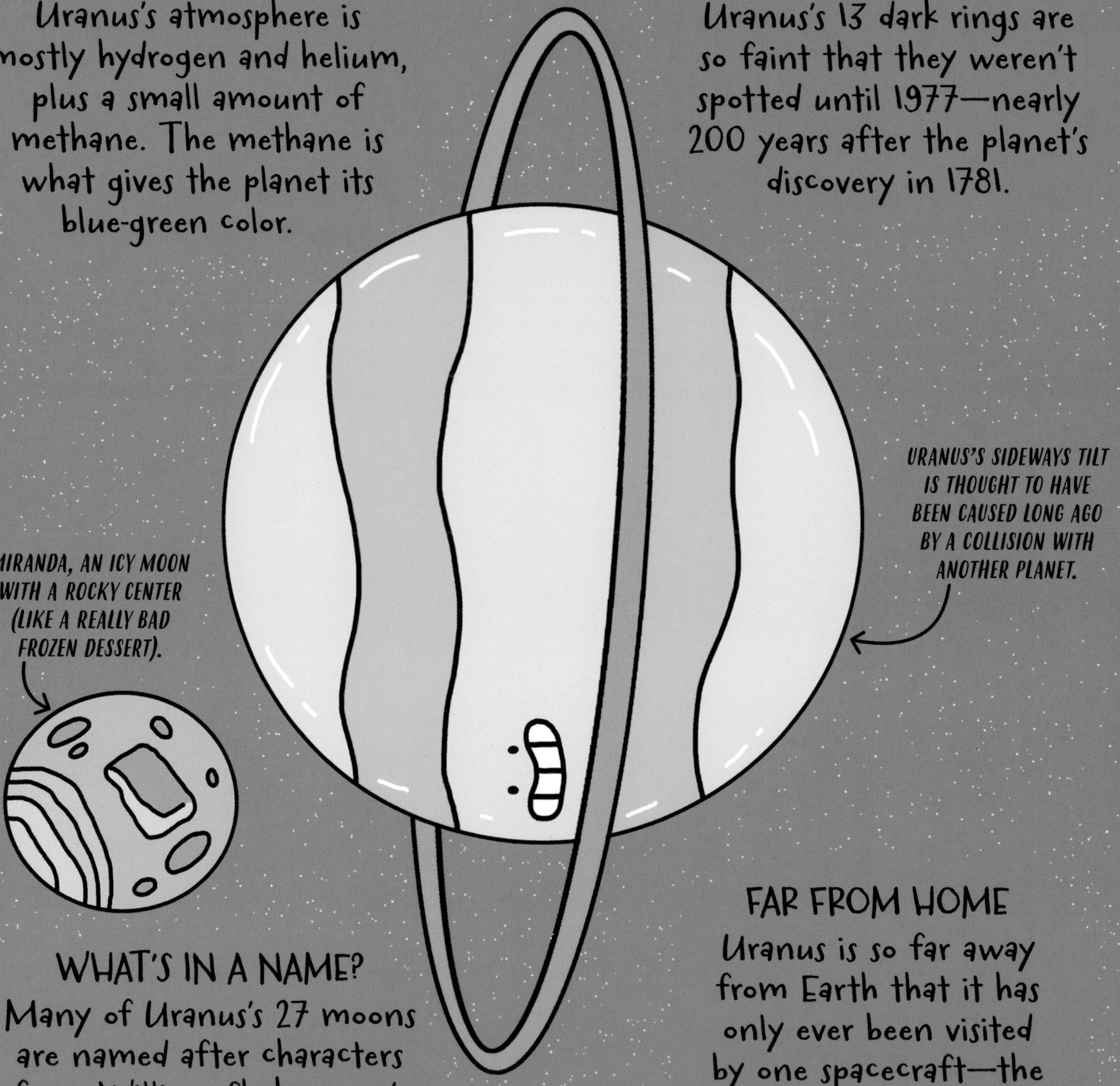

URANUS'S SIDEWAYS TILT IS THOUGHT TO HAVE BEEN CAUSED LONG AGO BY A COLLISION WITH ANOTHER PLANET.
MIRANDA, AN ICY MOON WITH A ROCKY CENTER (LIKE A REALLY BAD FROZEN DESSERT).

WHAT'S IN A NAME?

Many of Uranus's 27 moons are named after characters from William Shakespeare's plays, including Juliet, Oberon, Puck, and Miranda.

FAR FROM HOME

Uranus is so far away from Earth that it has only ever been visited by one spacecraft—the Voyager 2 probe in 1986.

THE BIGGER PICTURE

LONELY PLANET

At 2.8 billion miles from the Sun, Neptune is the eighth and most distant planet in the Solar System. This ice giant's orbit is so huge that it lasts 165 Earth years. Neptune's distance from the Sun also makes it the Solar System's coldest planet, at −328°F.

BLUE TOO

Like Uranus, Neptune's atmosphere contains the gas methane, making it appear eerily blue.

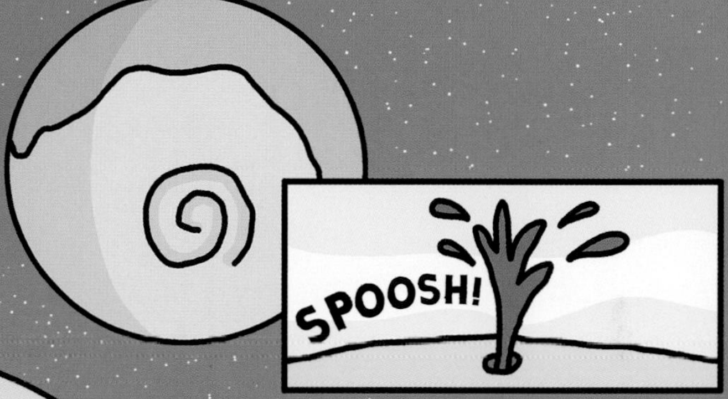
SPOOSH!

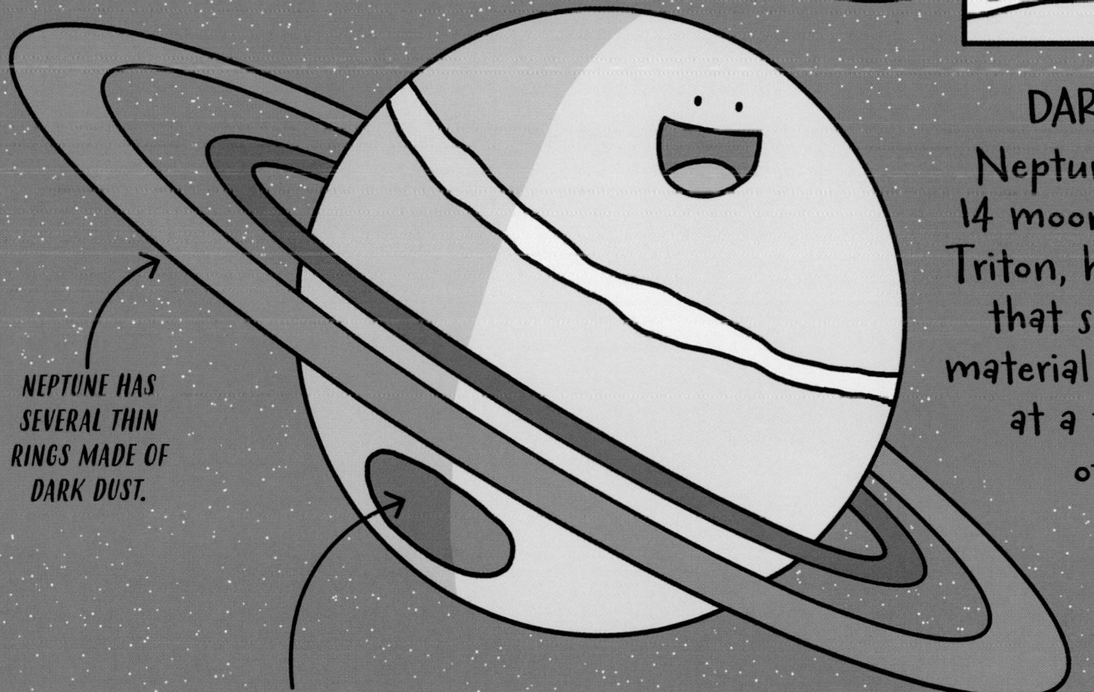

NEPTUNE HAS SEVERAL THIN RINGS MADE OF DARK DUST.

DARK STREAKS

Neptune has at least 14 moons. The largest, Triton, has huge geysers that shoot dark, icy material over its surface at a temperature of −391°F.

STORM WARNING

Neptune has the fastest winds in the Solar System, at over 1,200 miles per hour. Its "Great Dark Spot" of 1989 was a raging storm the size of Earth.

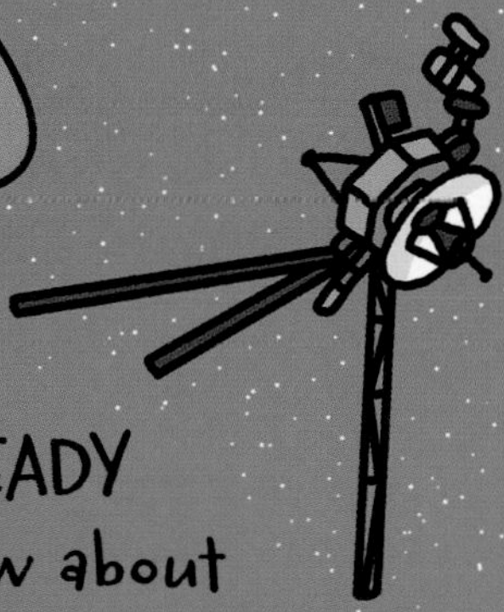

MISSING YOU ALREADY

Most of what we know about Neptune comes from Voyager 2, which flew past the planet in 1989 before disappearing out of the Solar System forever.

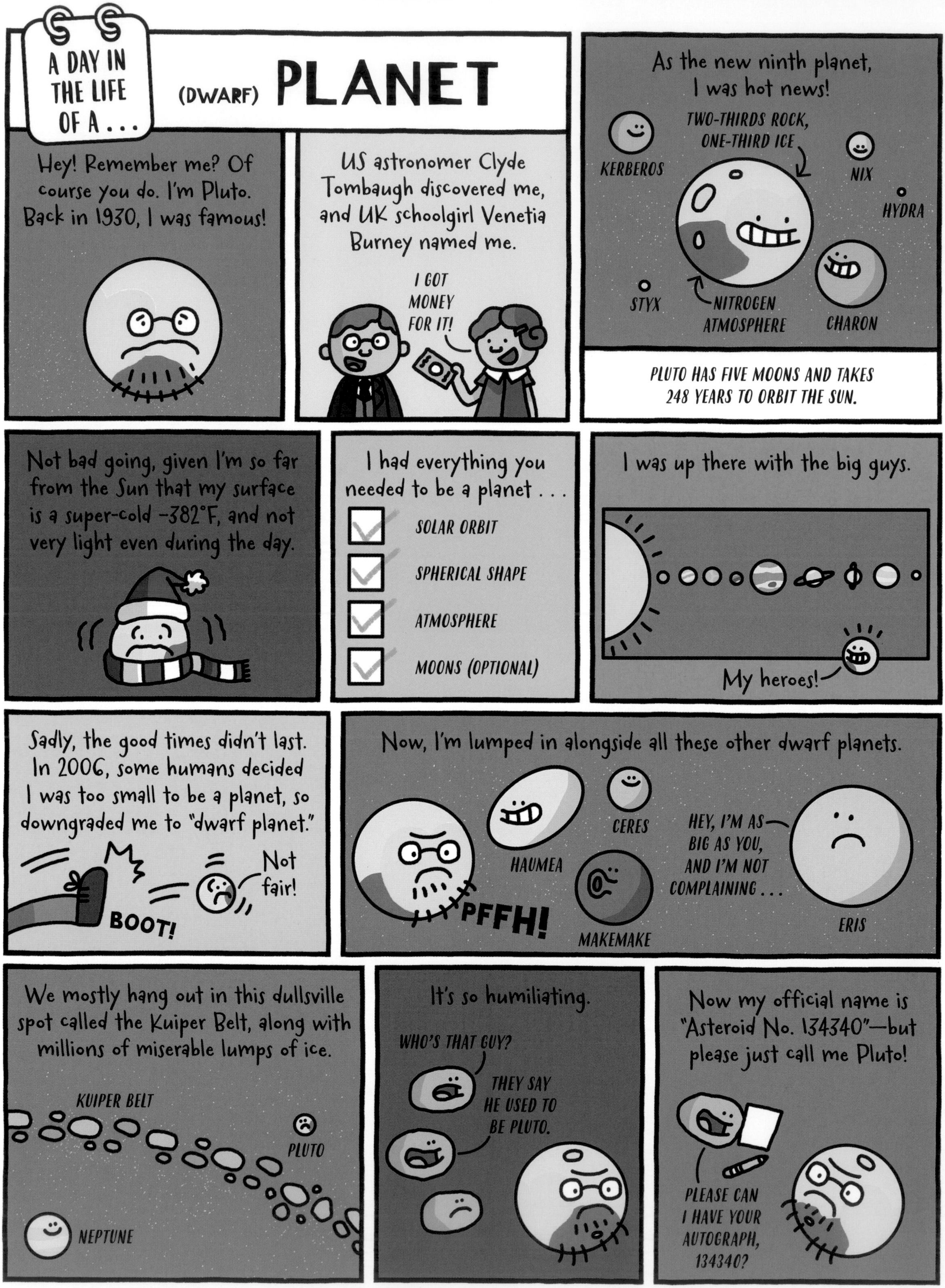
A DAY IN THE LIFE OF A . . .
(DWARF) PLANET
Hey! Remember me? Of course you do. I'm Pluto. Back in 1930, I was famous!
US astronomer Clyde Tombaugh discovered me, and UK schoolgirl Venetia Burney named me.
I GOT MONEY FOR IT!
As the new ninth planet, I was hot news!
TWO-THIRDS ROCK, ONE-THIRD ICE
KERBEROS
NIX
HYDRA
STYX
NITROGEN ATMOSPHERE
CHARON
PLUTO HAS FIVE MOONS AND TAKES 248 YEARS TO ORBIT THE SUN.
Not bad going, given I'm so far from the Sun that my surface is a super-cold -382°F, and not very light even during the day.
I had everything you needed to be a planet . . .
SOLAR ORBIT
SPHERICAL SHAPE
ATMOSPHERE
MOONS (OPTIONAL)
I was up there with the big guys.
My heroes!
Sadly, the good times didn't last. In 2006, some humans decided I was too small to be a planet, so downgraded me to "dwarf planet."
BOOT!
Not fair!
Now, I'm lumped in alongside all these other dwarf planets.
HAUMEA
CERES
MAKEMAKE
PFFH!
HEY, I'M AS BIG AS YOU, AND I'M NOT COMPLAINING . . .
ERIS
We mostly hang out in this dullsville spot called the Kuiper Belt, along with millions of miserable lumps of ice.
KUIPER BELT
PLUTO
NEPTUNE
It's so humiliating.
WHO'S THAT GUY?
THEY SAY HE USED TO BE PLUTO.
Now my official name is "Asteroid No. 134340"—but please just call me Pluto!
PLEASE CAN I HAVE YOUR AUTOGRAPH, 134340?

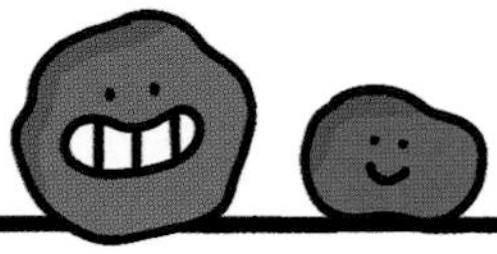

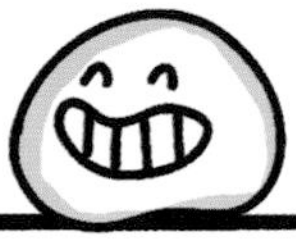

OUTER SPACE

Venture beyond Earth's Solar System, and you'll find comets and constellations, nebulae and neutron stars, plus most of the biggest mysteries in the universe.

Despite space probes and telescopes, human knowledge of what goes on in outer space remains full of holes—many of them black ones, sucking in everything that gets too close. Grab hold of something if you can . . . you're going in!

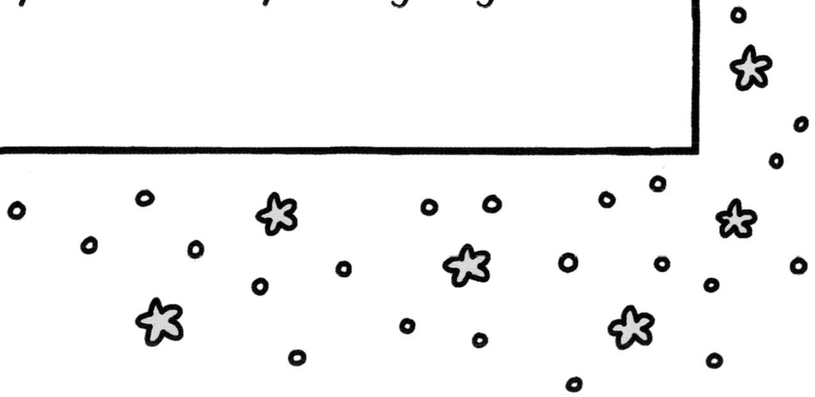

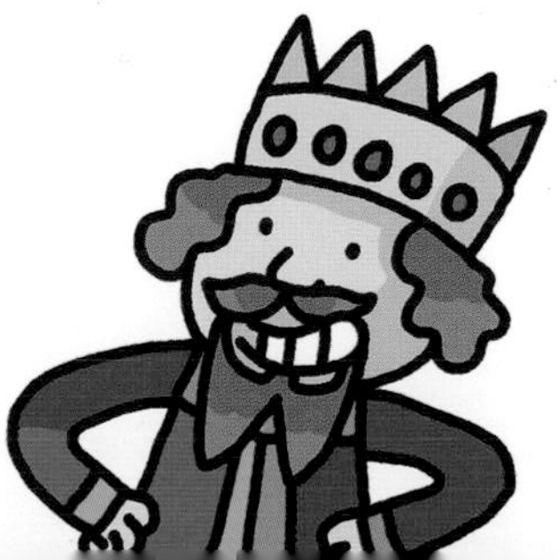

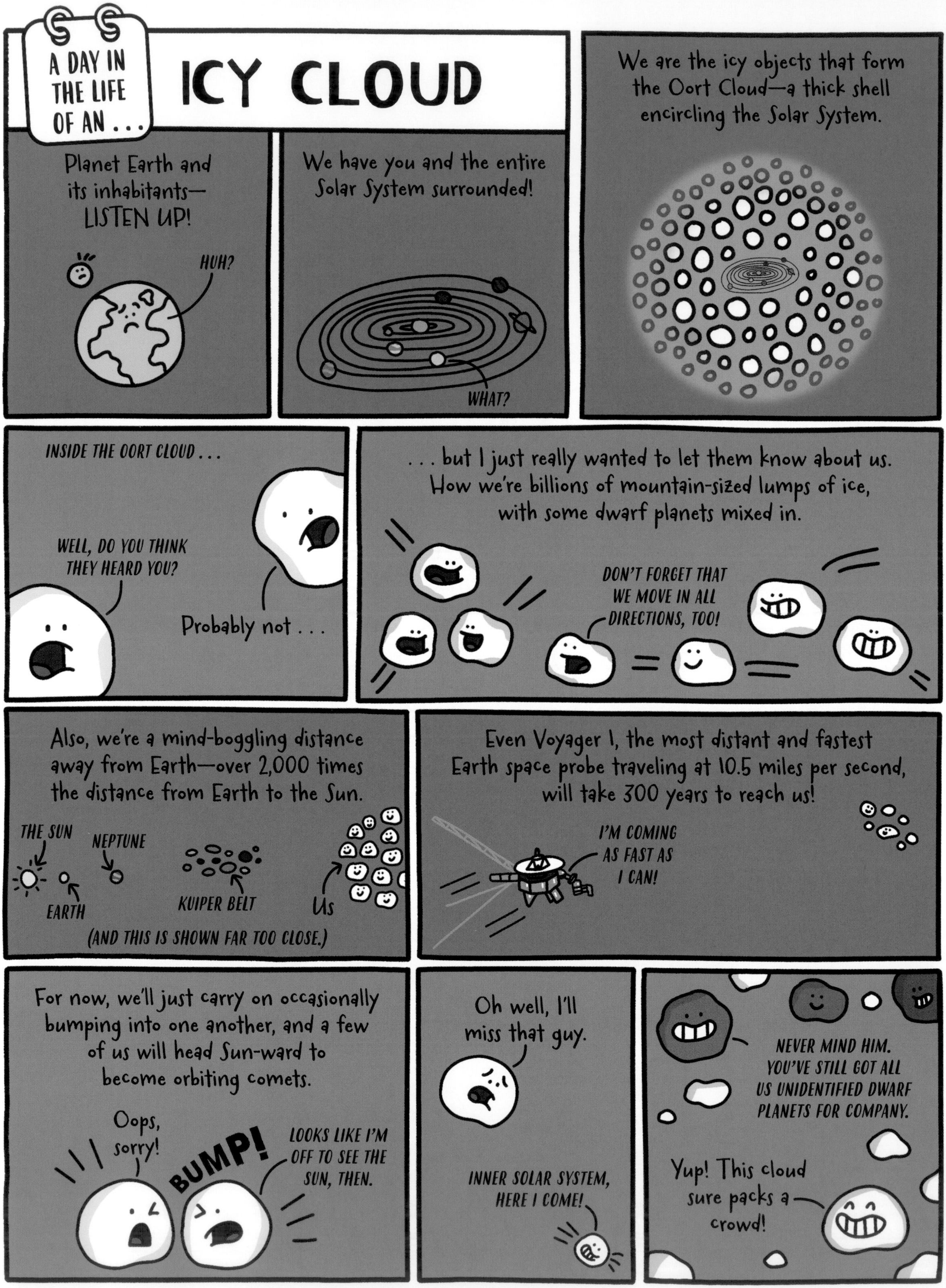
A DAY IN THE LIFE OF AN . . .
ICY CLOUD
Planet Earth and its inhabitants—LISTEN UP!
HUH?
We have you and the entire Solar System surrounded!
WHAT?
We are the icy objects that form the Oort Cloud—a thick shell encircling the Solar System.
INSIDE THE OORT CLOUD . . .
WELL, DO YOU THINK THEY HEARD YOU?
Probably not . . .
. . . but I just really wanted to let them know about us. How we're billions of mountain-sized lumps of ice, with some dwarf planets mixed in.
DON'T FORGET THAT WE MOVE IN ALL DIRECTIONS, TOO!
Also, we're a mind-boggling distance away from Earth—over 2,000 times the distance from Earth to the Sun.
THE SUN
NEPTUNE
EARTH
KUIPER BELT
Us
(AND THIS IS SHOWN FAR TOO CLOSE.)
Even Voyager 1, the most distant and fastest Earth space probe traveling at 10.5 miles per second, will take 300 years to reach us!
I'M COMING AS FAST AS I CAN!
For now, we'll just carry on occasionally bumping into one another, and a few of us will head Sun-ward to become orbiting comets.
Oops, sorry!
BUMP!
LOOKS LIKE I'M OFF TO SEE THE SUN, THEN.
Oh well, I'll miss that guy.
INNER SOLAR SYSTEM, HERE I COME!
NEVER MIND HIM. YOU'VE STILL GOT ALL US UNIDENTIFIED DWARF PLANETS FOR COMPANY.
Yup! This cloud sure packs a crowd!

THE BIGGER PICTURE

SNOWBALL FLIGHT

Early humans considered comets to be mysterious, frightening objects moving across the sky. Today, we know that they are giant, dirty snowballs made of frozen gases, rock, and dust from the formation of the Solar System. If a comet's orbit brings it close enough to the Sun, it develops a "tail" that can be bright enough to be seen from Earth, even during the day!

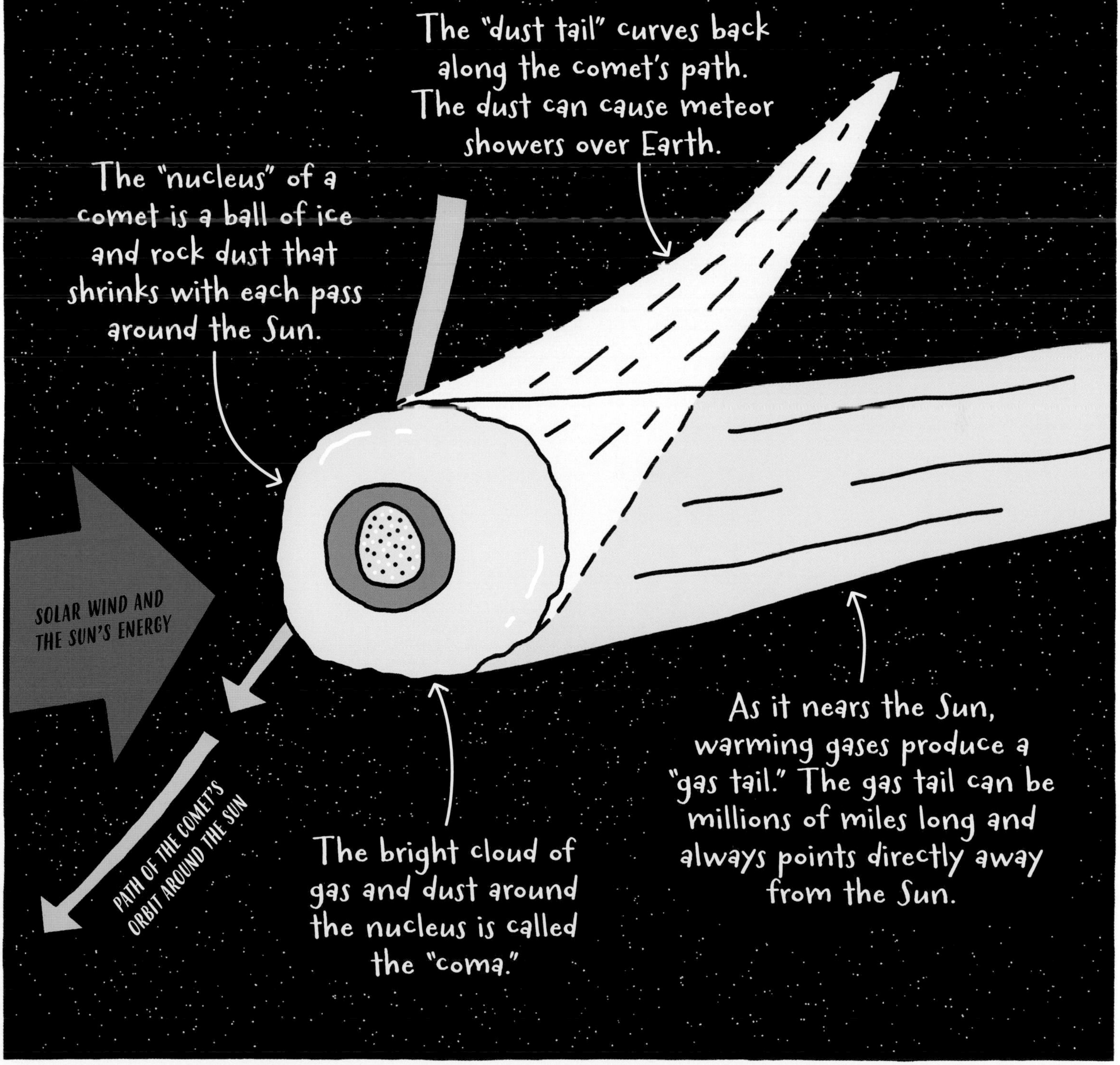

The "dust tail" curves back along the comet's path. The dust can cause meteor showers over Earth.
The "nucleus" of a comet is a ball of ice and rock dust that shrinks with each pass around the Sun.
SOLAR WIND AND THE SUN'S ENERGY
PATH OF THE COMET'S ORBIT AROUND THE SUN
The bright cloud of gas and dust around the nucleus is called the "coma."
As it nears the Sun, warming gases produce a "gas tail." The gas tail can be millions of miles long and always points directly away from the Sun.

The secret diary of a

HAIRY STAR

Extracts from the diary of "Hal," a comet* visible from Earth every 75–76 years

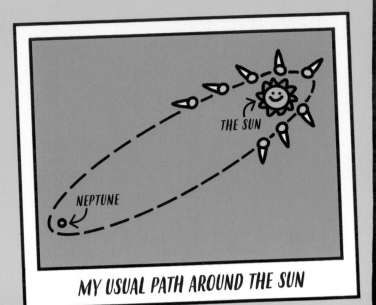

MY USUAL PATH AROUND THE SUN

FEBRUARY 1066

Well, after several thousand years swinging out into space beyond Neptune and then back around the Sun, I've decided to keep a diary. Sadly, some people down on Earth seem to think spotting me, as I pass close by, is a bad omen. In England, their new king, Harold, is particularly upset about seeing me, as he is preparing to face a likely invasion led by a Norman duke called William. I guess I'll find out what happened when I come back in at least 75 years' time!

SEPTEMBER 1222

Oops! I seem to have missed a diary entry—but I can tell you that Harold lost that battle. Still, it was a good result for me. William became King William I, and I was included in a lovely piece of art called the Bayeux Tapestry. It shows me passing right over Harold's head! Isn't that great? I just wish people down there would stop describing me as a "hairy star," though.

40

*SEE PAGE 39.

MAY 1759

At last, I've been given a proper name! A few years ago, a clever British astronomer called Edmond Halley realized that I'm the same "hairy star" passing over Earth roughly every 75–76 years. As a result, I was named after him and I'm now known as "Halley's Comet."

EDMOND HALLEY

APRIL 1910

Those wild Earth people! This time they have realized that their planet will pass through my tail (well, it is 30 million miles long!) and some of them are worried that I'll poison them! Some people are even buying gas masks and "anti-comet" pills and umbrellas. If that's what they think, I'm not sure it's worth coming back!

LOOK OUT BELOW!

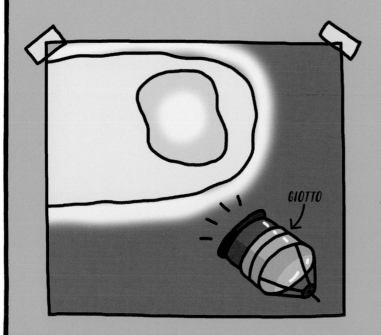

GIOTTO

MARCH 1986

Wow! What a reception! A fleet of spacecraft from Japan, Europe, the USA, the USSR, and others have come to meet me this time. A space probe called Giotto has shown my core to be a peanut-shaped lump about 9.3 miles long, so now they're calling me a "dirty snowball." I think I preferred "hairy star."

Bye for now—see you in 2061!

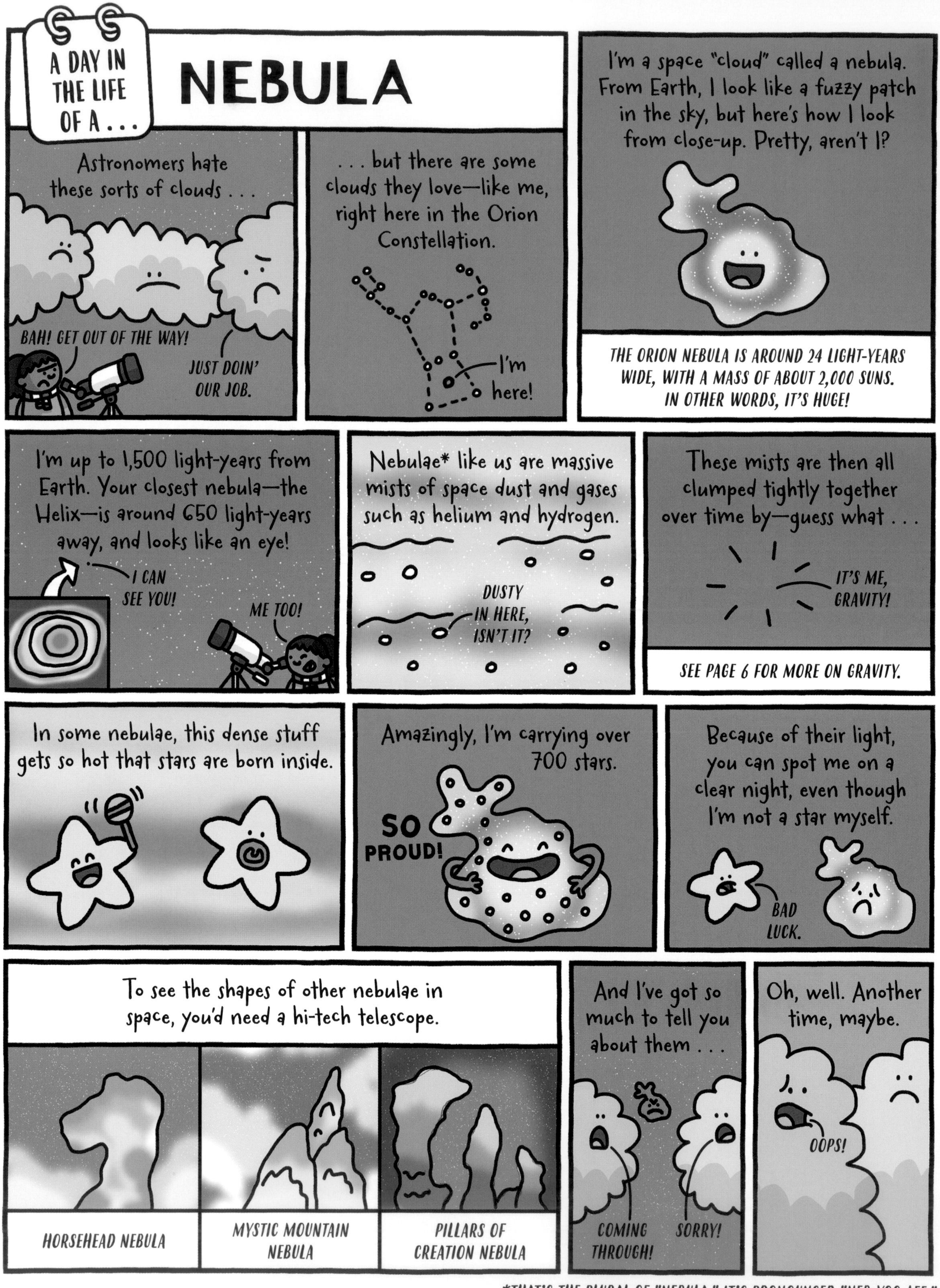
A DAY IN THE LIFE OF A . . .
NEBULA
Astronomers hate these sorts of clouds . . .
BAH! GET OUT OF THE WAY!
JUST DOIN' OUR JOB.
. . . but there are some clouds they love—like me, right here in the Orion Constellation.
I'm here!
I'm a space "cloud" called a nebula. From Earth, I look like a fuzzy patch in the sky, but here's how I look from close-up. Pretty, aren't I?
THE ORION NEBULA IS AROUND 24 LIGHT-YEARS WIDE, WITH A MASS OF ABOUT 2,000 SUNS. IN OTHER WORDS, IT'S HUGE!
I'm up to 1,500 light-years from Earth. Your closest nebula—the Helix—is around 650 light-years away, and looks like an eye!
I CAN SEE YOU!
ME TOO!
Nebulae* like us are massive mists of space dust and gases such as helium and hydrogen.
DUSTY IN HERE, ISN'T IT?
These mists are then all clumped tightly together over time by—guess what . . .
IT'S ME, GRAVITY!
SEE PAGE 6 FOR MORE ON GRAVITY.
In some nebulae, this dense stuff gets so hot that stars are born inside.
Amazingly, I'm carrying over 700 stars.
SO PROUD!
Because of their light, you can spot me on a clear night, even though I'm not a star myself.
BAD LUCK.
To see the shapes of other nebulae in space, you'd need a hi-tech telescope.
HORSEHEAD NEBULA
MYSTIC MOUNTAIN NEBULA
PILLARS OF CREATION NEBULA
And I've got so much to tell you about them . . .
COMING THROUGH!
SORRY!
Oh, well. Another time, maybe.
OOPS!

*THAT'S THE PLURAL OF "NEBULA." IT'S PRONOUNCED "NEB-YOO-LEE."

FABULOUS NEBULAE

Nebulae are some of the most complex and beautiful structures in the universe. The Hubble Space Telescope (see page 94) has observed hundreds of nebulae. Here are just a few of the most weird and wonderful:

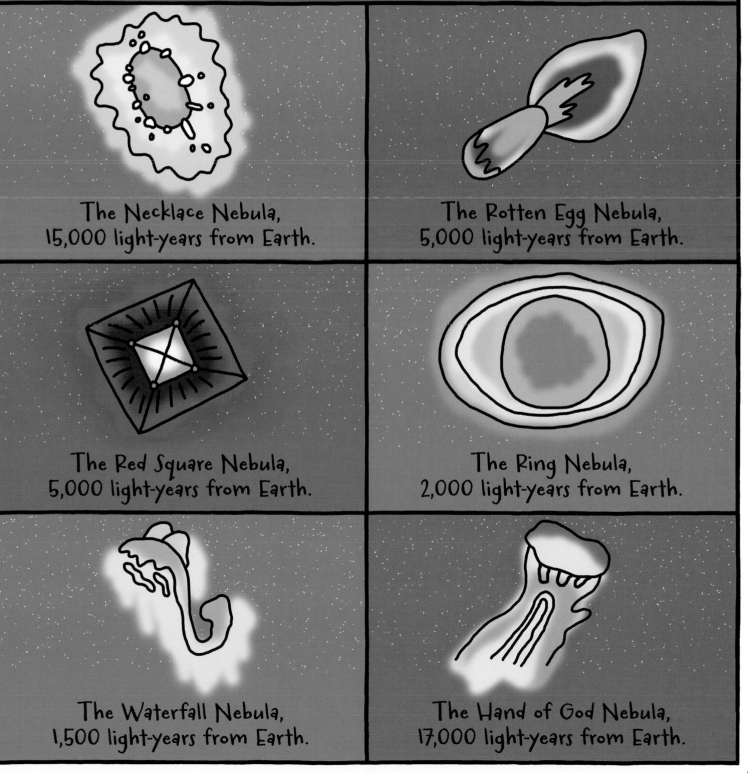

The Necklace Nebula, 15,000 light-years from Earth.

The Rotten Egg Nebula, 5,000 light-years from Earth.

The Red Square Nebula, 5,000 light-years from Earth.

The Ring Nebula, 2,000 light-years from Earth.

The Waterfall Nebula, 1,500 light-years from Earth.

The Hand of God Nebula, 17,000 light-years from Earth.

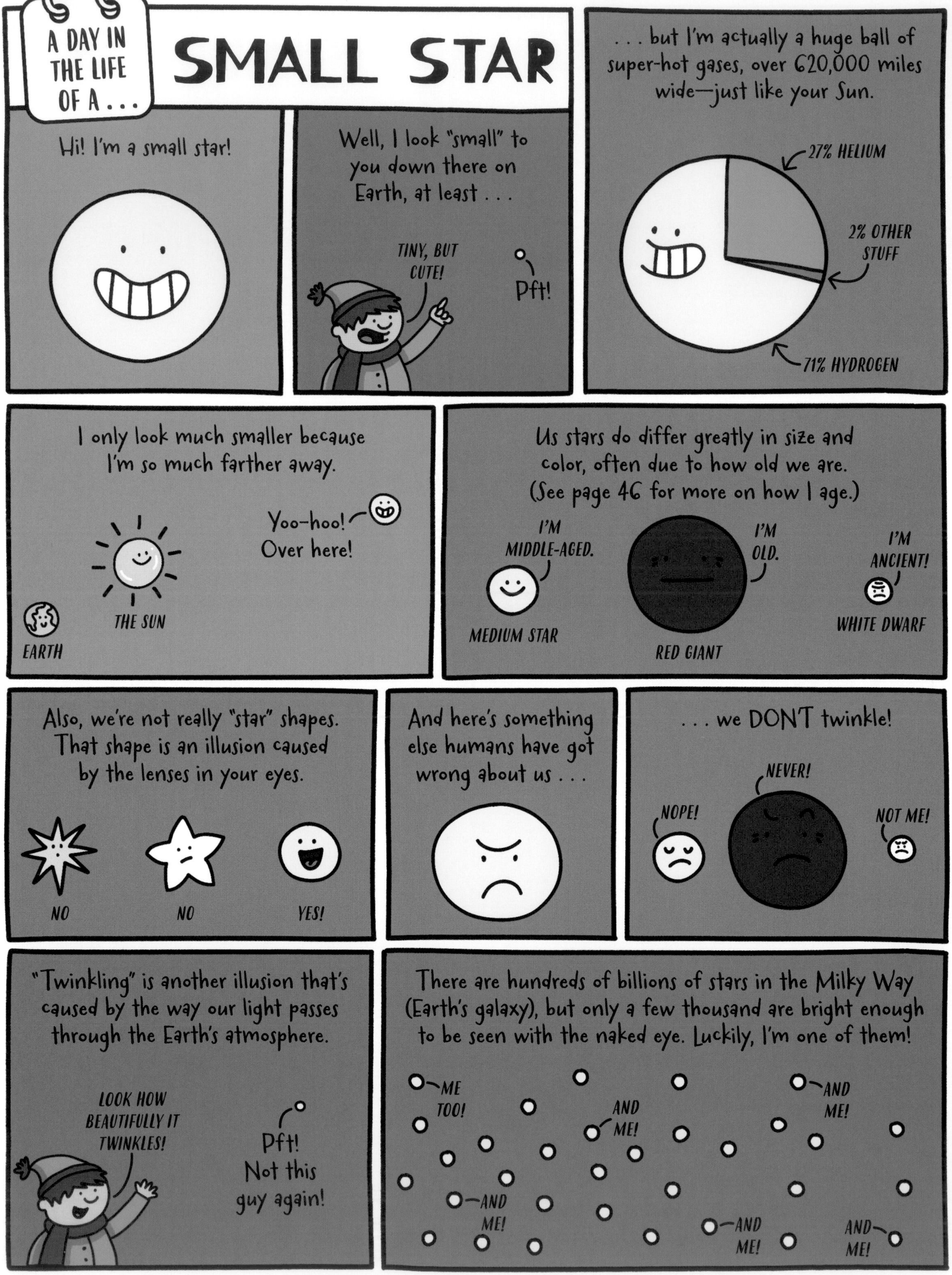
A DAY IN THE LIFE OF A . . .
SMALL STAR
Hi! I'm a small star!
Well, I look "small" to you down there on Earth, at least . . .
TINY, BUT CUTE!
Pft!
. . . but I'm actually a huge ball of super-hot gases, over 620,000 miles wide—just like your Sun.
27% HELIUM
2% OTHER STUFF
71% HYDROGEN
I only look much smaller because I'm so much farther away.
Yoo-hoo! Over here!
THE SUN
EARTH
Us stars do differ greatly in size and color, often due to how old we are. (See page 46 for more on how I age.)
I'M MIDDLE-AGED.
I'M OLD.
I'M ANCIENT!
MEDIUM STAR
RED GIANT
WHITE DWARF
Also, we're not really "star" shapes. That shape is an illusion caused by the lenses in your eyes.
NO
NO
YES!
And here's something else humans have got wrong about us . . .
. . . we DON'T twinkle!
NEVER!
NOPE!
NOT ME!
"Twinkling" is another illusion that's caused by the way our light passes through the Earth's atmosphere.
LOOK HOW BEAUTIFULLY IT TWINKLES!
Pft! Not this guy again!
There are hundreds of billions of stars in the Milky Way (Earth's galaxy), but only a few thousand are bright enough to be seen with the naked eye. Luckily, I'm one of them!
ME TOO!
AND ME!
AND ME!
AND ME!
AND ME!
AND ME!

STAR STORIES

The universe contains trillions of stars, all originally formed from gas and dust clumped together by gravity. The starting size of a star determines what happens to it as it ages. Read on to discover the different fates of the very smallest and the very largest stars.

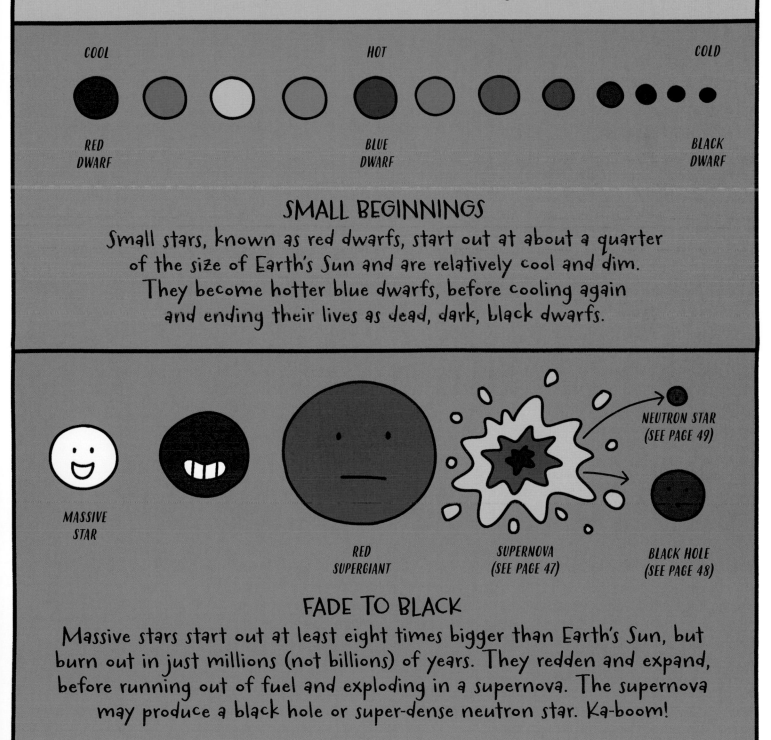

COOL

HOT

COLD

RED DWARF

BLUE DWARF

BLACK DWARF

SMALL BEGINNINGS

Small stars, known as red dwarfs, start out at about a quarter of the size of Earth's Sun and are relatively cool and dim. They become hotter blue dwarfs, before cooling again and ending their lives as dead, dark, black dwarfs.

MASSIVE STAR

RED SUPERGIANT

SUPERNOVA (SEE PAGE 47)

NEUTRON STAR (SEE PAGE 49)

BLACK HOLE (SEE PAGE 48)

FADE TO BLACK

Massive stars start out at least eight times bigger than Earth's Sun, but burn out in just millions (not billions) of years. They redden and expand, before running out of fuel and exploding in a supernova. The supernova may produce a black hole or super-dense neutron star. Ka-boom!

NOW TURN TO PAGE 46 FOR THE STORY OF A MEDIUM-SIZED STAR LIKE EARTH'S SUN.

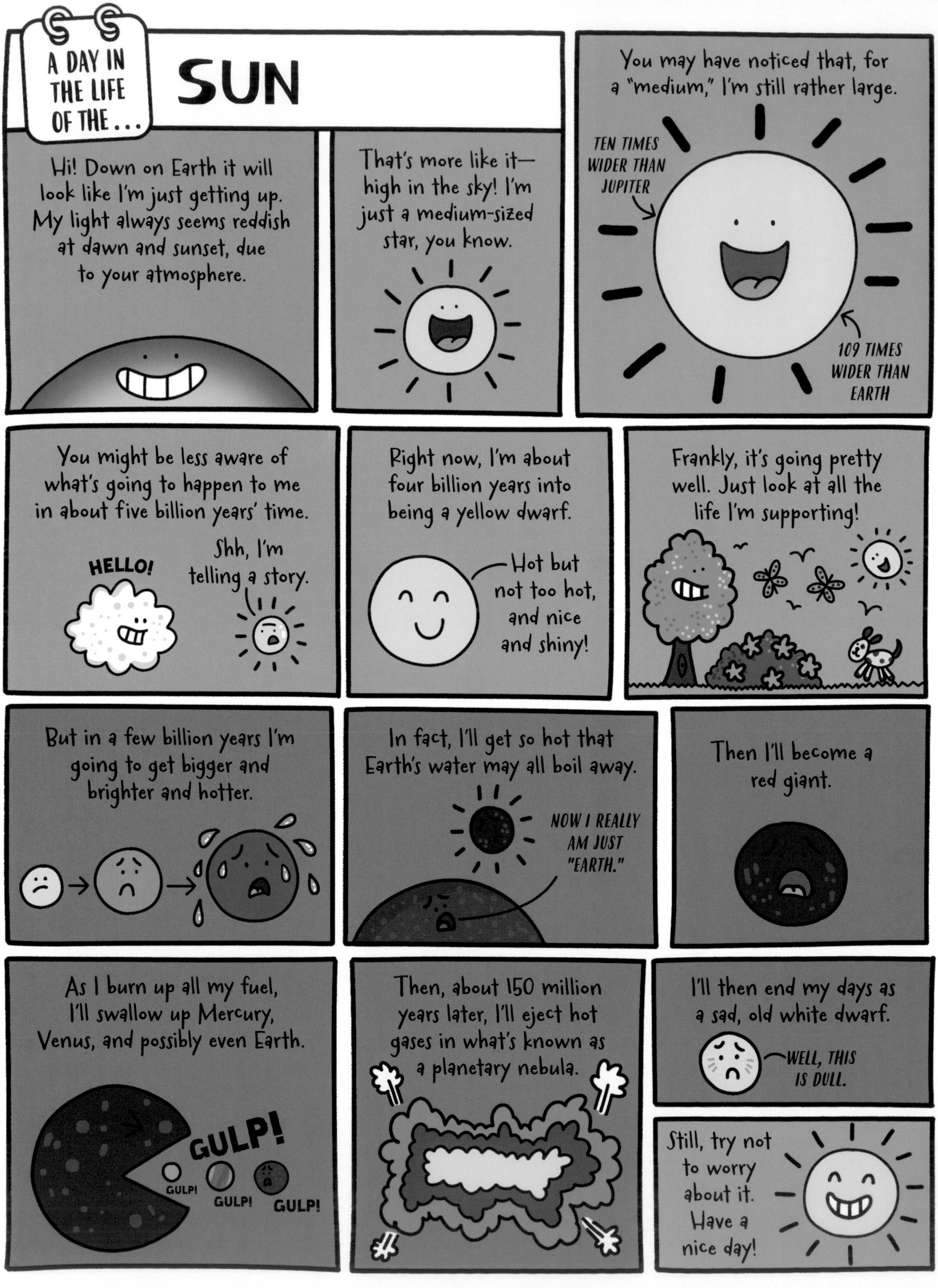

A DAY IN THE LIFE OF THE . . .
SUN
Hi! Down on Earth it will look like I'm just getting up. My light always seems reddish at dawn and sunset, due to your atmosphere.
That's more like it—high in the sky! I'm just a medium-sized star, you know.
You may have noticed that, for a "medium," I'm still rather large.
TEN TIMES WIDER THAN JUPITER
109 TIMES WIDER THAN EARTH
You might be less aware of what's going to happen to me in about five billion years' time.
HELLO!
Shh, I'm telling a story.
Right now, I'm about four billion years into being a yellow dwarf.
Hot but not too hot, and nice and shiny!
Frankly, it's going pretty well. Just look at all the life I'm supporting!
But in a few billion years I'm going to get bigger and brighter and hotter.
In fact, I'll get so hot that Earth's water may all boil away.
NOW I REALLY AM JUST "EARTH."
Then I'll become a red giant.
As I burn up all my fuel, I'll swallow up Mercury, Venus, and possibly even Earth.
GULP!
GULP!
GULP!
GULP!
Then, about 150 million years later, I'll eject hot gases in what's known as a planetary nebula.
I'll then end my days as a sad, old white dwarf.
WELL, THIS IS DULL.
Still, try not to worry about it. Have a nice day!

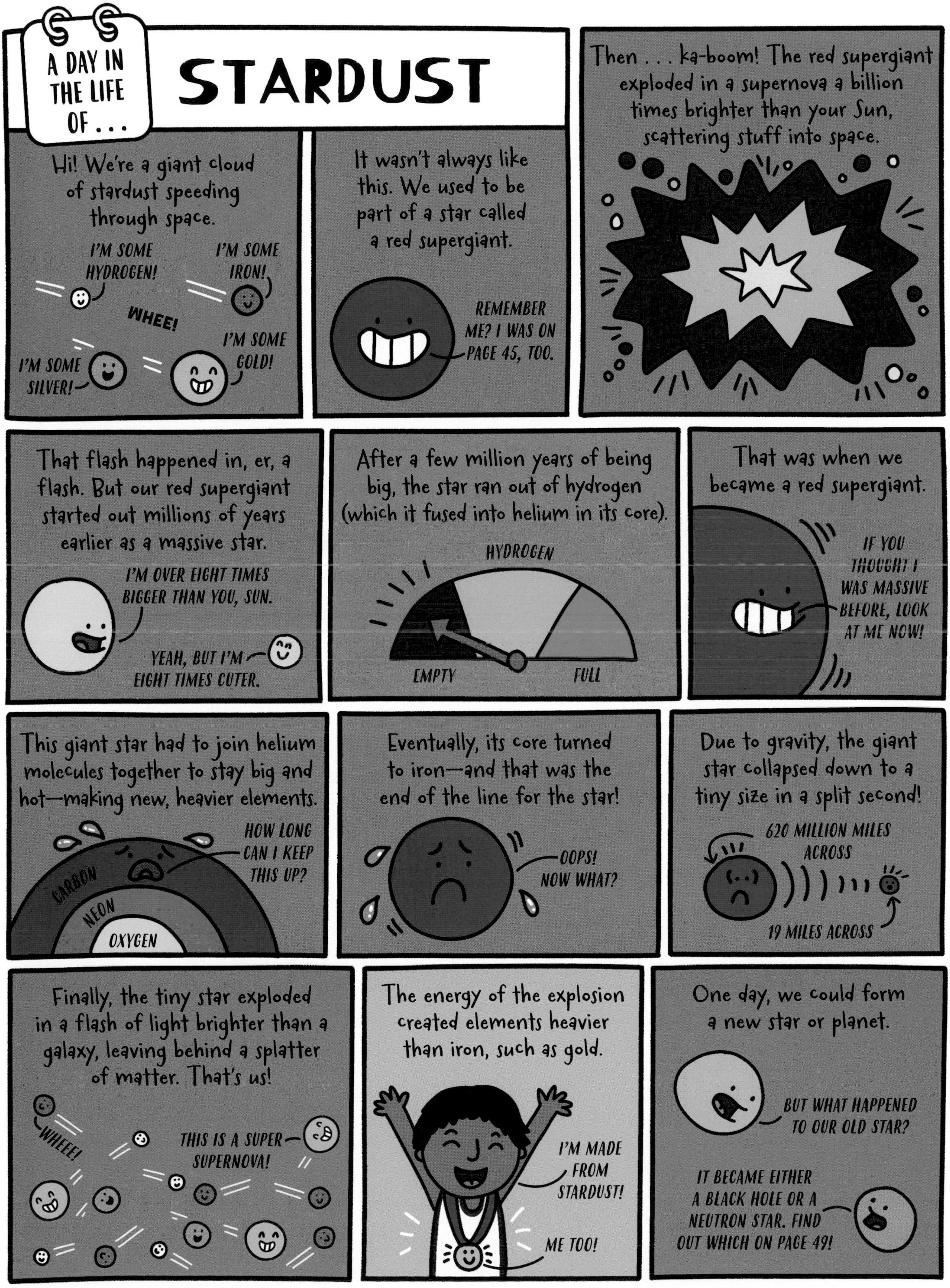
A DAY IN THE LIFE OF . . .
STARDUST
Hi! We're a giant cloud of stardust speeding through space.
I'M SOME HYDROGEN!
I'M SOME IRON!
WHEE!
I'M SOME SILVER!
I'M SOME GOLD!
It wasn't always like this. We used to be part of a star called a red supergiant.
REMEMBER ME? I WAS ON PAGE 45, TOO.
Then . . . ka-boom! The red supergiant exploded in a supernova a billion times brighter than your Sun, scattering stuff into space.
That flash happened in, er, a flash. But our red supergiant started out millions of years earlier as a massive star.
I'M OVER EIGHT TIMES BIGGER THAN YOU, SUN.
YEAH, BUT I'M EIGHT TIMES CUTER.
After a few million years of being big, the star ran out of hydrogen (which it fused into helium in its core).
HYDROGEN
EMPTY
FULL
That was when we became a red supergiant.
IF YOU THOUGHT I WAS MASSIVE BEFORE, LOOK AT ME NOW!
This giant star had to join helium molecules together to stay big and hot—making new, heavier elements.
HOW LONG CAN I KEEP THIS UP?
CARBON
NEON
OXYGEN
Eventually, its core turned to iron—and that was the end of the line for the star!
OOPS! NOW WHAT?
Due to gravity, the giant star collapsed down to a tiny size in a split second!
620 MILLION MILES ACROSS
19 MILES ACROSS
Finally, the tiny star exploded in a flash of light brighter than a galaxy, leaving behind a splatter of matter. That's us!
WHEEE!
THIS IS A SUPER SUPERNOVA!
The energy of the explosion created elements heavier than iron, such as gold.
I'M MADE FROM STARDUST!
ME TOO!
One day, we could form a new star or planet.
BUT WHAT HAPPENED TO OUR OLD STAR?
IT BECAME EITHER A BLACK HOLE OR A NEUTRON STAR. FIND OUT WHICH ON PAGE 49!

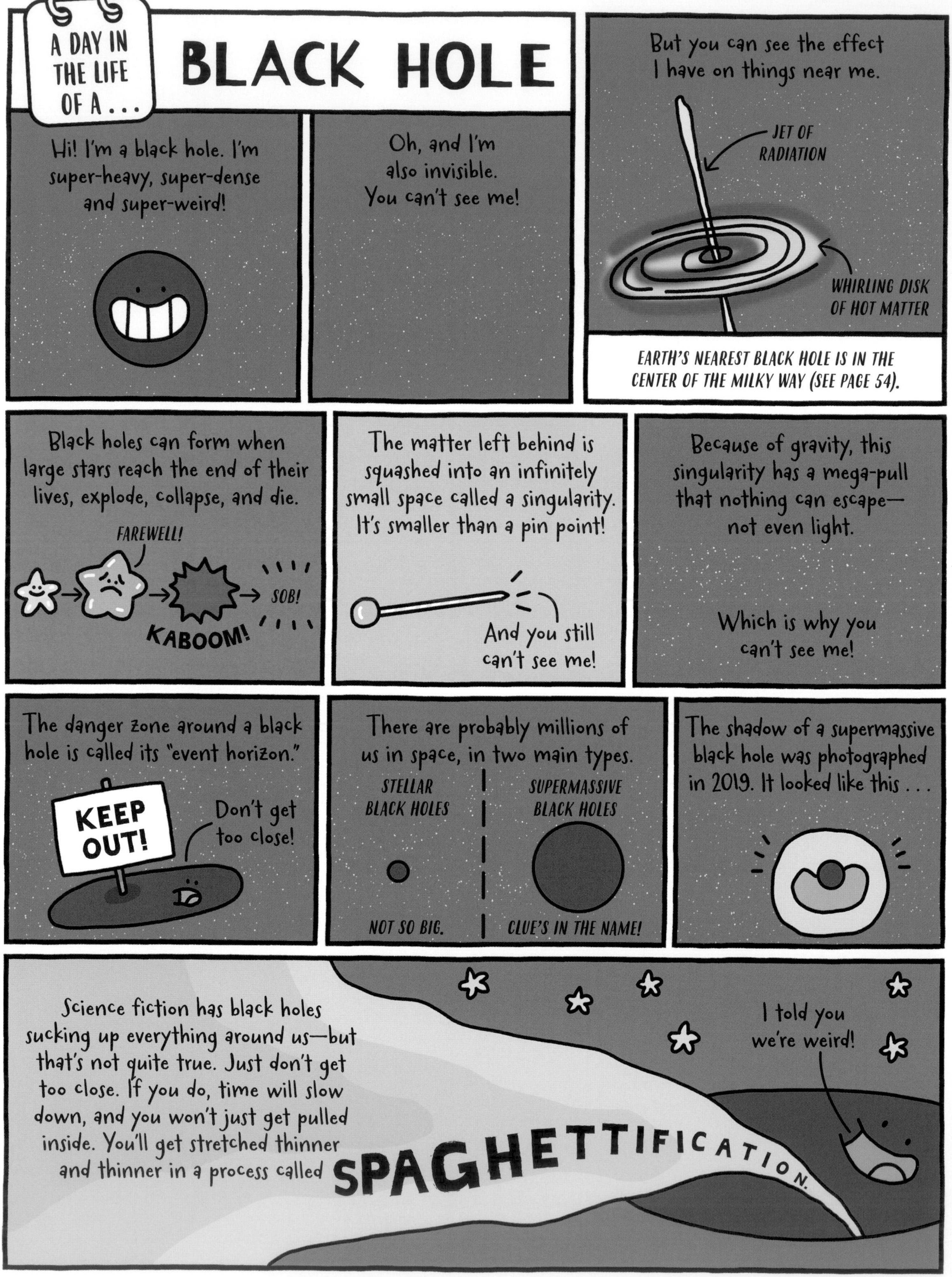
A DAY IN THE LIFE OF A . . .
BLACK HOLE
Hi! I'm a black hole. I'm super-heavy, super-dense and super-weird!
Oh, and I'm also invisible. You can't see me!
But you can see the effect I have on things near me.
JET OF RADIATION
WHIRLING DISK OF HOT MATTER
EARTH'S NEAREST BLACK HOLE IS IN THE CENTER OF THE MILKY WAY (SEE PAGE 54).
Black holes can form when large stars reach the end of their lives, explode, collapse, and die.
FAREWELL!
KABOOM!
SOB!
The matter left behind is squashed into an infinitely small space called a singularity. It's smaller than a pin point!
And you still can't see me!
Because of gravity, this singularity has a mega-pull that nothing can escape—not even light.
Which is why you can't see me!
The danger zone around a black hole is called its "event horizon."
KEEP OUT!
Don't get too close!
There are probably millions of us in space, in two main types.
STELLAR BLACK HOLES
SUPERMASSIVE BLACK HOLES
NOT SO BIG.
CLUE'S IN THE NAME!
The shadow of a supermassive black hole was photographed in 2019. It looked like this . . .
Science fiction has black holes sucking up everything around us—but that's not quite true. Just don't get too close. If you do, time will slow down, and you won't just get pulled inside. You'll get stretched thinner and thinner in a process called SPAGHETTIFICATION.
I told you we're weird!

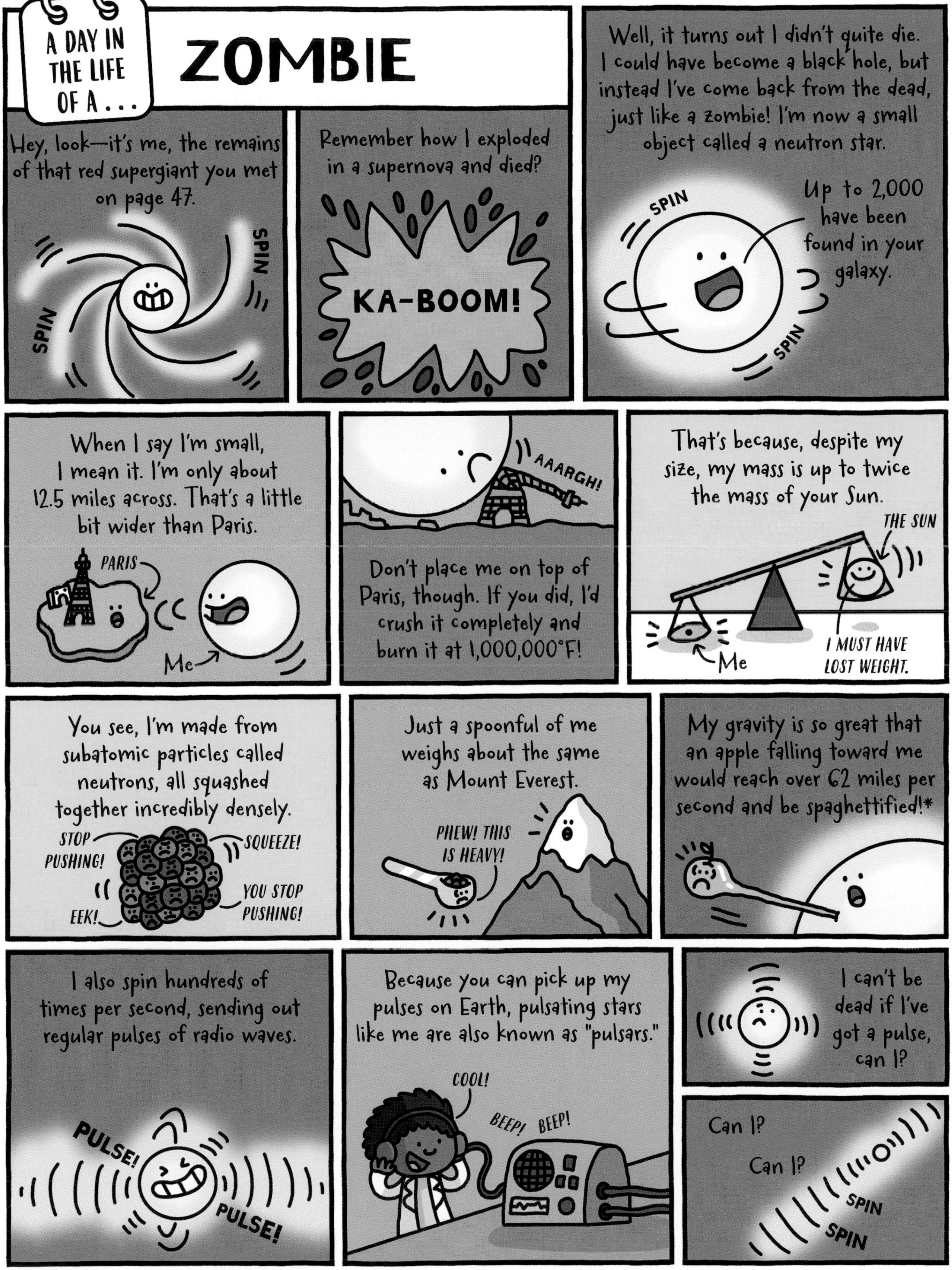
A DAY IN THE LIFE OF A . . .
ZOMBIE
Hey, look—it's me, the remains of that red supergiant you met on page 47.
SPIN
SPIN
Remember how I exploded in a supernova and died?
KA-BOOM!
Well, it turns out I didn't quite die. I could have become a black hole, but instead I've come back from the dead, just like a zombie! I'm now a small object called a neutron star.
SPIN
Up to 2,000 have been found in your galaxy.
SPIN
When I say I'm small, I mean it. I'm only about 12.5 miles across. That's a little bit wider than Paris.
PARIS
Me
AAAARGH!
Don't place me on top of Paris, though. If you did, I'd crush it completely and burn it at 1,000,000°F!
That's because, despite my size, my mass is up to twice the mass of your Sun.
THE SUN
Me
I MUST HAVE LOST WEIGHT.
You see, I'm made from subatomic particles called neutrons, all squashed together incredibly densely.
STOP PUSHING!
SQUEEZE!
EEK!
YOU STOP PUSHING!
Just a spoonful of me weighs about the same as Mount Everest.
PHEW! THIS IS HEAVY!
My gravity is so great that an apple falling toward me would reach over 62 miles per second and be spaghettified!*
I also spin hundreds of times per second, sending out regular pulses of radio waves.
PULSE!
PULSE!
Because you can pick up my pulses on Earth, pulsating stars like me are also known as "pulsars."
COOL!
BEEP! BEEP!
I can't be dead if I've got a pulse, can I?
Can I?
Can I?
SPIN
SPIN

*SEE PAGE 48 FOR MORE ON SPAGHETTIFICATION.

GIANT DOT-TO-DOT

Hello again! Remember me from page 42? I'm the Orion Nebula, and this is the Orion Constellation. You can find me here, along with lots of stars. Together we're like a giant dot-to-dot puzzle in the sky. If you join us all up, you'll see a picture of a hunter with a club and shield.

ORION'S CLUB

ORION'S SHIELD

BELLATRIX

BETELGEUSE

ORION'S BELT

Me

RIGEL

SAIPH

ORION'S SWORD

ORION ACTUALLY INCLUDES MANY MORE STARS. THE DARKER THE NIGHT SKY, THE MORE YOU MIGHT SEE.

The outline of a hunter in the sky was first imagined by the ancient Greeks. We're really all just unconnected spots of light, like this . . .

The Orion Constellation (and me!) can be seen from both the northern and southern hemispheres, depending on the time of year.

ORION

NORTHERN HEMISPHERE

EQUATOR

SOUTHERN HEMISPHERE

Our constellation seems to rise and set in the sky, but this is actually due to the Earth turning.

UP!

DOWN!

One of our brightest stars is Betelgeuse—a red supergiant (see page 47) that may explode as a supernova in about 100,000 years.

WHAT A WAY TO GO!

SEE PAGE 47 FOR MORE ON SUPERNOVAS.

It'll be a pity to lose Orion's shoulder, but at least he'll still have the three stars that make up his belt.

ALNITAK

MINTAKA

ALNILAM

And he'll still have his sword—which is the best bit because it has me in it!

See you tonight! Don't be late. Bye!

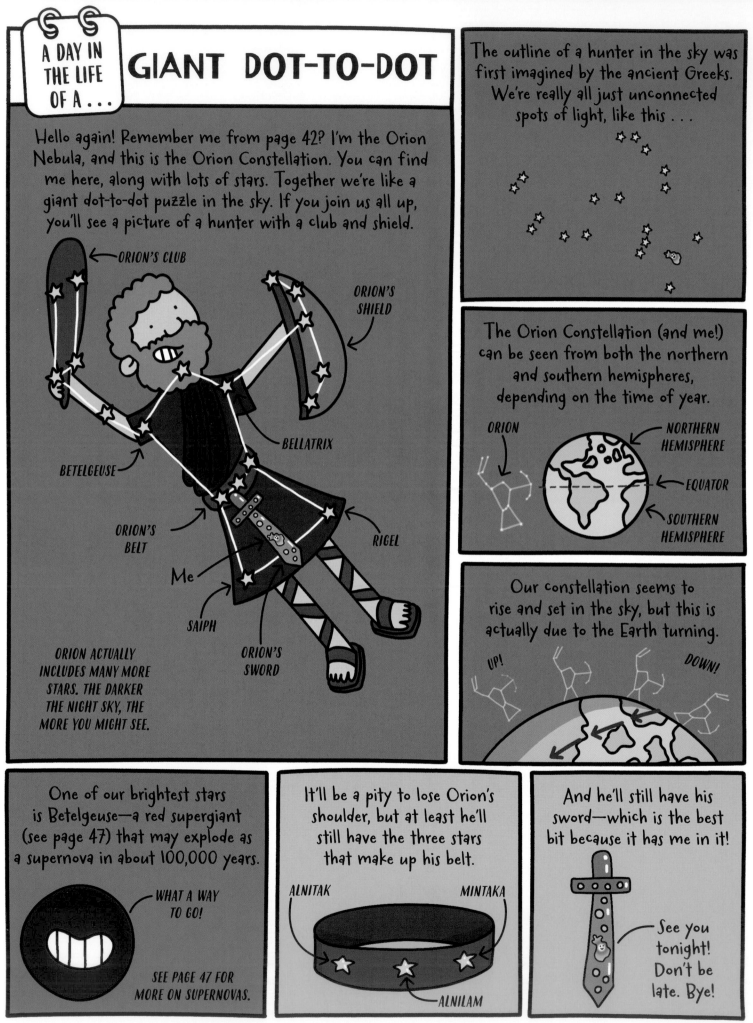

THE BIGGER PICTURE

STAR TURNS

The 88 officially recognized constellations include the 12 signs of the western zodiac. These are star patterns that occupy an imaginary ring in the night sky called "the ecliptic." Seen from Earth, the Sun seems to travel through these constellations in the course of a year. This is what gave rise to the ancient practice of astrology—a belief that the stars influence human lives. While astrology and horoscopes can be fun, they have no scientific foundation—unlike astronomy. However, as some of the first star patterns ever studied by humans, constellations remain fascinating and beautiful.

WHAT'S IN A NAME?

The scientific names of the constellations are given in Latin. For example, "Capricornus" is "Capricorn," also known as the Sea Goat. "Scorpius" is "Scorpio."

NIGHT LIGHTS

The stars of the ecliptic cannot be seen from Earth during daylight because of the light from the Sun.

ARIES
PISCES
TAURUS
AQUARIUS
GEMINI
CAPRICORNUS
THE SUN
EARTH
CANCER
SAGITTARIUS
LEO
SCORPIUS
VIRGO
LIBRA

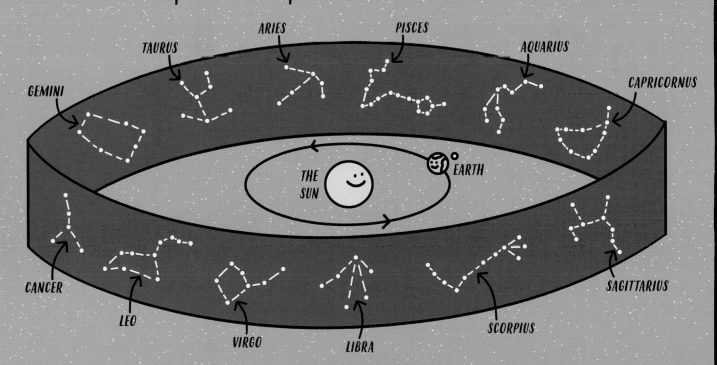

UNLUCKY 13

The zodiac should really include a thirteenth constellation called Ophiuchus. Sadly for Ophiuchus, it was dropped by astrologers because it's easier to divide a year into twelve similar-sized months.

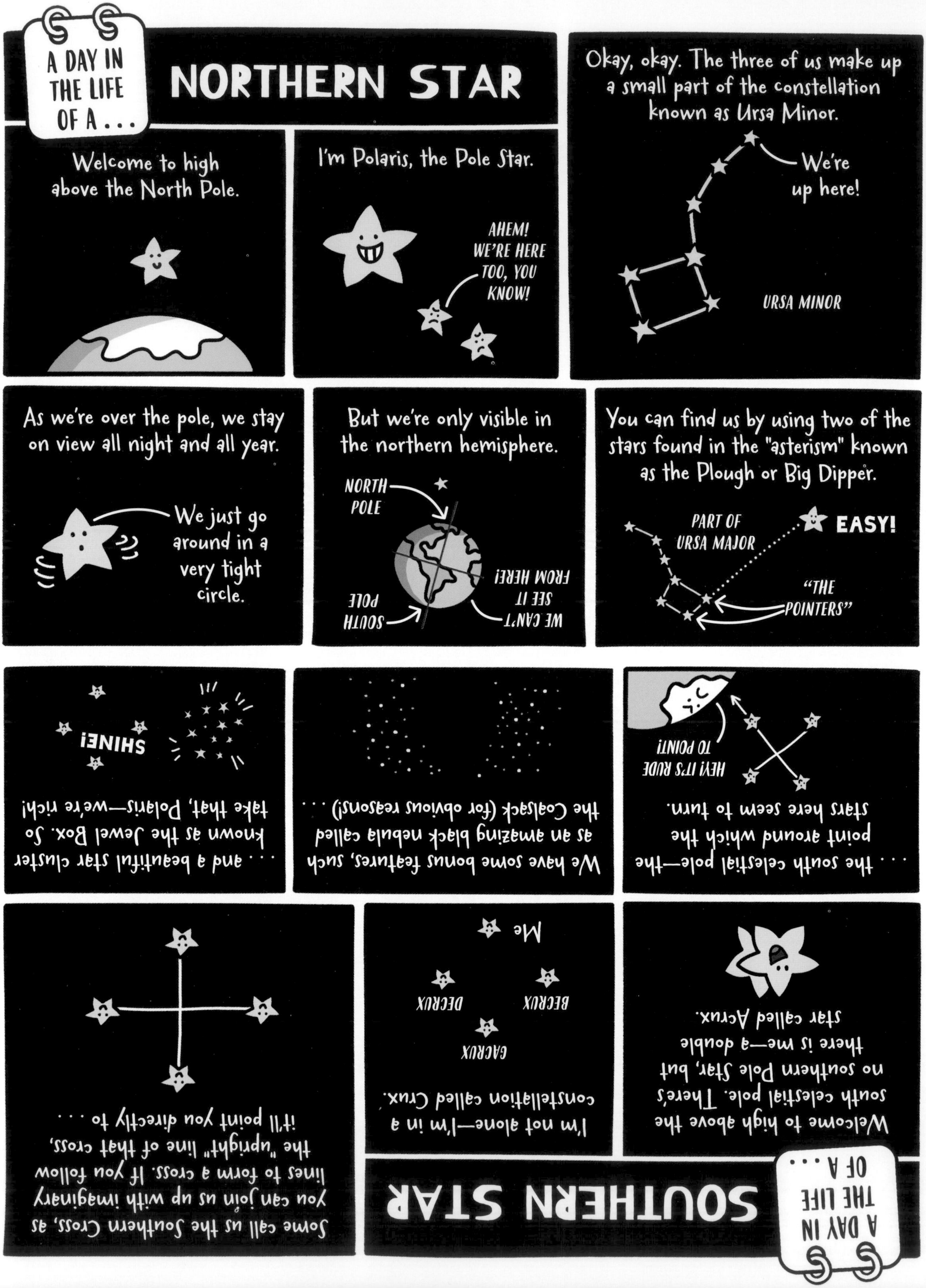
A DAY IN THE LIFE OF A . . .
NORTHERN STAR
Welcome to high above the North Pole.
I'm Polaris, the Pole Star.
AHEM! WE'RE HERE TOO, YOU KNOW!
Okay, okay. The three of us make up a small part of the constellation known as Ursa Minor.
We're up here!
URSA MINOR
As we're over the pole, we stay on view all night and all year.
We just go around in a very tight circle.
But we're only visible in the northern hemisphere.
NORTH POLE
SOUTH POLE
WE CAN'T SEE IT FROM HERE!
You can find us by using two of the stars found in the "asterism" known as the Plough or Big Dipper.
PART OF URSA MAJOR
EASY!
"THE POINTERS"
A DAY IN THE LIFE OF A . . .
SOUTHERN STAR
Welcome to high above the south celestial pole. There's no southern Pole Star, but there is me—a double star called Acrux.
I'm not alone—I'm in a constellation called Crux.
Me
BECRUX
DECRUX
GACRUX
Some call us the Southern Cross, as you can join us up with imaginary lines to form a cross. If you follow the "upright" line of that cross, it'll point you directly to . . .
. . . the south celestial pole—the point around which the stars here seem to turn.
HEY! IT'S RUDE TO POINT!
We have some bonus features, such as an amazing black nebula called the Coalsack (for obvious reasons) . . .
. . . and a beautiful star cluster known as the Jewel Box. So take that, Polaris—we're rich!
SHINE!

THE BIGGER PICTURE

PARTNERS IN SHINE

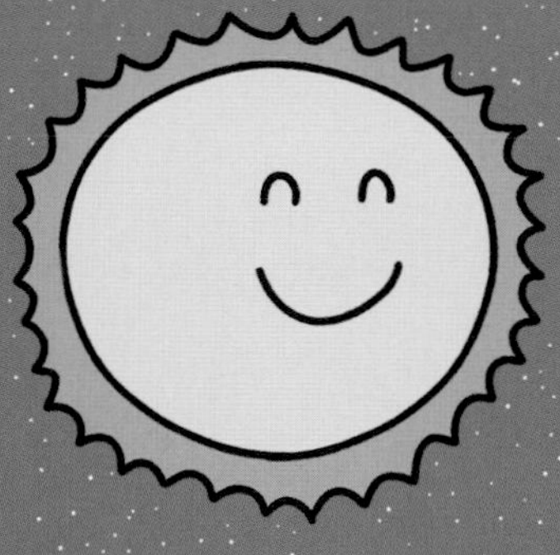

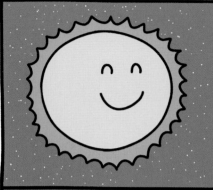

Earth's Sun is fairly unusual in that it is a solitary star. Many other stars appear in pairs orbiting around each other. These are known as binary star systems. There are also systems with three or more orbiting stars, as well as larger clusters making up whole galaxies.

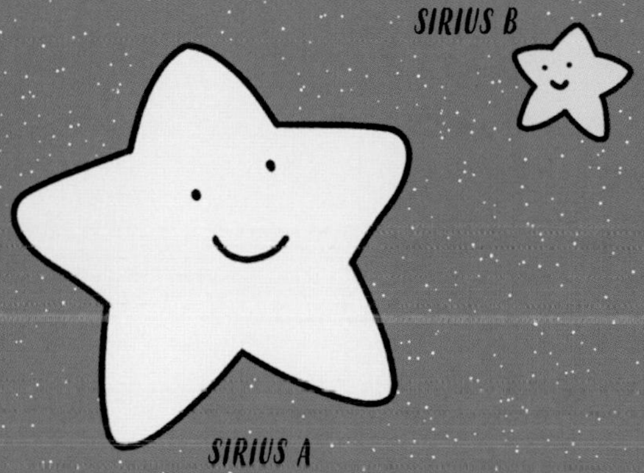
SIRIUS B
SIRIUS A

TWO'S COMPANY

Sirius A—nicknamed the Dog Star—is the brightest star in Earth's night sky. It is in a binary system with Sirius B, a dim and distant white dwarf. Sirius A and Sirius B orbit each other.

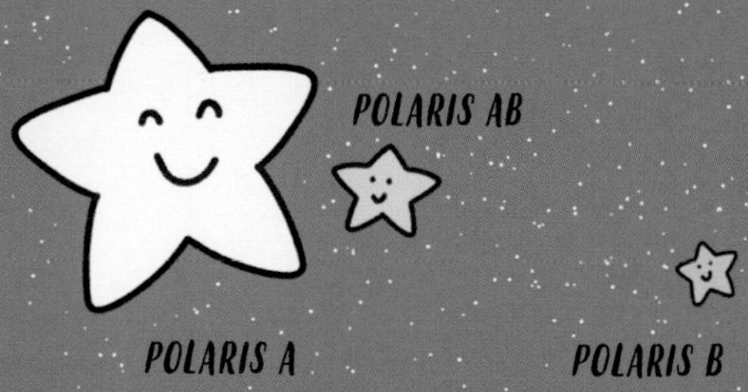
POLARIS AB
POLARIS A
POLARIS B

THREE'S ALLOWED

For centuries, travelers in the northern hemisphere have been using Polaris, also known as the Pole Star, to help them find their way at night. That's because Polaris currently lies over the North Pole. However, what was once thought to be a single star is in fact a "trinary" system made up of three different stars.

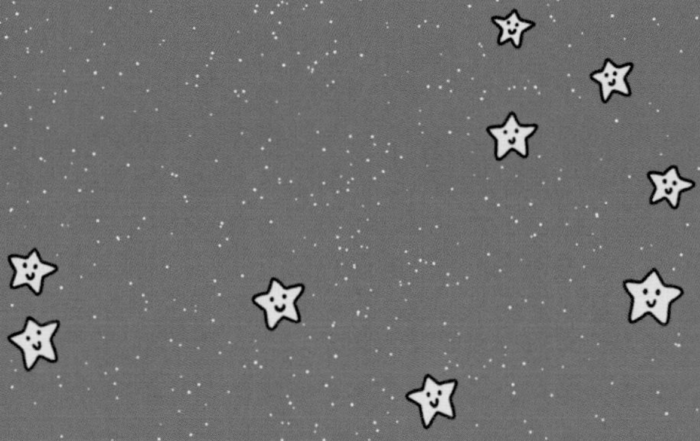

SEVEN UP

The Pleiades, also known as the Seven Sisters, is a cluster of several stars that can be easily seen in the night sky. The cluster actually contains over 1,000 stars, though nine of them (not seven!) are particularly bright.

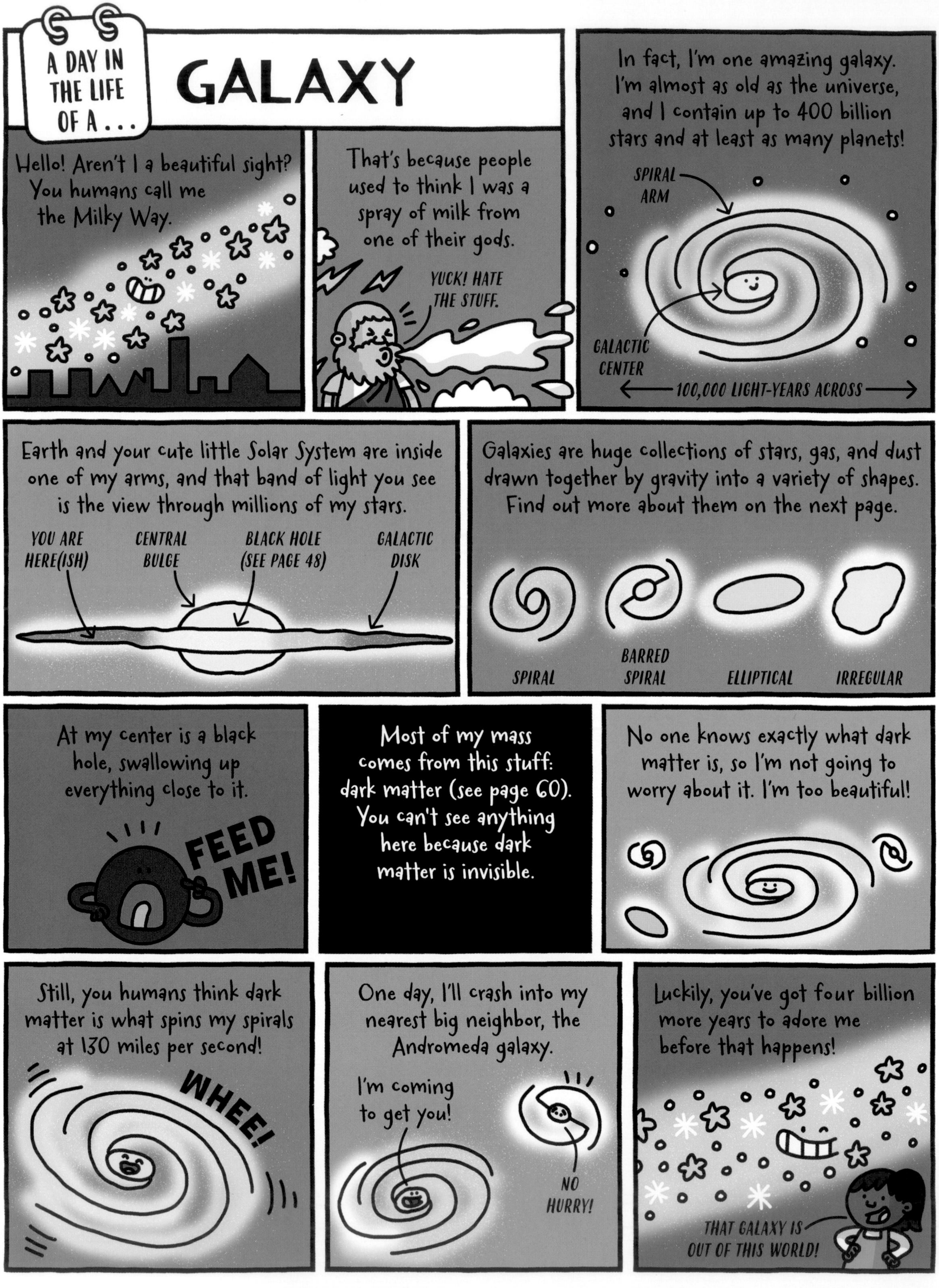
A DAY IN THE LIFE OF A . . .
GALAXY
Hello! Aren't I a beautiful sight? You humans call me the Milky Way.
That's because people used to think I was a spray of milk from one of their gods.
YUCK! HATE THE STUFF.
In fact, I'm one amazing galaxy. I'm almost as old as the universe, and I contain up to 400 billion stars and at least as many planets!
SPIRAL ARM
GALACTIC CENTER
100,000 LIGHT-YEARS ACROSS
Earth and your cute little Solar System are inside one of my arms, and that band of light you see is the view through millions of my stars.
YOU ARE HERE(ISH)
CENTRAL BULGE
BLACK HOLE (SEE PAGE 48)
GALACTIC DISK
Galaxies are huge collections of stars, gas, and dust drawn together by gravity into a variety of shapes. Find out more about them on the next page.
SPIRAL
BARRED SPIRAL
ELLIPTICAL
IRREGULAR
At my center is a black hole, swallowing up everything close to it.
FEED ME!
Most of my mass comes from this stuff: dark matter (see page 60). You can't see anything here because dark matter is invisible.
No one knows exactly what dark matter is, so I'm not going to worry about it. I'm too beautiful!
Still, you humans think dark matter is what spins my spirals at 130 miles per second!
WHEE!
One day, I'll crash into my nearest big neighbor, the Andromeda galaxy.
I'm coming to get you!
NO HURRY!
Luckily, you've got four billion more years to adore me before that happens!
THAT GALAXY IS OUT OF THIS WORLD!

THE BIGGER PICTURE	GALAXY QUEST

Thanks to technology such as the Hubble Space Telescope (see page 94), tens of thousands of galaxies have been spotted outside our own Milky Way. That's just a fraction of the 200 billion galaxies that are believed to exist. They come in different shapes and sizes, with the largest galaxies thought to contain over 100 trillion stars.

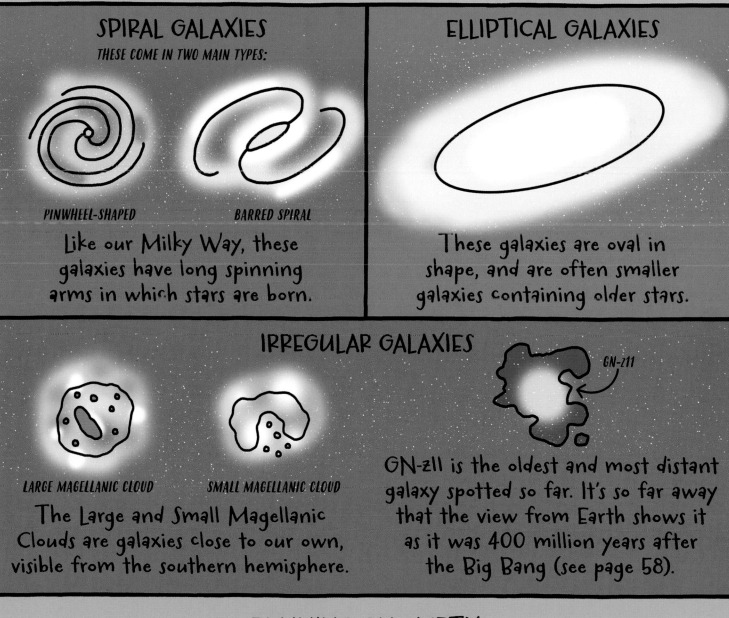

SPIRAL GALAXIES
THESE COME IN TWO MAIN TYPES:

PINWHEEL-SHAPED

BARRED SPIRAL

Like our Milky Way, these galaxies have long spinning arms in which stars are born.

ELLIPTICAL GALAXIES

These galaxies are oval in shape, and are often smaller galaxies containing older stars.

IRREGULAR GALAXIES

GN-z11

LARGE MAGELLANIC CLOUD

SMALL MAGELLANIC CLOUD

The Large and Small Magellanic Clouds are galaxies close to our own, visible from the southern hemisphere.

GN-z11 is the oldest and most distant galaxy spotted so far. It's so far away that the view from Earth shows it as it was 400 million years after the Big Bang (see page 58).

RUNNING ON EMPTY
The space between galaxies, called the Intergalactic Medium, is almost a perfect vacuum, containing as little as one atom per cubic meter of space. In other words, there's almost nothing there!

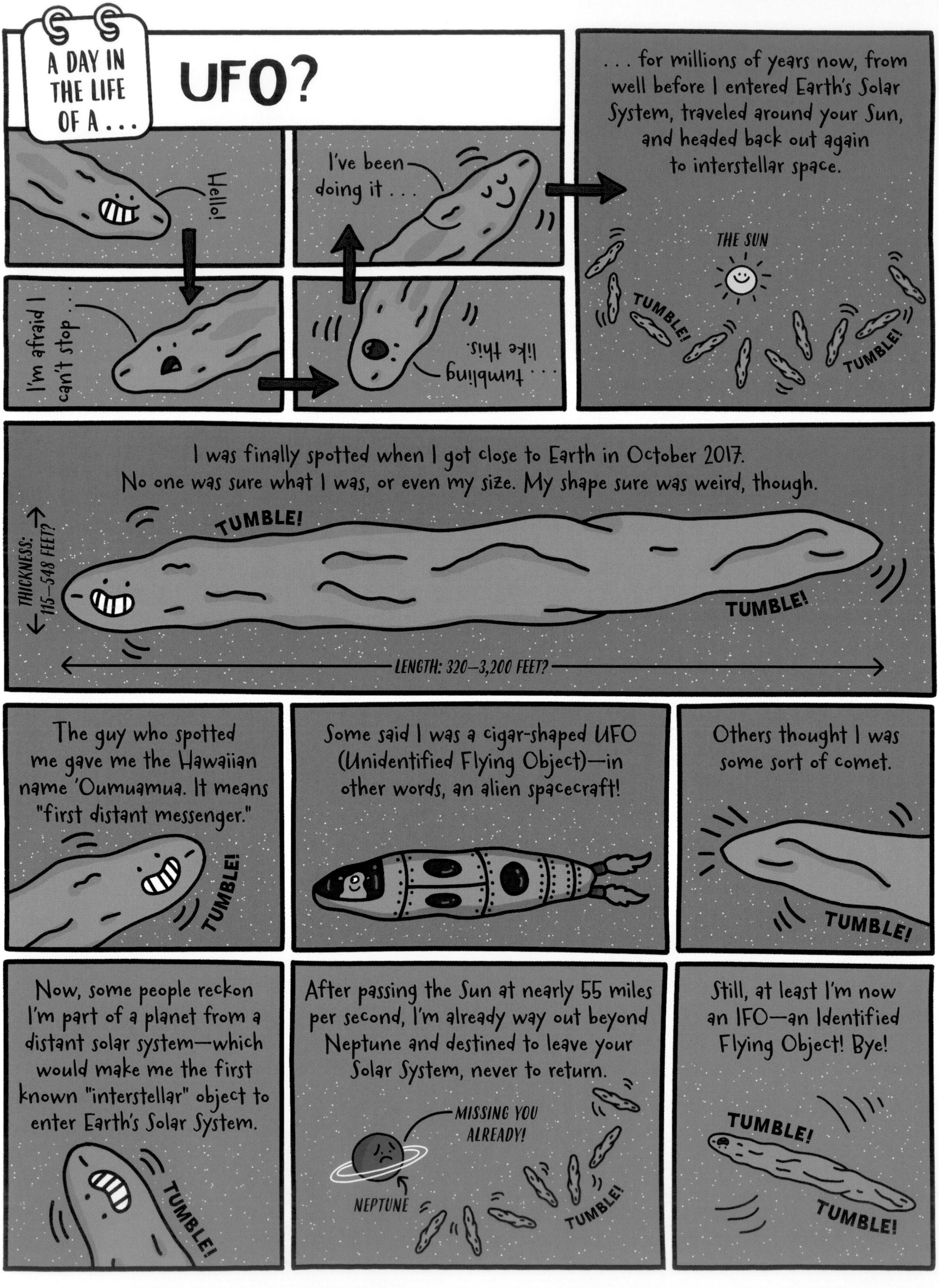
A DAY IN THE LIFE OF A . . .
UFO?
Hello!
I'm afraid I can't stop . . .
I've been doing it . . .
. . . tumbling like this.
. . . for millions of years now, from well before I entered Earth's Solar System, traveled around your Sun, and headed back out again to interstellar space.
THE SUN
TUMBLE!
TUMBLE!
I was finally spotted when I got close to Earth in October 2017. No one was sure what I was, or even my size. My shape sure was weird, though.
THICKNESS: 115–548 FEET?
TUMBLE!
TUMBLE!
LENGTH: 320–3,200 FEET?
The guy who spotted me gave me the Hawaiian name 'Oumuamua. It means "first distant messenger."
TUMBLE!
Some said I was a cigar-shaped UFO (Unidentified Flying Object)—in other words, an alien spacecraft!
Others thought I was some sort of comet.
TUMBLE!
Now, some people reckon I'm part of a planet from a distant solar system—which would make me the first known "interstellar" object to enter Earth's Solar System.
TUMBLE!
After passing the Sun at nearly 55 miles per second, I'm already way out beyond Neptune and destined to leave your Solar System, never to return.
MISSING YOU ALREADY!
NEPTUNE
TUMBLE!
Still, at least I'm now an IFO—an Identified Flying Object! Bye!
TUMBLE!
TUMBLE!

THE BIGGER PICTURE

CLOSE TO HOME

Over 65 million years ago an asteroid struck Earth, dooming the dinosaurs and changing life on this planet. Today, astronomers monitor over 25,000 Near-Earth Objects (NEOs)—mostly asteroids—just in case any of them look to be coming too close for comfort. Here are a few of them:

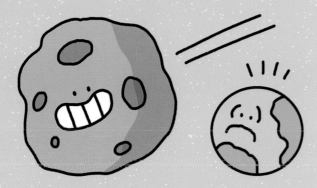

4581 ASCLEPIUS

More than half a mile wide, this asteroid was first spotted in late March 1989—several days after its closest approach to Earth! The date March 23 is now known to some NEO fans as Near Miss Day. Gulp!

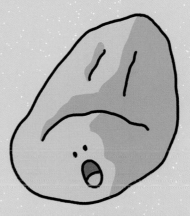

1036 GANYMED

At over 18 miles wide, this distant asteroid is the largest of the Potentially Harmful Objects (PHOs) currenlly being tracked. Luckily, Ganymed's orbit doesn't cross with Earth's, and is mostly found closer to Jupiter.

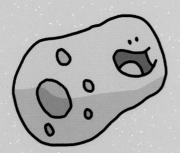

1999 AN10

This small asteroid is next due to come within 243,000 miles of Earth in 2027. If you're not too nervous, you can follow it using binoculars.

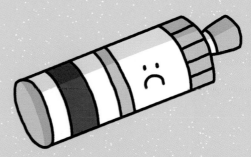

J002E3

This NEO is thought to be a booster rocket left over from the Apollo 12 mission to the Moon in 1969. Ironically, it may one day collide with the Moon!

The secret diary of a
BIG BANG!

Extracts from the 13.8-billion-year-old diary of "Una," an expanding universe

1
NO TIME AT ALL

Sorry, I've no idea of the date, as time itself doesn't exist yet. I'm just an infinitely small, infinitely dense dot of energy—smaller than an atom—with a temperature of over 212 nonillion°F (that's 212,000,000, 000,000,000,000,000,000,000, 000°F). That said, I do hope to achieve big things one day . . . perhaps soon!

2
ONE BILLIONTH OF A SECOND LATER

For reasons that even I don't understand, I've expanded into something trillions of times bigger. I'm made of all these weird particles, many of which keep bumping into each other and disappearing. I hope they don't all vanish!

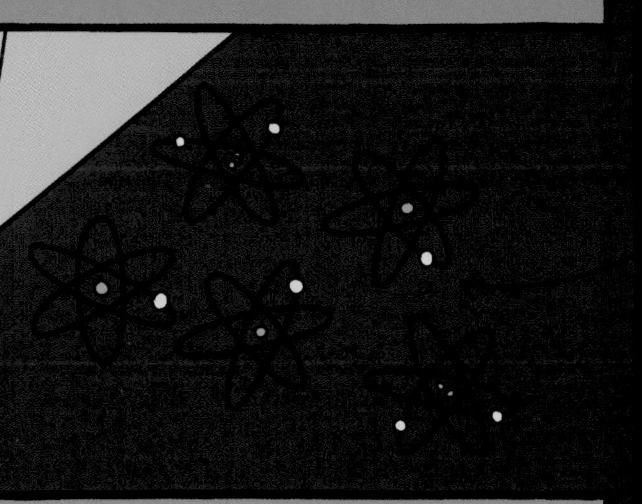

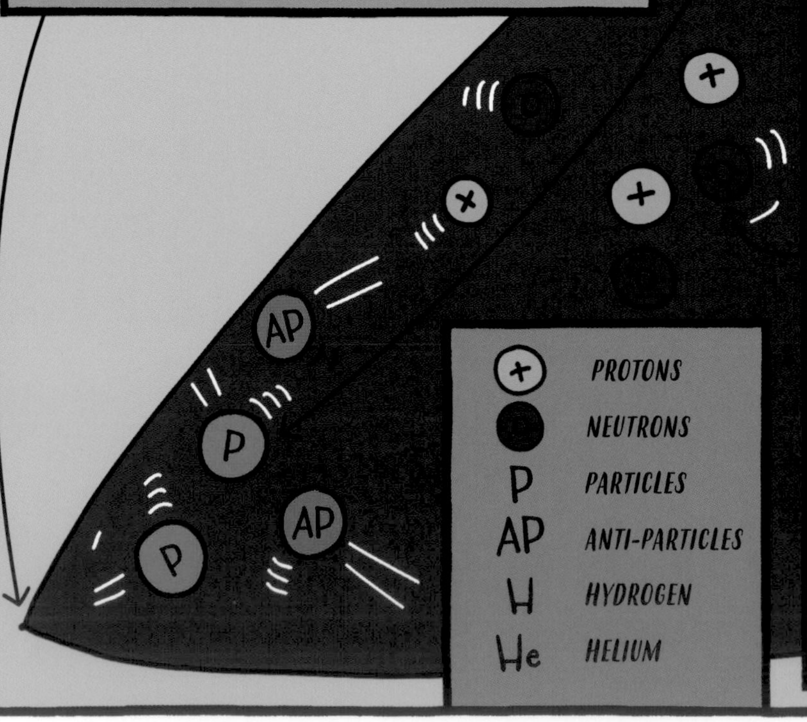

3
ONE MILLIONTH OF A SECOND LATER

Hurrah! They didn't vanish! The remaining particles have created something I'm calling "matter." Some are tiny things with positive electrical charges, and the rest have no charge at all. I'm naming them protons (+) and neutrons (0).

⊕	PROTONS
●	NEUTRONS
P	PARTICLES
AP	ANTI-PARTICLES
H	HYDROGEN
He	HELIUM

4

400,000 YEARS LATER

Now that time finally exists, it certainly seems to fly! I've cooled down enough to combine those protons and neutrons with tiny little electrons (–) to make atoms. Ta-daaah! I've also released lots of light energy.

6

ONE BILLION YEARS LATER

Incredible! Thanks to gravity, those clumps have been pulled into billions of galaxies with stars igniting inside. It's just as well that I'm still expanding or I don't think I'd have room for all this stuff!

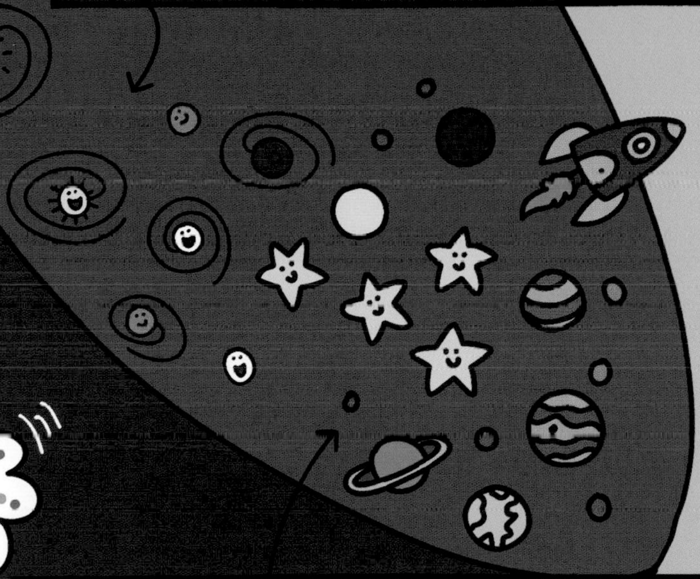

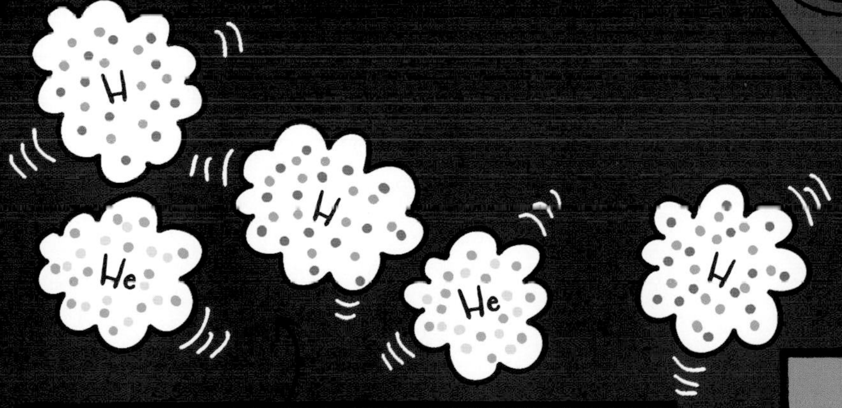

H
H
He
He
H

5

500 MILLION YEARS LATER

Those atoms have formed the gases hydrogen and helium—the lightest elements of all. Despite this, something called gravity has started pulling them into clumps. This is all out of my control now. Yikes!

7

13.8 BILLION YEARS LATER

Wow! What a journey! I now contain stars, planets, galaxies, and even LIFE! Plus I'm still getting bigger, and at a faster rate! But how and why? Maybe one day the humans in that Solar System I made over four billion years ago will work it out. I sure hope so!

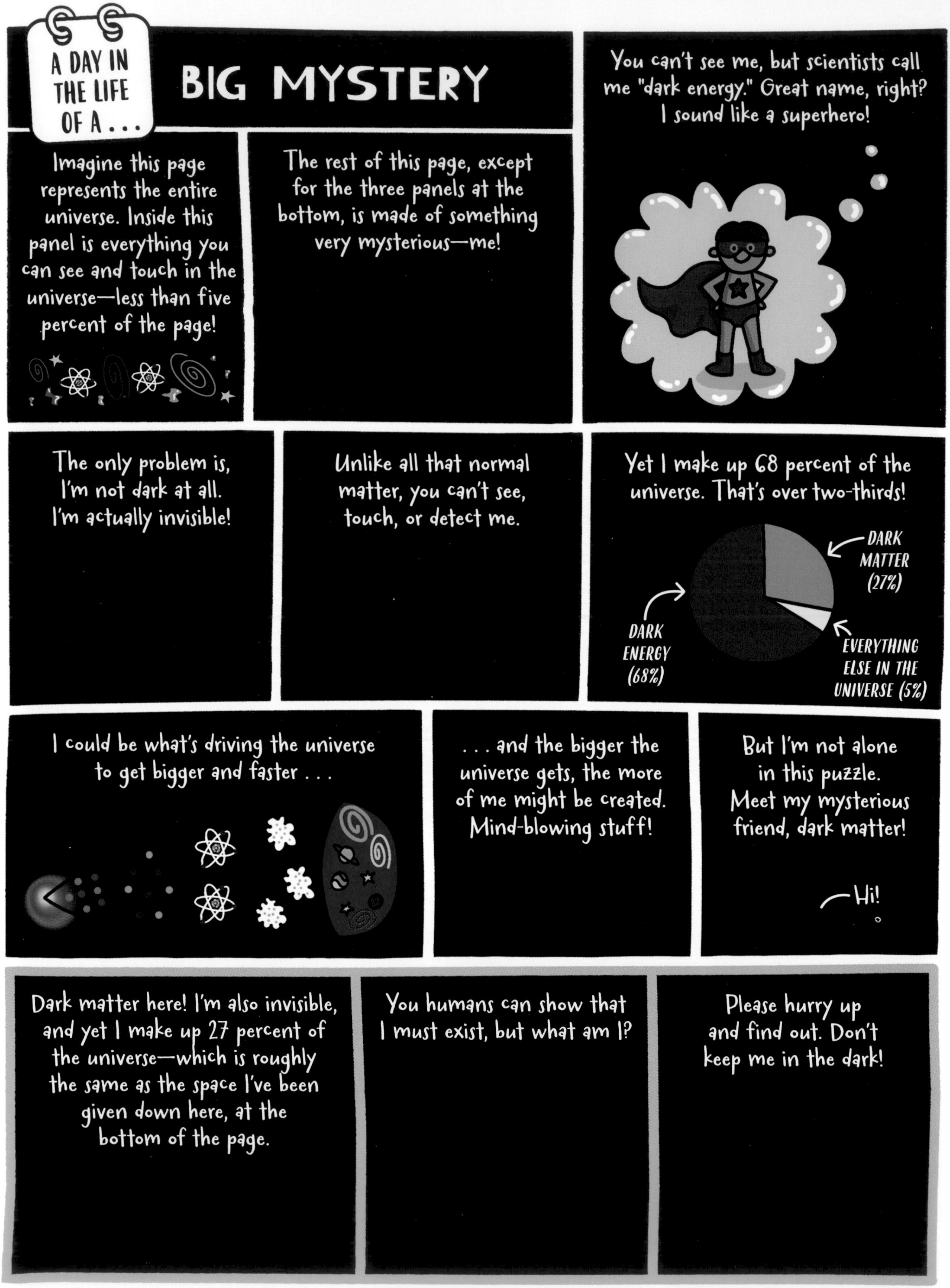
A DAY IN THE LIFE OF A . . .
BIG MYSTERY
Imagine this page represents the entire universe. Inside this panel is everything you can see and touch in the universe—less than five percent of the page!
The rest of this page, except for the three panels at the bottom, is made of something very mysterious—me!
You can't see me, but scientists call me "dark energy." Great name, right? I sound like a superhero!
The only problem is, I'm not dark at all. I'm actually invisible!
Unlike all that normal matter, you can't see, touch, or detect me.
Yet I make up 68 percent of the universe. That's over two-thirds!
DARK MATTER (27%)
DARK ENERGY (68%)
EVERYTHING ELSE IN THE UNIVERSE (5%)
I could be what's driving the universe to get bigger and faster . . .
. . . and the bigger the universe gets, the more of me might be created. Mind-blowing stuff!
But I'm not alone in this puzzle. Meet my mysterious friend, dark matter!
—Hi!
Dark matter here! I'm also invisible, and yet I make up 27 percent of the universe—which is roughly the same as the space I've been given down here, at the bottom of the page.
You humans can show that I must exist, but what am I?
Please hurry up and find out. Don't keep me in the dark!

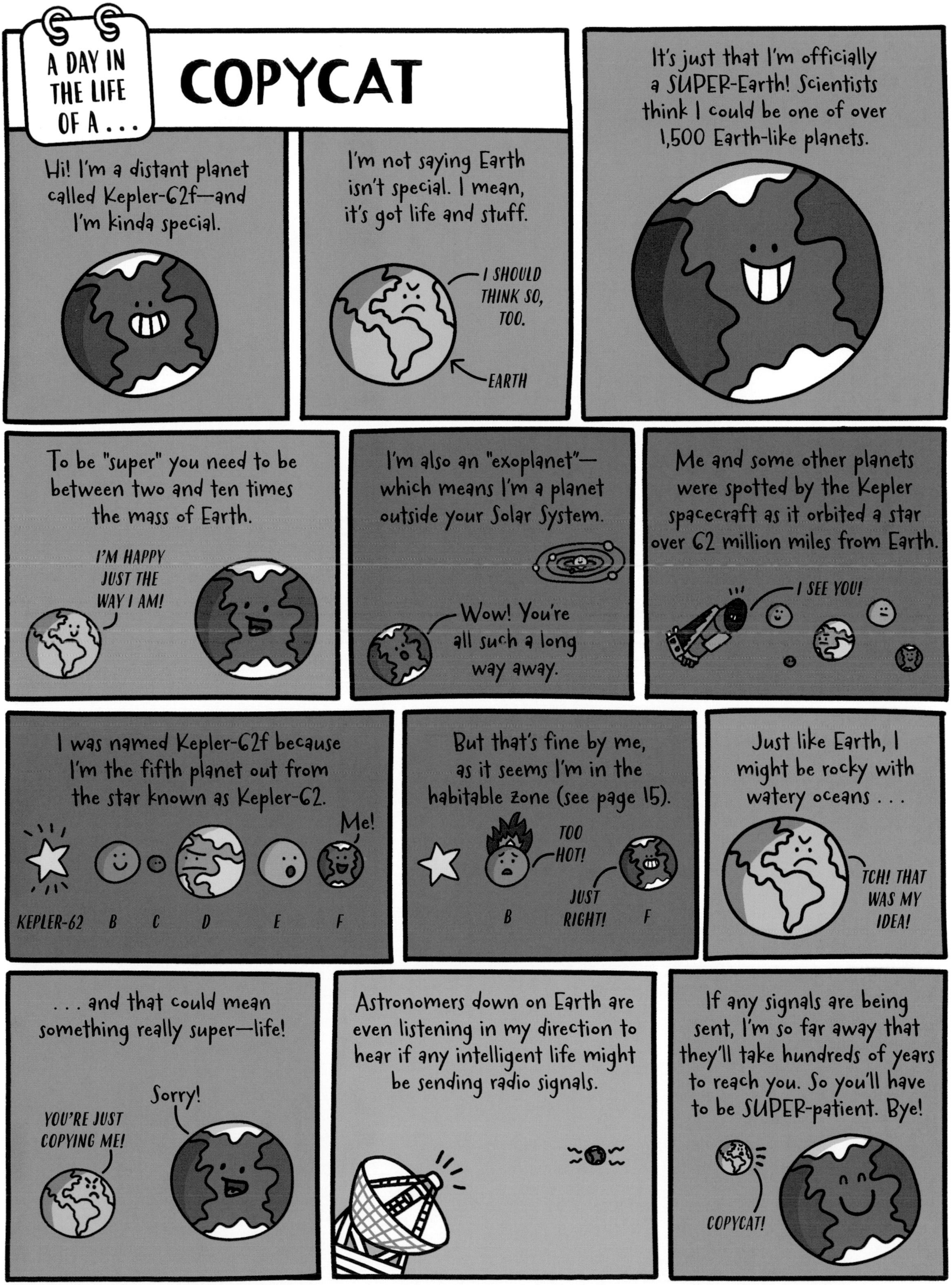
A DAY IN THE LIFE OF A . . .
COPYCAT
Hi! I'm a distant planet called Kepler-62f—and I'm kinda special.
I'm not saying Earth isn't special. I mean, it's got life and stuff.
I SHOULD THINK SO, TOO.
EARTH
It's just that I'm officially a SUPER-Earth! Scientists think I could be one of over 1,500 Earth-like planets.
To be "super" you need to be between two and ten times the mass of Earth.
I'M HAPPY JUST THE WAY I AM!
I'm also an "exoplanet"—which means I'm a planet outside your Solar System.
Wow! You're all such a long way away.
Me and some other planets were spotted by the Kepler spacecraft as it orbited a star over 62 million miles from Earth.
I SEE YOU!
I was named Kepler-62f because I'm the fifth planet out from the star known as Kepler-62.
Me!
KEPLER-62
B
C
D
E
F
But that's fine by me, as it seems I'm in the habitable zone (see page 15).
TOO HOT!
JUST RIGHT!
B
F
Just like Earth, I might be rocky with watery oceans . . .
TCH! THAT WAS MY IDEA!
. . . and that could mean something really super—life!
YOU'RE JUST COPYING ME!
Sorry!
Astronomers down on Earth are even listening in my direction to hear if any intelligent life might be sending radio signals.
If any signals are being sent, I'm so far away that they'll take hundreds of years to reach you. So you'll have to be SUPER-patient. Bye!
COPYCAT!

ARE WE NEARLY THERE YET?

Space is a great place to visit. Imagine if you could jump in a car and drive to the Moon and beyond at a steady 62 miles per hour. Here's how long it might take you to reach some of the universe's top attractions. Just remember to pack some snacks!

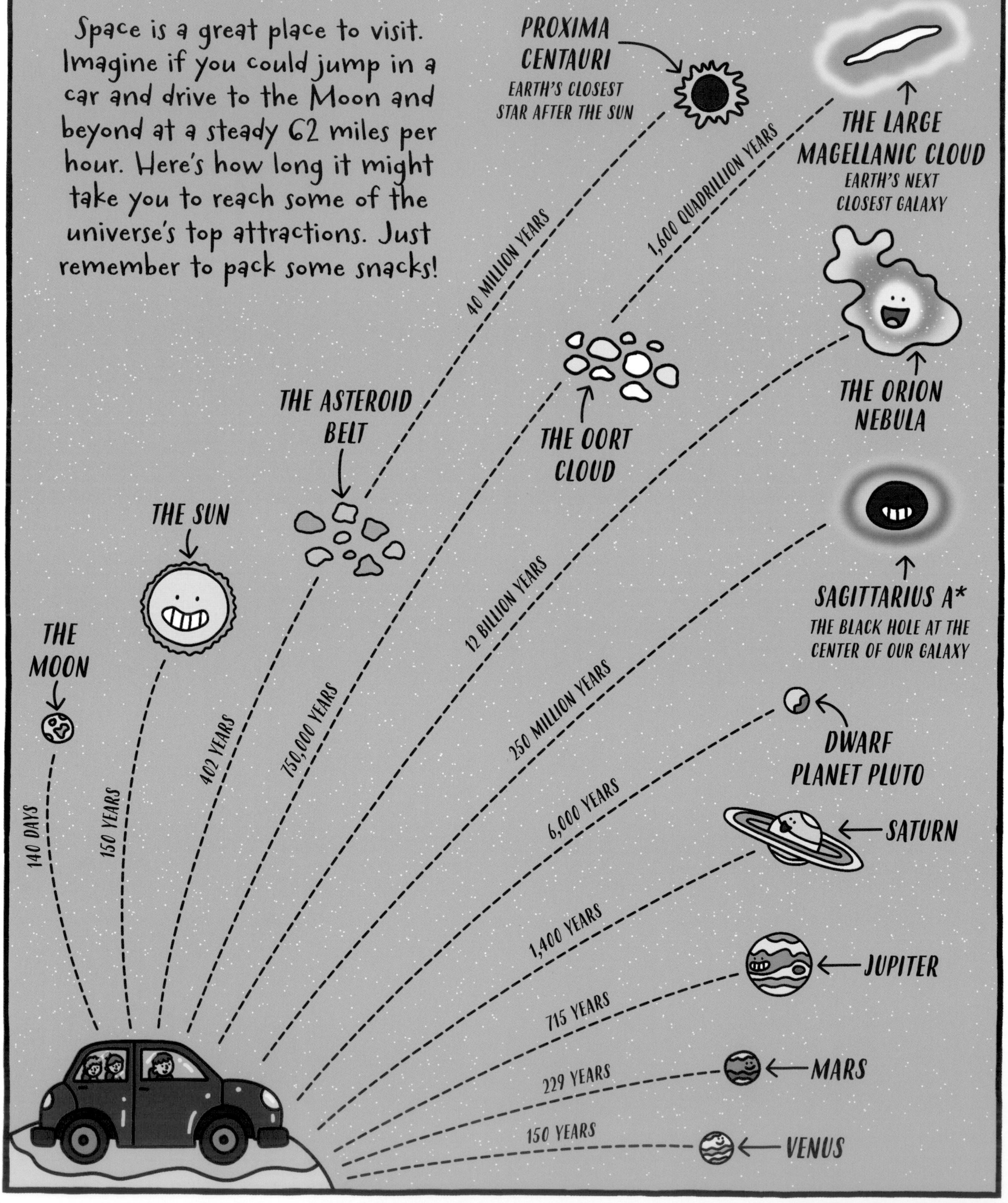

PROXIMA CENTAURI
EARTH'S CLOSEST STAR AFTER THE SUN
40 MILLION YEARS
THE LARGE MAGELLANIC CLOUD
EARTH'S NEXT CLOSEST GALAXY
1,600 QUADRILLION YEARS
THE ORION NEBULA
THE OORT CLOUD
THE ASTEROID BELT
THE SUN
THE MOON
SAGITTARIUS A*
THE BLACK HOLE AT THE CENTER OF OUR GALAXY
12 BILLION YEARS
250 MILLION YEARS
750,000 YEARS
402 YEARS
150 YEARS
140 DAYS
DWARF PLANET PLUTO
6,000 YEARS
SATURN
1,400 YEARS
JUPITER
715 YEARS
MARS
229 YEARS
VENUS
150 YEARS

ALL TIMES GIVEN ARE AVERAGES.

SPACE TRAVEL

Humans have been on Earth for around 300,000 years, but have only been venturing into space for the last six decades. Amazingly, those 60 or so years have seen people walk on the Moon, set up space stations, and even eye up Mars as a future holiday destination.

In this section, you'll discover how people have pursued their dreams of exploring the cosmos. It's one giant leap for humankind!

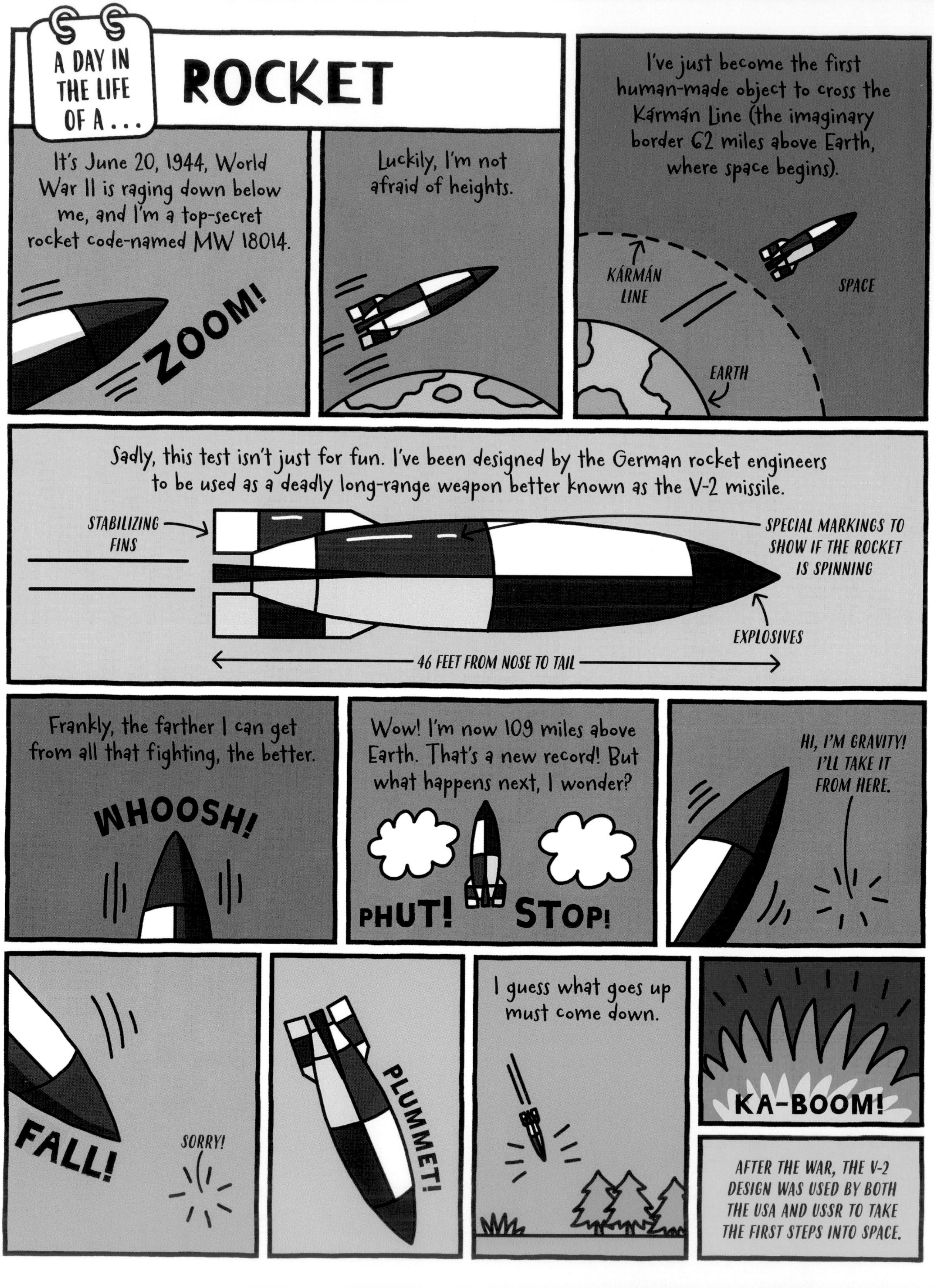
A DAY IN THE LIFE OF A . . .
ROCKET
It's June 20, 1944, World War II is raging down below me, and I'm a top-secret rocket code-named MW 18014.
ZOOM!
Luckily, I'm not afraid of heights.
I've just become the first human-made object to cross the Kármán Line (the imaginary border 62 miles above Earth, where space begins).
KÁRMÁN LINE
SPACE
EARTH
Sadly, this test isn't just for fun. I've been designed by the German rocket engineers to be used as a deadly long-range weapon better known as the V-2 missile.
STABILIZING FINS
SPECIAL MARKINGS TO SHOW IF THE ROCKET IS SPINNING
EXPLOSIVES
46 FEET FROM NOSE TO TAIL
Frankly, the farther I can get from all that fighting, the better.
WHOOSH!
Wow! I'm now 109 miles above Earth. That's a new record! But what happens next, I wonder?
PHUT!
STOP!
HI, I'M GRAVITY! I'LL TAKE IT FROM HERE.
FALL!
SORRY!
PLUMMET!
I guess what goes up must come down.
KA-BOOM!
AFTER THE WAR, THE V-2 DESIGN WAS USED BY BOTH THE USA AND USSR TO TAKE THE FIRST STEPS INTO SPACE.

THE BIGGER PICTURE

TAKING OFF

Rockets have been on the rise since the Chinese invented gunpowder over 1,000 years ago. Here's a pocket history:

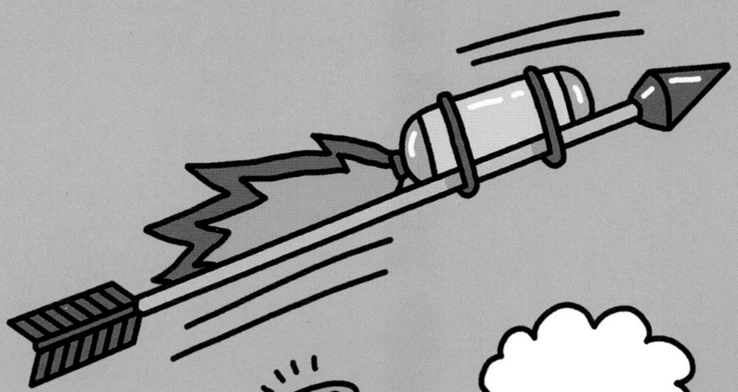

FIREPOWER!

Chinese soldiers used "fire arrows" (arrows with fireworks attached) as early as 1232 CE.

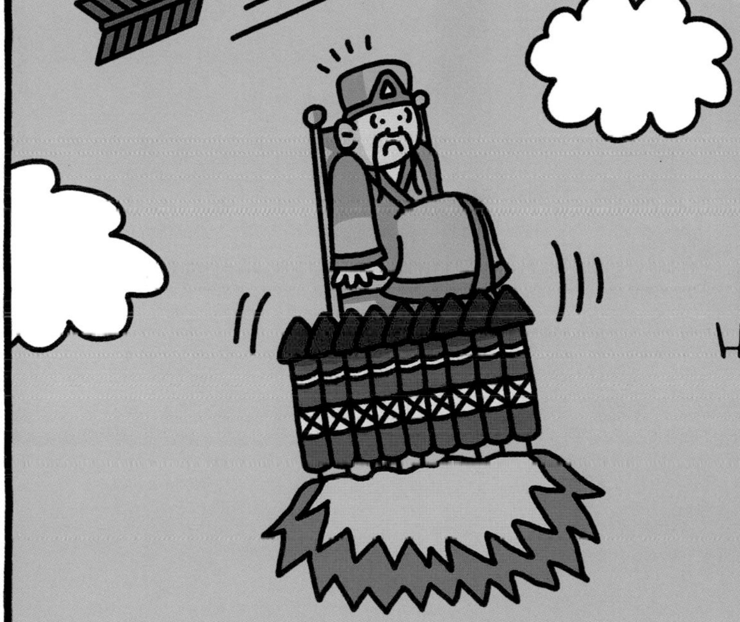

IN THE HOT SEAT

Legend has it that a Chinese court official called Wan Hu tried to fire himself into space around 1500 CE. His attempt involved sitting in a chair with 47 fireworks attached to it. The fireworks exploded and Wan Hu was never seen again!

ROCKET MAN 1

Inspired by sci-fi stories, Russian math teacher Konstantin Tsiolkovsky proposed using rockets to explore space back in 1903. His rules of rocketry are still used today.

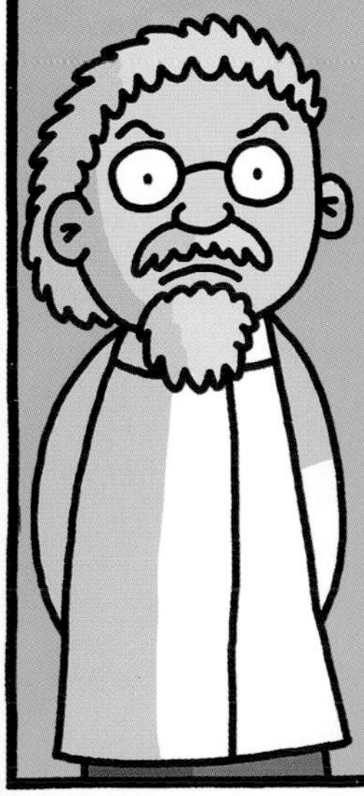

ROCKET MAN 2

American rocketeer Robert Goddard launched the first modern-style liquid-fueled rocket (nicknamed "Nell") in 1926. Nell's flight lasted just two-and-a-half seconds before crashing in a cabbage field.

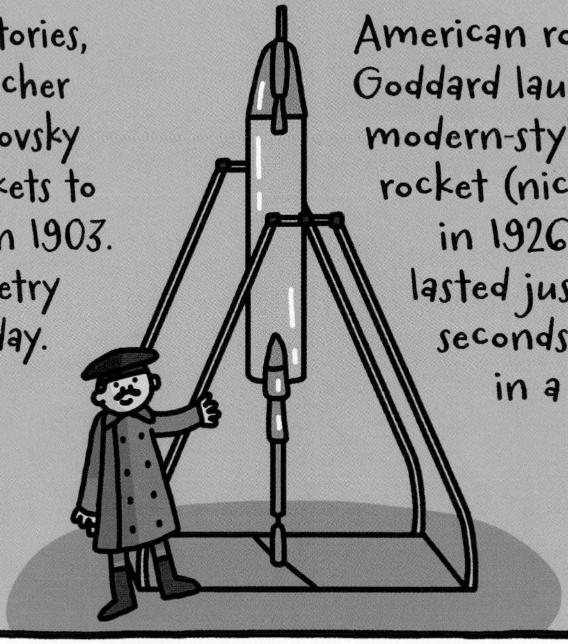

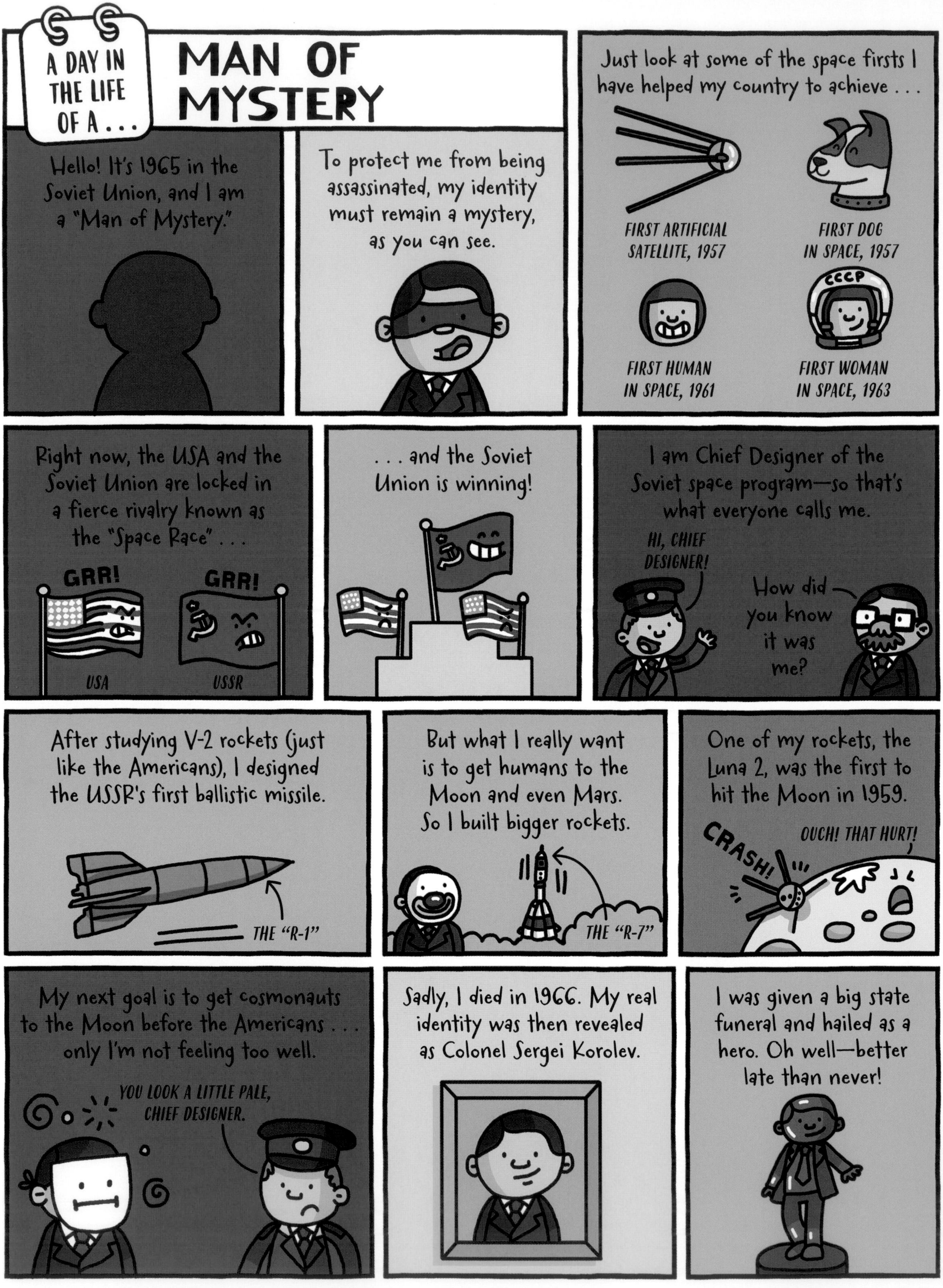
A DAY IN THE LIFE OF A . . .
MAN OF MYSTERY
Hello! It's 1965 in the Soviet Union, and I am a "Man of Mystery."
To protect me from being assassinated, my identity must remain a mystery, as you can see.
Just look at some of the space firsts I have helped my country to achieve . . .
FIRST ARTIFICIAL SATELLITE, 1957
FIRST DOG IN SPACE, 1957
CCCP
FIRST HUMAN IN SPACE, 1961
FIRST WOMAN IN SPACE, 1963
Right now, the USA and the Soviet Union are locked in a fierce rivalry known as the "Space Race" . . .
GRR!
GRR!
USA
USSR
. . . and the Soviet Union is winning!
I am Chief Designer of the Soviet space program—so that's what everyone calls me.
HI, CHIEF DESIGNER!
How did you know it was me?
After studying V-2 rockets (just like the Americans), I designed the USSR's first ballistic missile.
THE "R-1"
But what I really want is to get humans to the Moon and even Mars. So I built bigger rockets.
THE "R-7"
One of my rockets, the Luna 2, was the first to hit the Moon in 1959.
CRASH!
OUCH! THAT HURT!
My next goal is to get cosmonauts to the Moon before the Americans . . . only I'm not feeling too well.
YOU LOOK A LITTLE PALE, CHIEF DESIGNER.
Sadly, I died in 1966. My real identity was then revealed as Colonel Sergei Korolev.
I was given a big state funeral and hailed as a hero. Oh well—better late than never!

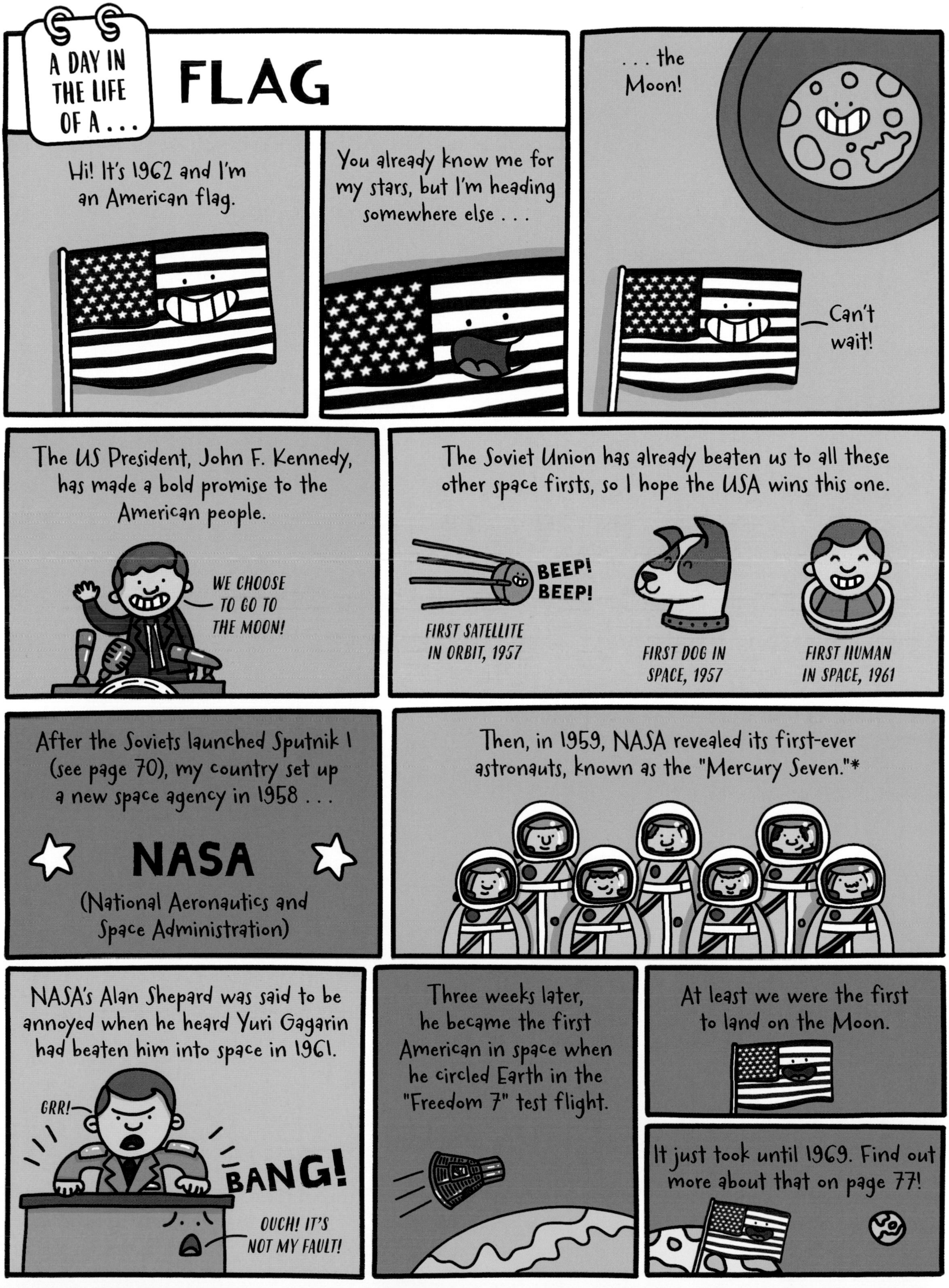
A DAY IN THE LIFE OF A . . .
FLAG
Hi! It's 1962 and I'm an American flag.
You already know me for my stars, but I'm heading somewhere else . . .
. . . the Moon!
Can't wait!
The US President, John F. Kennedy, has made a bold promise to the American people.
WE CHOOSE TO GO TO THE MOON!
The Soviet Union has already beaten us to all these other space firsts, so I hope the USA wins this one.
BEEP! BEEP!
FIRST SATELLITE IN ORBIT, 1957
FIRST DOG IN SPACE, 1957
FIRST HUMAN IN SPACE, 1961
After the Soviets launched Sputnik I (see page 70), my country set up a new space agency in 1958 . . .
NASA
(National Aeronautics and Space Administration)
Then, in 1959, NASA revealed its first-ever astronauts, known as the "Mercury Seven."*
NASA's Alan Shepard was said to be annoyed when he heard Yuri Gagarin had beaten him into space in 1961.
GRR!
BANG!
OUCH! IT'S NOT MY FAULT!
Three weeks later, he became the first American in space when he circled Earth in the "Freedom 7" test flight.
At least we were the first to land on the Moon.
It just took until 1969. Find out more about that on page 77!

*THE MERCURY SEVEN WERE: ALAN SHEPARD, GUS GRISSOM, GORDON COOPER, DEKE SLAYTON, WALLY SCHIRRA, JOHN GLENN, AND SCOTT CARPENTER.

MEET THE FAMILY

Sergei Korolev (see page 66) designed a range of increasingly powerful rockets, helping the Soviet Union to achieve many historic space firsts. A group of rocket designs such as this is known as a "family." It's time to meet some of this family's members:

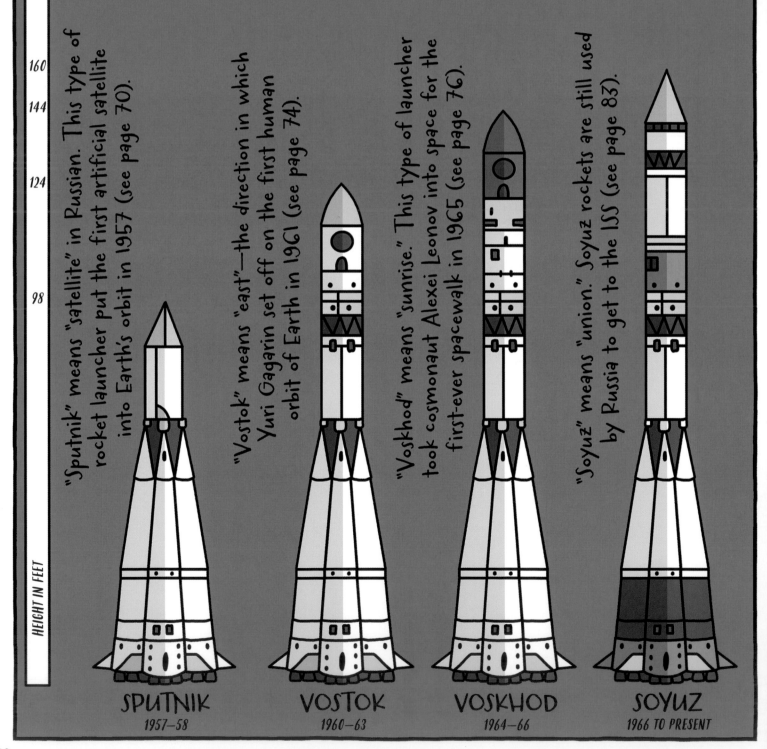

HEIGHT IN FEET

160
144
124
98

"Sputnik" means "satellite" in Russian. This type of rocket launcher put the first artificial satellite into Earth's orbit in 1957 (see page 70).

"Vostok" means "east"—the direction in which Yuri Gagarin set off on the first human orbit of Earth in 1961 (see page 74).

"Voskhod" means "sunrise." This type of launcher took cosmonaut Alexei Leonov into space for the first-ever spacewalk in 1965 (see page 76).

"Soyuz" means "union." Soyuz rockets are still used by Russia to get to the ISS (see page 83).

SPUTNIK
1957–58

VOSTOK
1960–63

VOSKHOD
1964–66

SOYUZ
1966 TO PRESENT

UP, UP, AND AWAY

The size of NASA's rockets has grown with the size of the space agency's ambitions. From the single-person Mercury to the mighty Saturn V, this is America's Apollo-era rocket family:

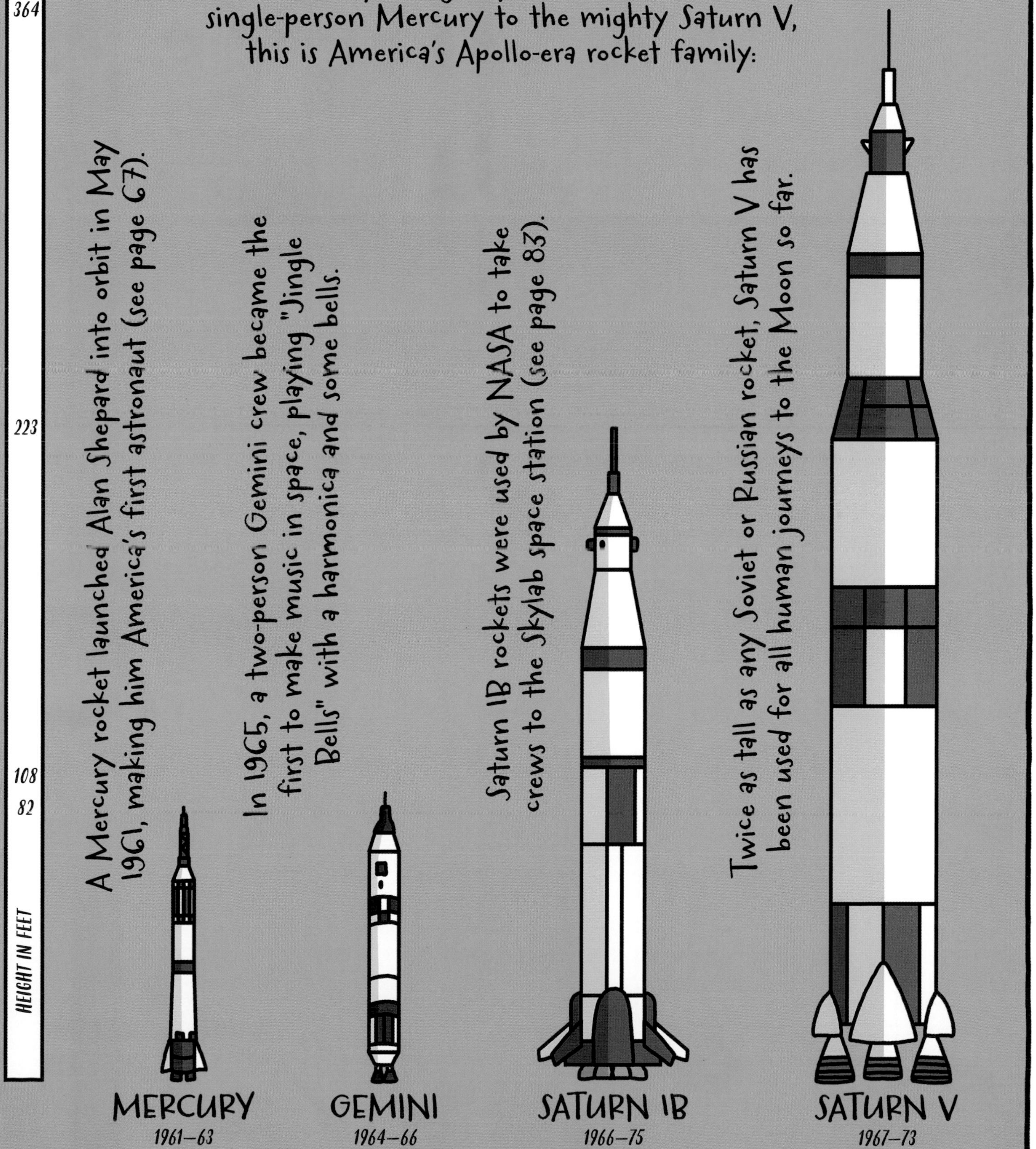
HEIGHT IN FEET
364
223
108
82
A Mercury rocket launched Alan Shepard into orbit in May 1961, making him America's first astronaut (see page 67).
In 1965, a two-person Gemini crew became the first to make music in space, playing "Jingle Bells" with a harmonica and some bells.
Saturn IB rockets were used by NASA to take crews to the Skylab space station (see page 83).
Twice as tall as any Soviet or Russian rocket, Saturn V has been used for all human journeys to the Moon so far.
MERCURY
1961–63
GEMINI
1964–66
SATURN IB
1966–75
SATURN V
1967–73

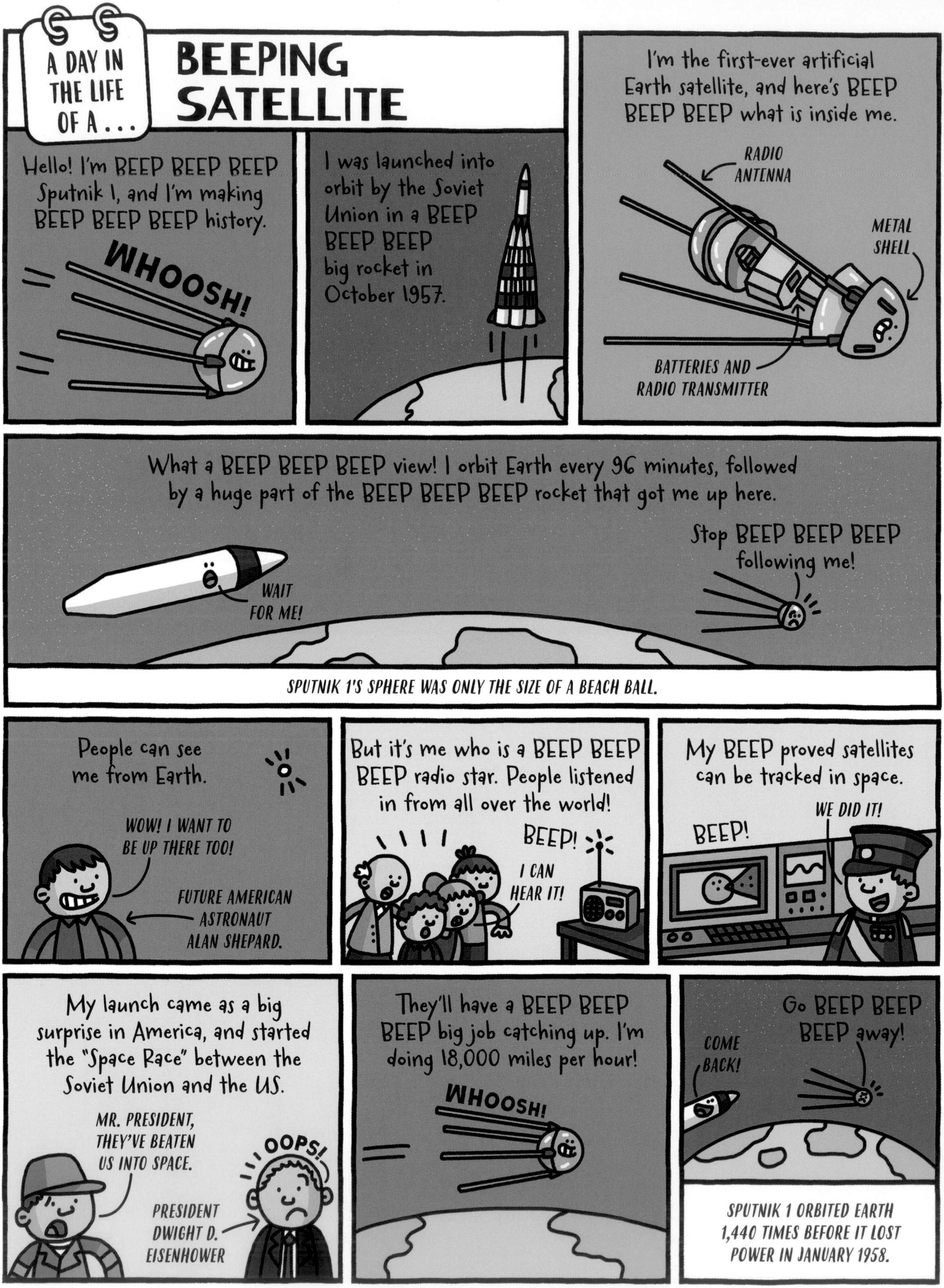
A DAY IN THE LIFE OF A . . .
BEEPING SATELLITE
Hello! I'm BEEP BEEP BEEP Sputnik 1, and I'm making BEEP BEEP BEEP history.
WHOOSH!
I was launched into orbit by the Soviet Union in a BEEP BEEP BEEP big rocket in October 1957.
I'm the first-ever artificial Earth satellite, and here's BEEP BEEP BEEP what is inside me.
RADIO ANTENNA
METAL SHELL
BATTERIES AND RADIO TRANSMITTER
What a BEEP BEEP BEEP view! I orbit Earth every 96 minutes, followed by a huge part of the BEEP BEEP BEEP rocket that got me up here.
WAIT FOR ME!
Stop BEEP BEEP BEEP following me!
SPUTNIK 1'S SPHERE WAS ONLY THE SIZE OF A BEACH BALL.
People can see me from Earth.
WOW! I WANT TO BE UP THERE TOO!
FUTURE AMERICAN ASTRONAUT ALAN SHEPARD.
But it's me who is a BEEP BEEP BEEP radio star. People listened in from all over the world!
BEEP!
I CAN HEAR IT!
My BEEP proved satellites can be tracked in space.
BEEP!
WE DID IT!
My launch came as a big surprise in America, and started the "Space Race" between the Soviet Union and the US.
MR. PRESIDENT, THEY'VE BEATEN US INTO SPACE.
OOPS!
PRESIDENT DWIGHT D. EISENHOWER
They'll have a BEEP BEEP BEEP big job catching up. I'm doing 18,000 miles per hour!
WHOOSH!
Go BEEP BEEP BEEP away!
COME BACK!
SPUTNIK 1 ORBITED EARTH 1,440 TIMES BEFORE IT LOST POWER IN JANUARY 1958.

THE BIGGER PICTURE

LIFE ~~ON~~ OFF EARTH

Animals have been helping humans to research the risks of space travel for 75 years (without any choice in the matter, of course). The dangers of liftoff, weightlessness, and space radiation were all tested on other species first. Here are some notable astro-animals:

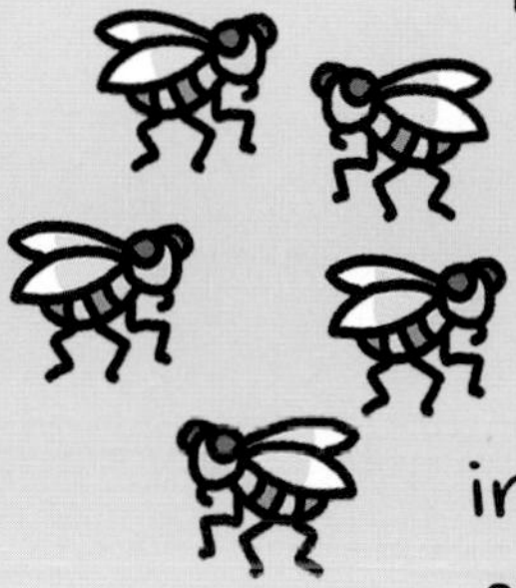

HIGH FLYERS

Tiny flies were the first species in space. Fruit flies were flown 68 miles above the Earth by the USA in 1947, in the nose cone of a captured V-2 rocket.

CANINE COSMONAUT

Moscow street stray Laika became the first animal to orbit Earth in November 1957. She sadly died during her mission, angering many animal-lovers.

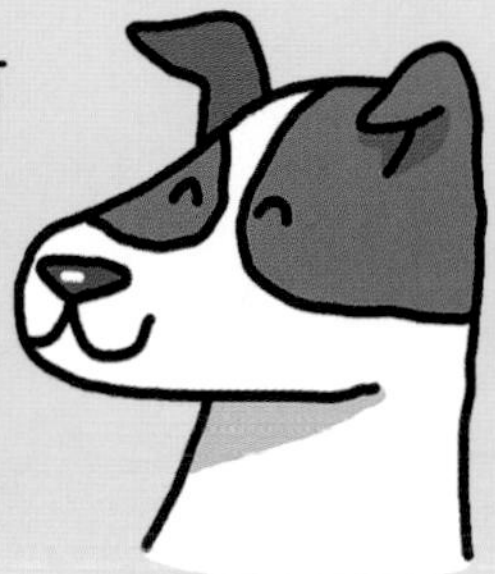

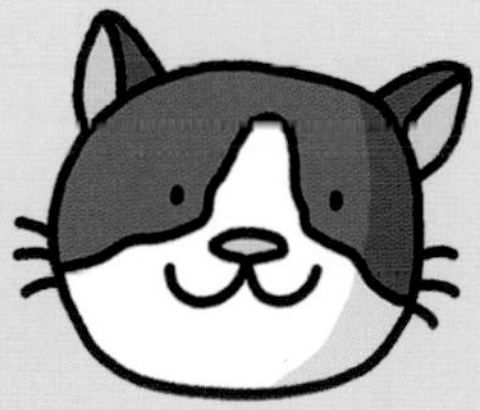

PURRFECT LANDING

Félicette became the first (and so far only) astro-cat in 1963, when she was launched into space by the French. She returned to Earth safely and was hailed a heroine!

TURBO TORTOISES

The Soviets sent two tortoises (plus some fruit-fly eggs) around the Moon in 1968. They became the first animals to complete a lunar orbit.

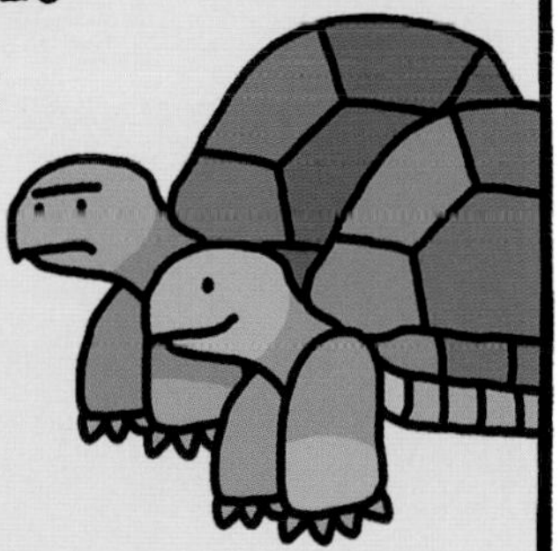

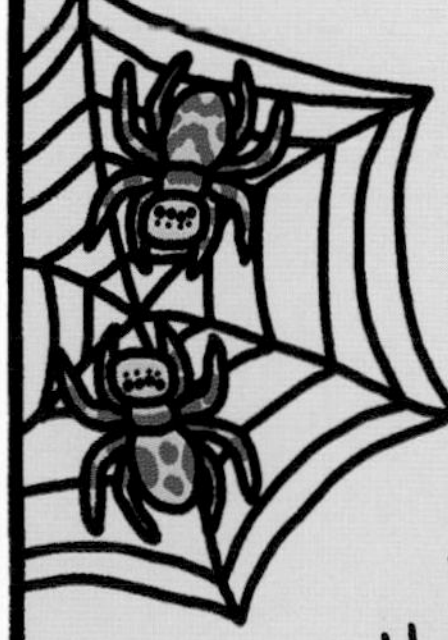

ASTRO ARACHNIDS

Anita and Arabella—two garden spiders—were flown aboard NASA's Skylab space station in 1973 to see if weightlessness would affect their webs. It did at first, but the spiders very soon got back to spinning tip-top traps.

SPACE SURVIVORS

In 2007, some microscopic mini-beasts named tardigrades spent 12 days in open space on a satellite. Amazingly, some survived (find out more on page 104).

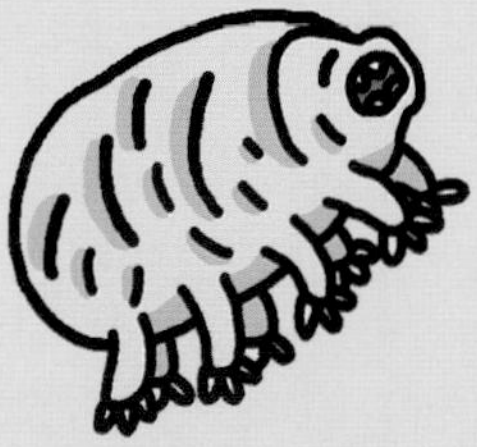

The secret diary of a

SPACE MONKEY

Extracts from the diary of "Miss Baker," a space-race-era squirrel monkey

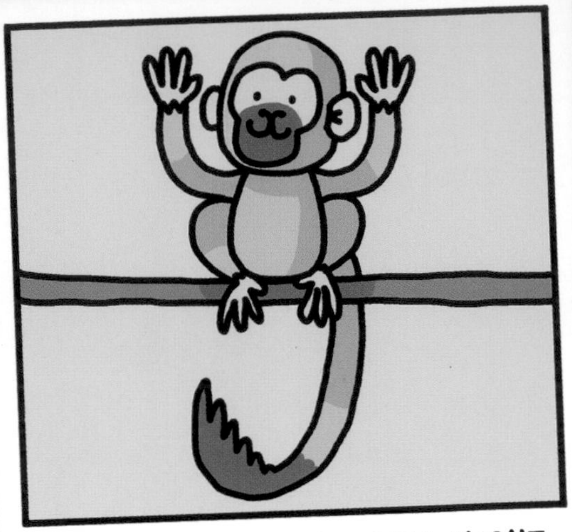

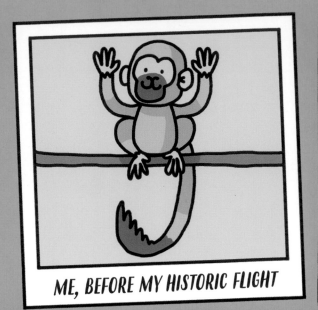

ME, BEFORE MY HISTORIC FLIGHT

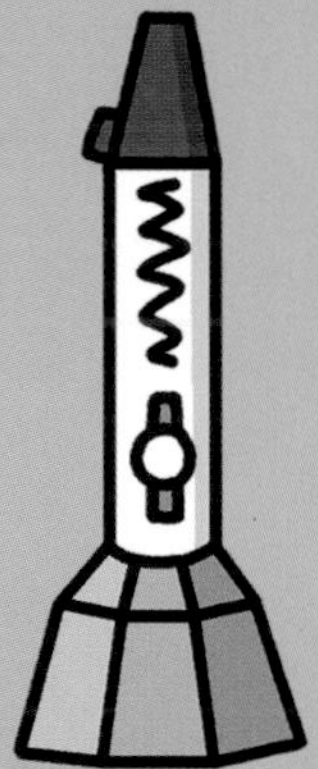

JUPITER MISSILE

EARLY 1959

Sorry, but I'm not sure what the date is. I've just been brought (against my will!) all the way from my home in Peru to a pet shop in Florida, USA. Worse still, it seems like me and 25 other squirrel monkeys are now on the move again. We've all been sold to the American space agency NASA. Who knows what they could want us for? Space-banana research?

ONE WEEK LATER

Now I know why NASA wants us. We're being prepared to go into space on one of their Jupiter missiles. The only "space" I want to see is a nice green space with lots of trees. My plan is to be super-nice to the scientists, so they choose one of the other monkeys instead.

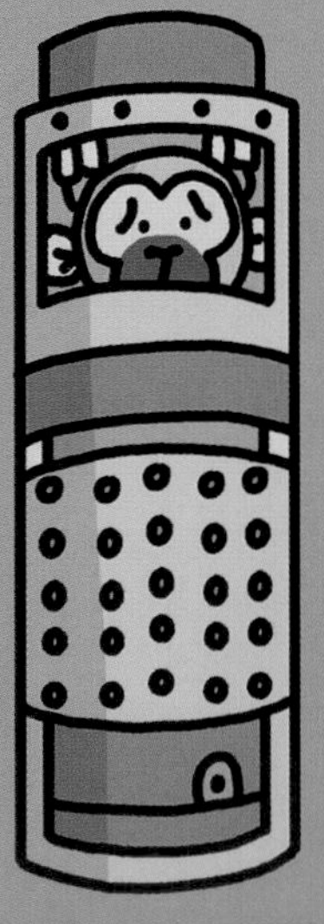

ME IN MY CAPSULE

NEXT DAY

Well, that plan backfired. The scientists ended up picking me because I'm so nice and gentle to work with. I've already been measured for a special capsule and given a tiny space helmet with electrodes attached to monitor my body. This is so unfair!

MAY 28, 1959 (VERY EARLY)

Looks like I'm about to make another unwanted journey. Before dawn this morning, me and a larger rhesus macaque monkey were placed in our capsules inside the nose cone of a Jupiter rocket. She's been given the name "Able," and they're calling me "Miss Baker." Also on board are some human blood samples, yeast, bacteria, mustard seeds, and some onions. But no bananas. Bah!

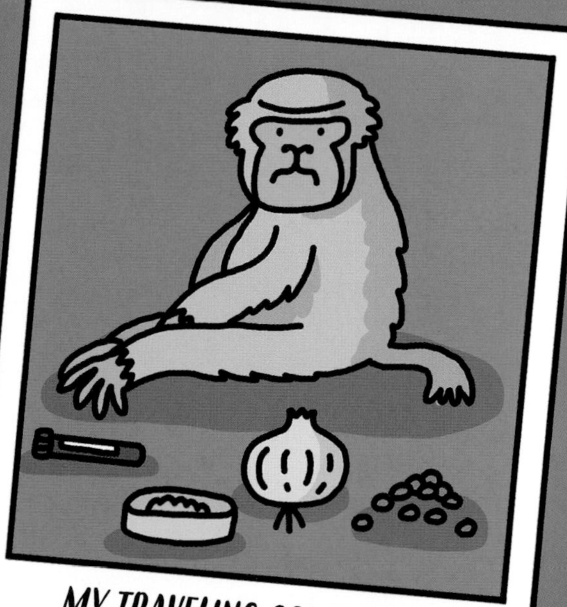

MY TRAVELING COMPANIONS

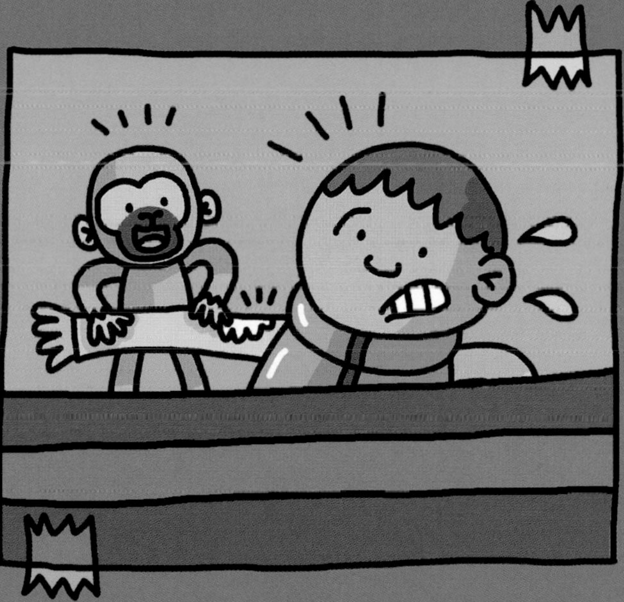

MAY 28, 1959 (LATER)

Hurray! We all survived! The flight went 298 miles up and lasted just 16 minutes, with nine minutes of weightlessness. After landing in the ocean, we were rescued by some people in a big ship. I bit my "rescuer" on the arm. Serves him right, too. I didn't ask to go into space!

NEXT DAY

I'm a celebrity! The press are calling me and Able "monkeynauts," and I had my picture taken on top of a model rocket. Given their rivalry with the Soviet Union, NASA are very pleased that we survived. I am too! Now, where are those space-bananas?

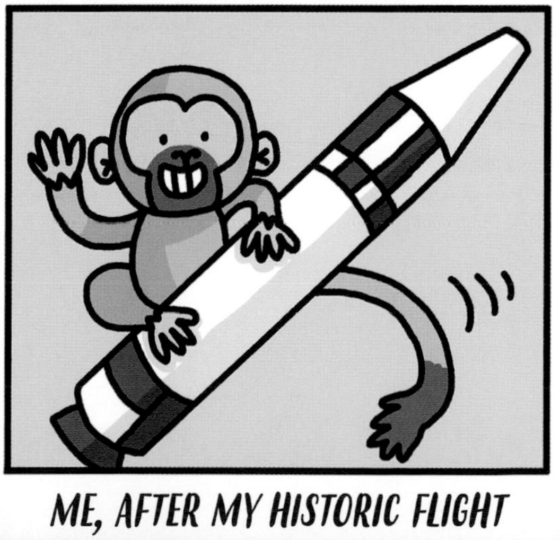

ME, AFTER MY HISTORIC FLIGHT

MISS BAKER LIVED TO BE 27 YEARS OLD (A SQUIRREL MONKEY RECORD!) AND WAS TREATED TO BANANAS TOPPED WITH STRAWBERRY JELLY ON THE TWENTY-FIFTH ANNIVERSARY OF HER FLIGHT.

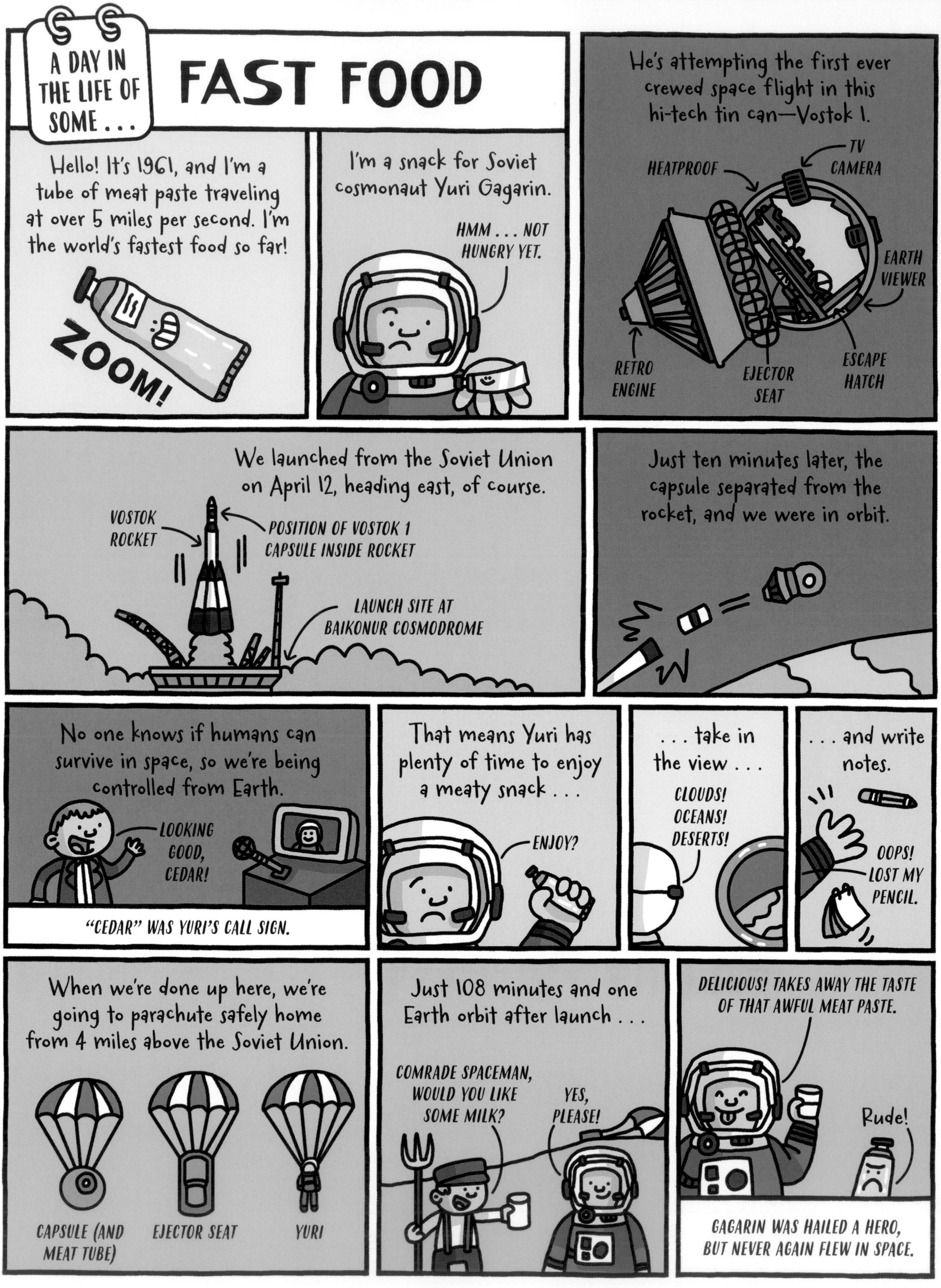
A DAY IN THE LIFE OF SOME . . .
FAST FOOD
Hello! It's 1961, and I'm a tube of meat paste traveling at over 5 miles per second. I'm the world's fastest food so far!
ZOOM!
I'm a snack for Soviet cosmonaut Yuri Gagarin.
HMM . . . NOT HUNGRY YET.
He's attempting the first ever crewed space flight in this hi-tech tin can—Vostok 1.
HEATPROOF
TV CAMERA
EARTH VIEWER
RETRO ENGINE
EJECTOR SEAT
ESCAPE HATCH
We launched from the Soviet Union on April 12, heading east, of course.
VOSTOK ROCKET
POSITION OF VOSTOK 1 CAPSULE INSIDE ROCKET
LAUNCH SITE AT BAIKONUR COSMODROME
Just ten minutes later, the capsule separated from the rocket, and we were in orbit.
No one knows if humans can survive in space, so we're being controlled from Earth.
LOOKING GOOD, CEDAR!
"CEDAR" WAS YURI'S CALL SIGN.
That means Yuri has plenty of time to enjoy a meaty snack . . .
ENJOY?
. . . take in the view . . .
CLOUDS! OCEANS! DESERTS!
. . . and write notes.
OOPS! LOST MY PENCIL.
When we're done up here, we're going to parachute safely home from 4 miles above the Soviet Union.
CAPSULE (AND MEAT TUBE)
EJECTOR SEAT
YURI
Just 108 minutes and one Earth orbit after launch . . .
COMRADE SPACEMAN, WOULD YOU LIKE SOME MILK?
YES, PLEASE!
DELICIOUS! TAKES AWAY THE TASTE OF THAT AWFUL MEAT PASTE.
Rude!
GAGARIN WAS HAILED A HERO, BUT NEVER AGAIN FLEW IN SPACE.

THE BIGGER PICTURE

SPACE'S ACES

Soviet Union cosmonaut Yuri Gagarin was the first person to fly in space, but here are some other historic human pioneers:

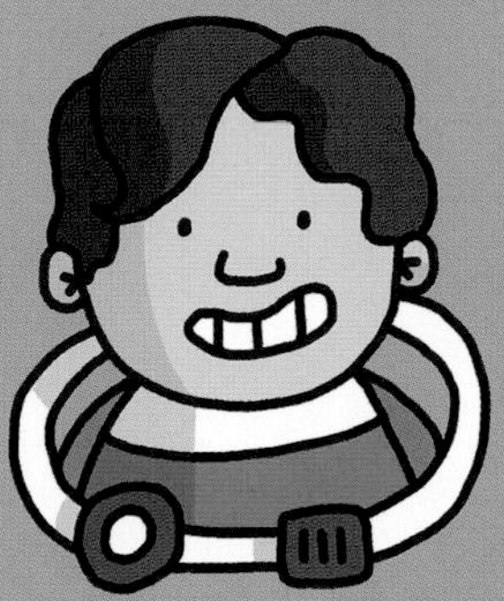

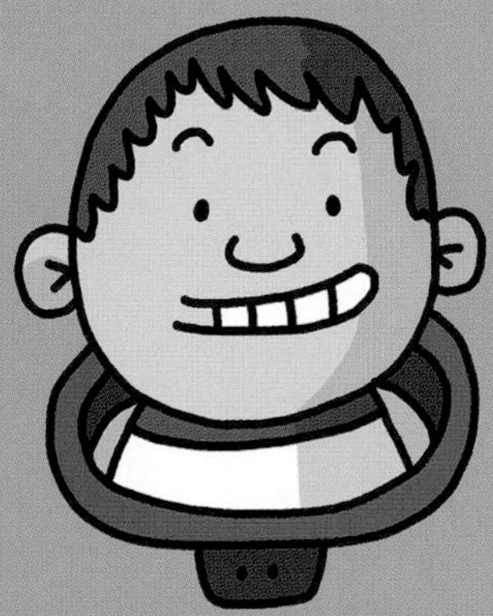

VALENTINA TERESHKOVA

Soviet cosmonaut Valentina was a skilled skydiver who became the first woman in space in 1963. Her code name was "Chaika" (Russian for "seagull"), and she remains the youngest woman ever to travel to space.

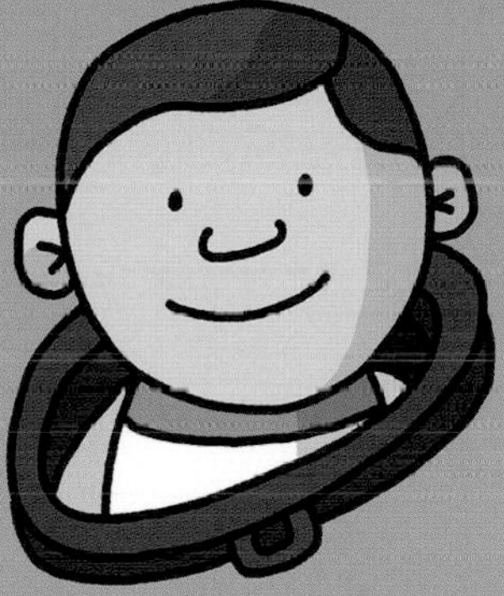

ALAN SHEPARD

In 1961, Alan became the first American in space (see page 67). Ten years later, he flew to the Moon, and to this day he remains the only person to have played golf on its surface.

NEIL ARMSTRONG

NASA astronaut Neil became the first human to walk on the Moon on July 20, 1969 (see page 77). He became so famous that his barber later kept his cut-off hair to sell to collectors.

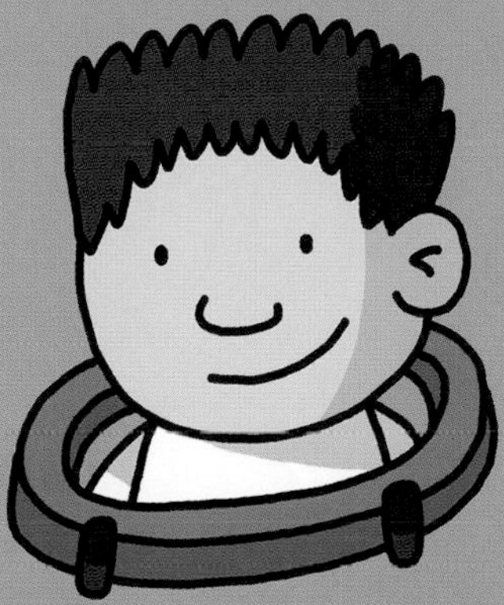

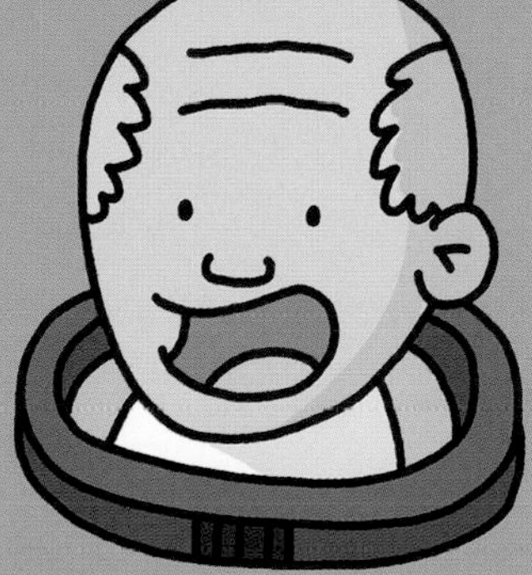

YANG LIWEI

Liwei became the first Chinese astronaut in 2003, on a mission that saw China become the third independent space nation (after the USA and USSR/Russia).

DENNIS TITO

American engineer Dennis became the first space tourist when, in 2001, he paid $20 million to spend eight days on the International Space Station.

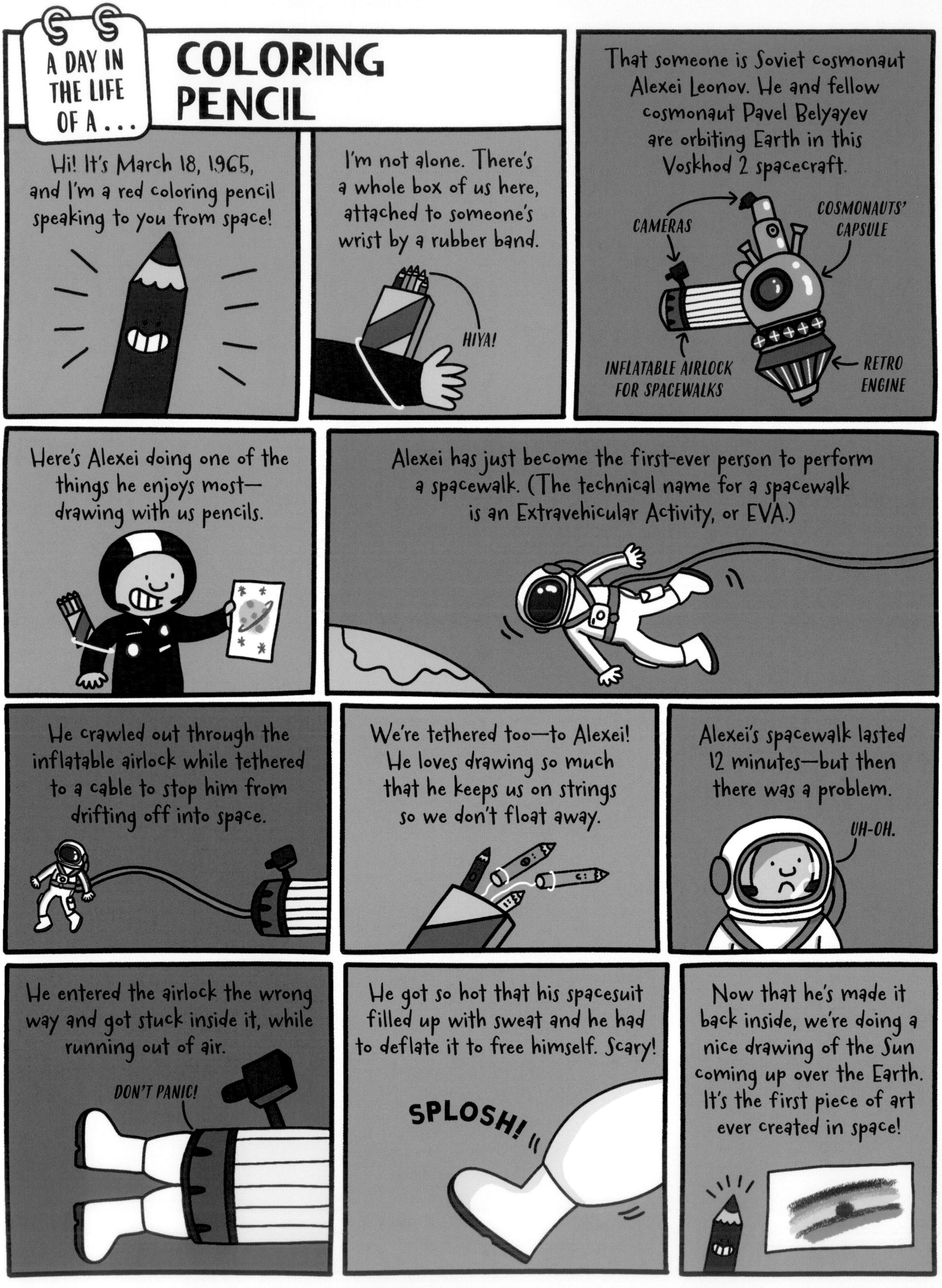
A DAY IN THE LIFE OF A . . .
COLORING PENCIL
Hi! It's March 18, 1965, and I'm a red coloring pencil speaking to you from space!
I'm not alone. There's a whole box of us here, attached to someone's wrist by a rubber band.
HIYA!
That someone is Soviet cosmonaut Alexei Leonov. He and fellow cosmonaut Pavel Belyayev are orbiting Earth in this Voskhod 2 spacecraft.
CAMERAS
COSMONAUTS' CAPSULE
INFLATABLE AIRLOCK FOR SPACEWALKS
RETRO ENGINE
Here's Alexei doing one of the things he enjoys most—drawing with us pencils.
Alexei has just become the first-ever person to perform a spacewalk. (The technical name for a spacewalk is an Extravehicular Activity, or EVA.)
He crawled out through the inflatable airlock while tethered to a cable to stop him from drifting off into space.
We're tethered too—to Alexei! He loves drawing so much that he keeps us on strings so we don't float away.
Alexei's spacewalk lasted 12 minutes—but then there was a problem.
UH-OH.
He entered the airlock the wrong way and got stuck inside it, while running out of air.
DON'T PANIC!
He got so hot that his spacesuit filled up with sweat and he had to deflate it to free himself. Scary!
SPLOSH!
Now that he's made it back inside, we're doing a nice drawing of the Sun coming up over the Earth. It's the first piece of art ever created in space!

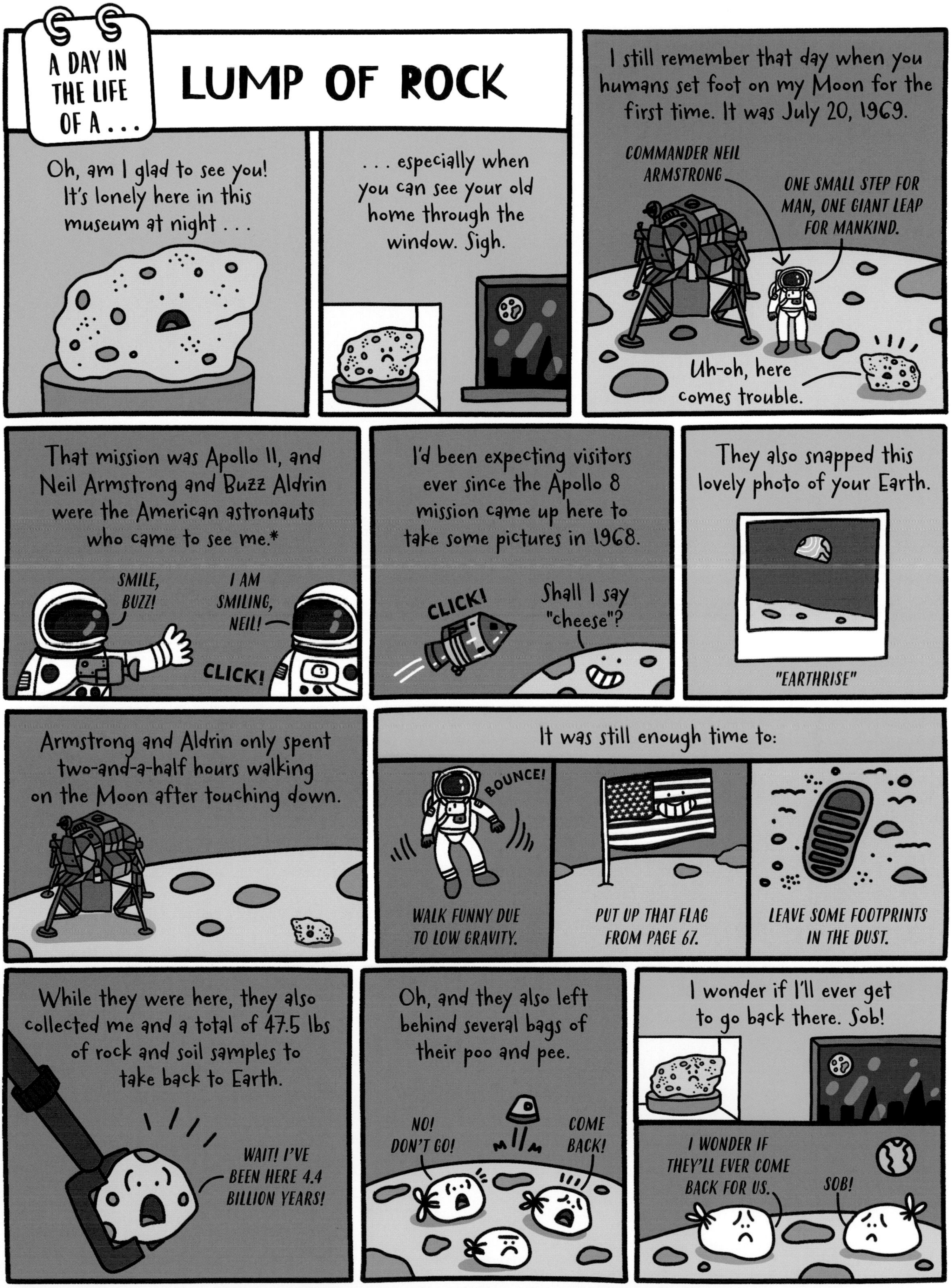
A DAY IN THE LIFE OF A . . .
LUMP OF ROCK
Oh, am I glad to see you! It's lonely here in this museum at night . . .
. . . especially when you can see your old home through the window. Sigh.
I still remember that day when you humans set foot on my Moon for the first time. It was July 20, 1969.
COMMANDER NEIL ARMSTRONG
ONE SMALL STEP FOR MAN, ONE GIANT LEAP FOR MANKIND.
Uh-oh, here comes trouble.
That mission was Apollo 11, and Neil Armstrong and Buzz Aldrin were the American astronauts who came to see me.*
SMILE, BUZZ!
I AM SMILING, NEIL!
CLICK!
I'd been expecting visitors ever since the Apollo 8 mission came up here to take some pictures in 1968.
CLICK!
Shall I say "cheese"?
They also snapped this lovely photo of your Earth.
"EARTHRISE"
Armstrong and Aldrin only spent two-and-a-half hours walking on the Moon after touching down.
It was still enough time to:
BOUNCE!
WALK FUNNY DUE TO LOW GRAVITY.
PUT UP THAT FLAG FROM PAGE 67.
LEAVE SOME FOOTPRINTS IN THE DUST.
While they were here, they also collected me and a total of 47.5 lbs of rock and soil samples to take back to Earth.
WAIT! I'VE BEEN HERE 4.4 BILLION YEARS!
Oh, and they also left behind several bags of their poo and pee.
NO! DON'T GO!
COME BACK!
I wonder if I'll ever get to go back there. Sob!
I WONDER IF THEY'LL EVER COME BACK FOR US.
SOB!

*A THIRD ASTRONAUT, MICHAEL COLLINS, REMAINED IN THE COMMAND MODULE WHILE ARMSTRONG AND ALDRIN VISITED THE MOON'S SURFACE.

From 1969 until 1972, NASA's Apollo missions landed a total of 12 people on the Moon. Pushed into space by a mighty Saturn V launch vehicle, each three-person crew was sent on a 1.5-million-km round trip. The missions used the gravity of the Earth and Moon to fly in a giant figure eight. In the early 1970s, the frequent blast-offs were watched on TV by millions of people worldwide.

ROCKET STAGES
The Saturn V was a stack of powerful rockets known as stages.

ESCAPE SYSTEM FOR EMERGENCIES

COMMAND MODULE (INSIDE HERE)

SERVICE MODULE (INSIDE HERE)

LUNAR MODULE (INSIDE HERE)

THIRD STAGE

SECOND STAGE

FIRST STAGE

LAUNCH ENGINES

THE APOLLO MISSIONS: FROM LIFTOFF TO SPLASHDOWN

1. From the launch site at Cape Canaveral in Florida, USA, the spacecraft is sent into orbit around Earth before heading toward the Moon.

2. The rocket stages fall away in turn as their fuel is used up.

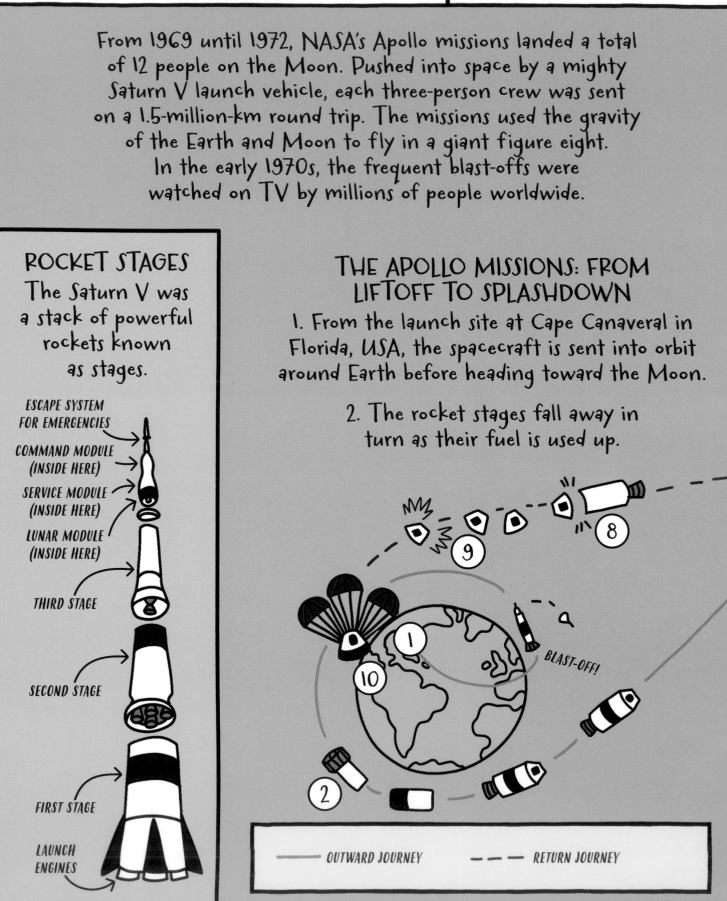

BLAST-OFF!

——— OUTWARD JOURNEY   – – – RETURN JOURNEY

TO THE MOON . . . AND BACK!

3. Set free from the third stage, the crewed command module and the service module turn and join with the lunar module.

4. Now combined, the command module, service module, and lunar module flip and enter the Moon's orbit.

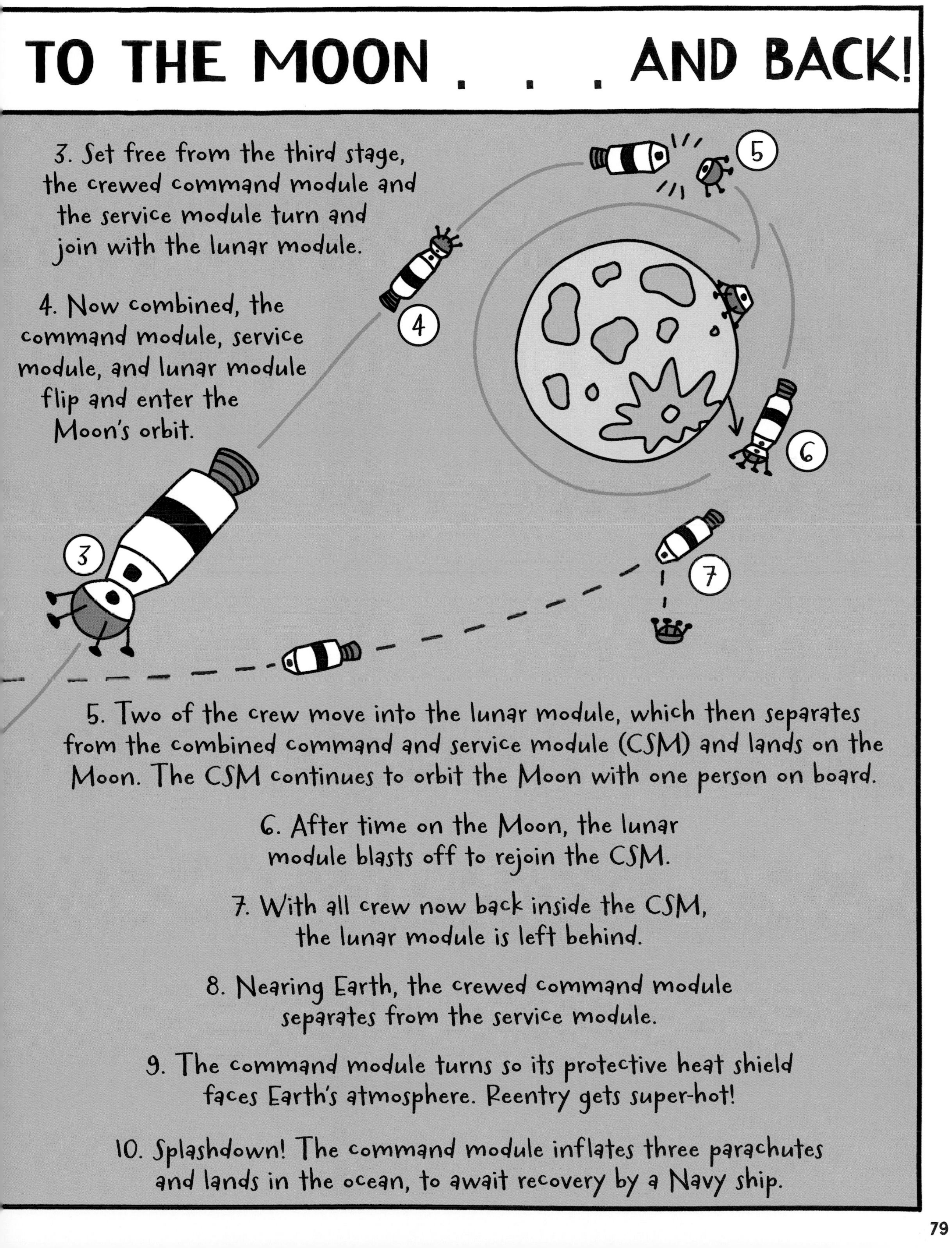

5
4
6
3
7

5. Two of the crew move into the lunar module, which then separates from the combined command and service module (CSM) and lands on the Moon. The CSM continues to orbit the Moon with one person on board.

6. After time on the Moon, the lunar module blasts off to rejoin the CSM.

7. With all crew now back inside the CSM, the lunar module is left behind.

8. Nearing Earth, the crewed command module separates from the service module.

9. The command module turns so its protective heat shield faces Earth's atmosphere. Reentry gets super-hot!

10. Splashdown! The command module inflates three parachutes and lands in the ocean, to await recovery by a Navy ship.

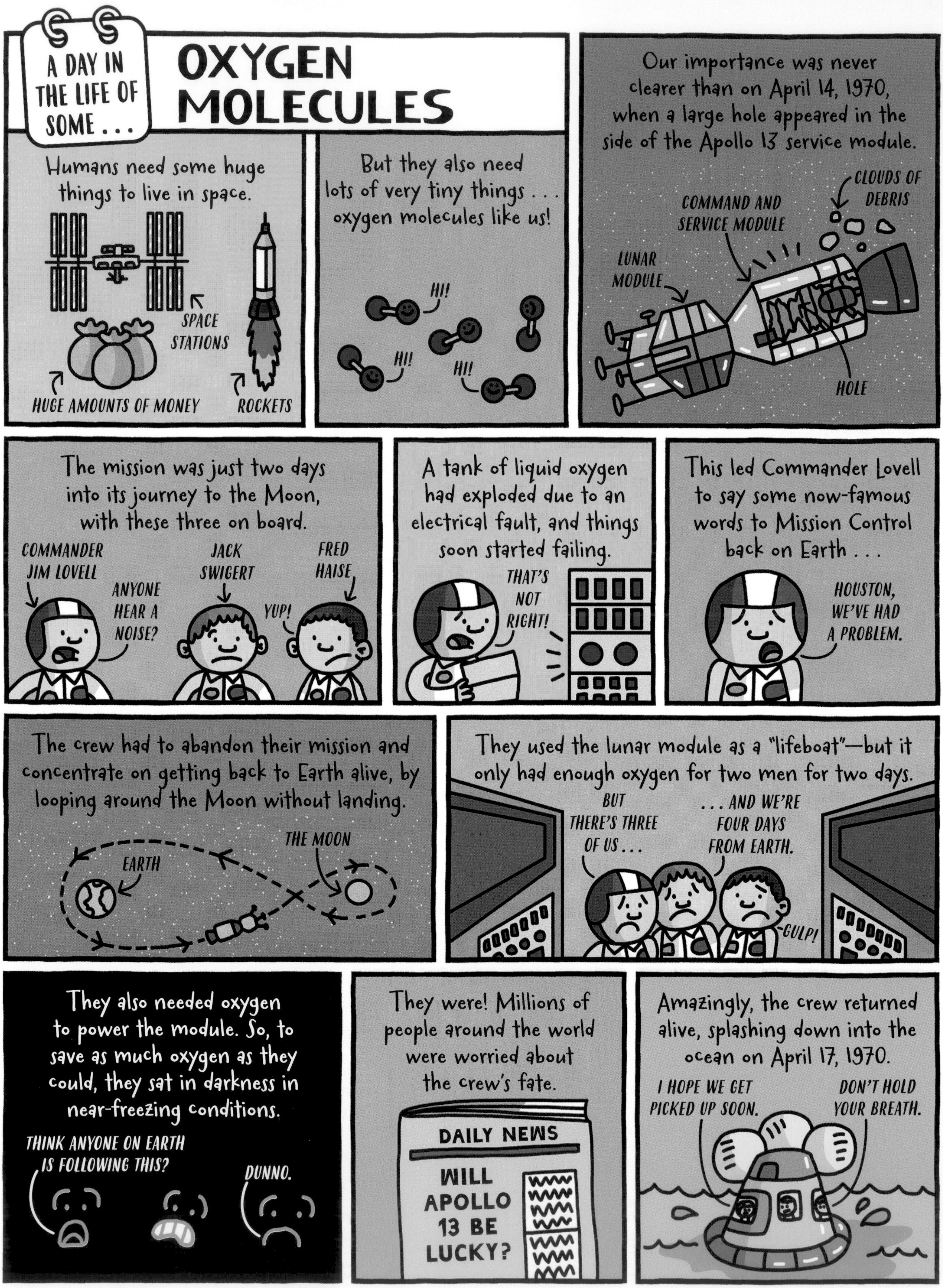
A DAY IN THE LIFE OF SOME . . .
OXYGEN MOLECULES
Humans need some huge things to live in space.
SPACE STATIONS
HUGE AMOUNTS OF MONEY
ROCKETS
But they also need lots of very tiny things . . . oxygen molecules like us!
HI!
HI!
HI!
Our importance was never clearer than on April 14, 1970, when a large hole appeared in the side of the Apollo 13 service module.
CLOUDS OF DEBRIS
COMMAND AND SERVICE MODULE
LUNAR MODULE
HOLE
The mission was just two days into its journey to the Moon, with these three on board.
COMMANDER JIM LOVELL
JACK SWIGERT
FRED HAISE
ANYONE HEAR A NOISE?
YUP!
A tank of liquid oxygen had exploded due to an electrical fault, and things soon started failing.
THAT'S NOT RIGHT!
This led Commander Lovell to say some now-famous words to Mission Control back on Earth . . .
HOUSTON, WE'VE HAD A PROBLEM.
The crew had to abandon their mission and concentrate on getting back to Earth alive, by looping around the Moon without landing.
THE MOON
EARTH
They used the lunar module as a "lifeboat"—but it only had enough oxygen for two men for two days.
BUT THERE'S THREE OF US . . .
. . . AND WE'RE FOUR DAYS FROM EARTH.
GULP!
They also needed oxygen to power the module. So, to save as much oxygen as they could, they sat in darkness in near-freezing conditions.
THINK ANYONE ON EARTH IS FOLLOWING THIS?
DUNNO.
They were! Millions of people around the world were worried about the crew's fate.
DAILY NEWS
WILL APOLLO 13 BE LUCKY?
Amazingly, the crew returned alive, splashing down into the ocean on April 17, 1970.
I HOPE WE GET PICKED UP SOON.
DON'T HOLD YOUR BREATH.

THE BIGGER PICTURE

OVER THE MOON

NASA's final three Apollo missions made walking on the Moon seem rather old-fashioned, with the introduction of their lunar roving vehicle (also known as an LRV or moon buggy). Here's a look at some of the most notable rovers to go for a drive on the Moon:

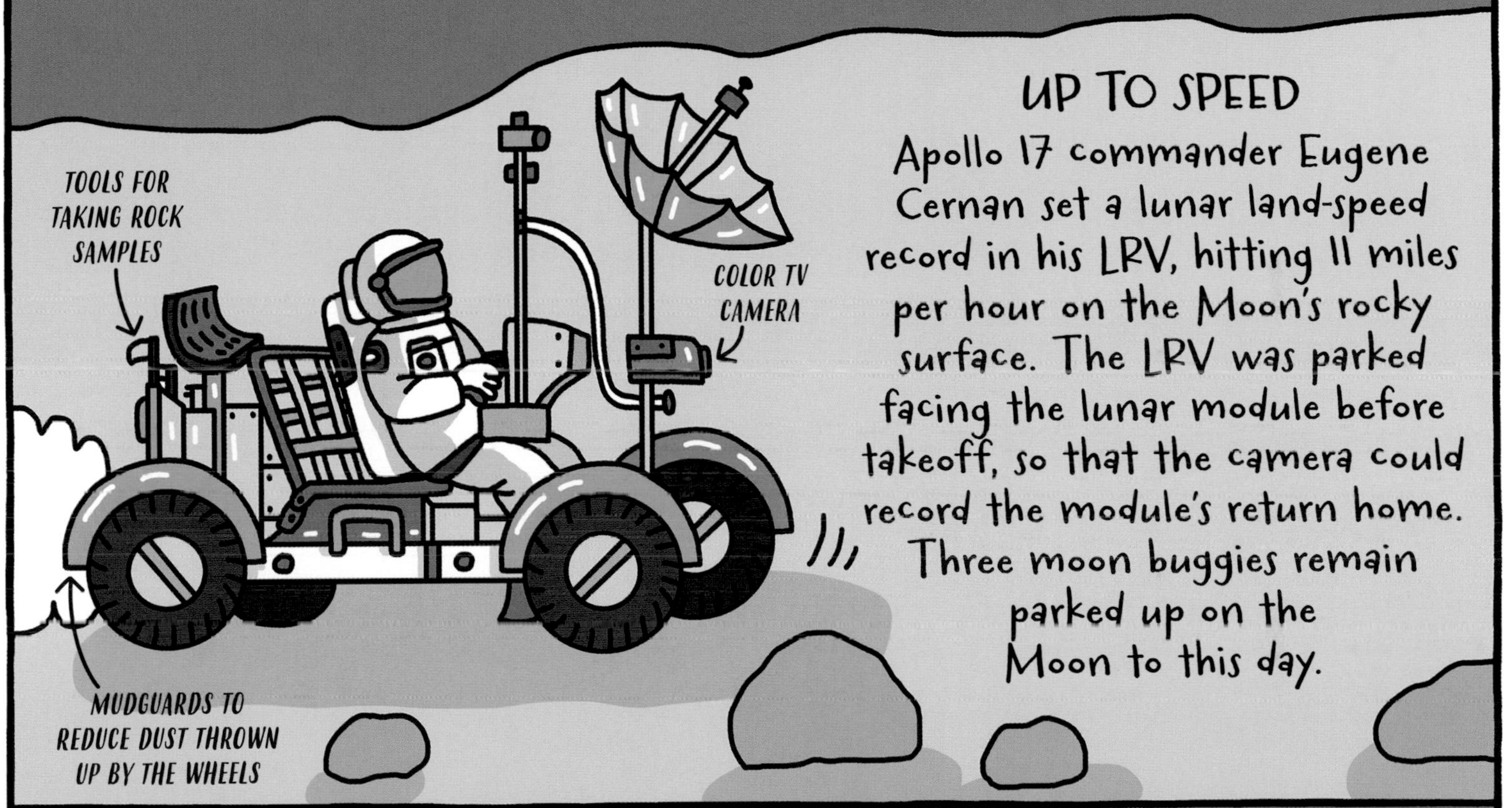

TOOLS FOR TAKING ROCK SAMPLES
COLOR TV CAMERA
MUDGUARDS TO REDUCE DUST THROWN UP BY THE WHEELS

UP TO SPEED

Apollo 17 commander Eugene Cernan set a lunar land-speed record in his LRV, hitting 11 miles per hour on the Moon's rocky surface. The LRV was parked facing the lunar module before takeoff, so that the camera could record the module's return home. Three moon buggies remain parked up on the Moon to this day.

ROLLING ALONG

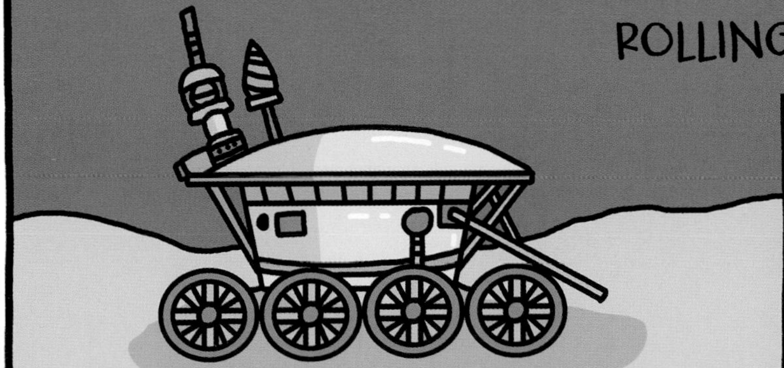

Looking a bit like a tin bath on wheels, the Soviet Union's remote-controlled Lunokhod 2 ("Moonwalker 2") rover landed in early 1973 and covered 24 miles—a lunar distance record!

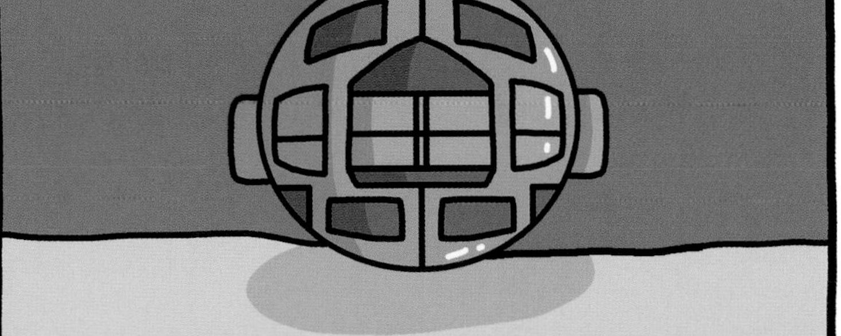

JAXA, the Japanese space agency, has plans to send a small, ball-shaped robot rover (just over 3 inches in diameter!) to explore the Moon's surface.

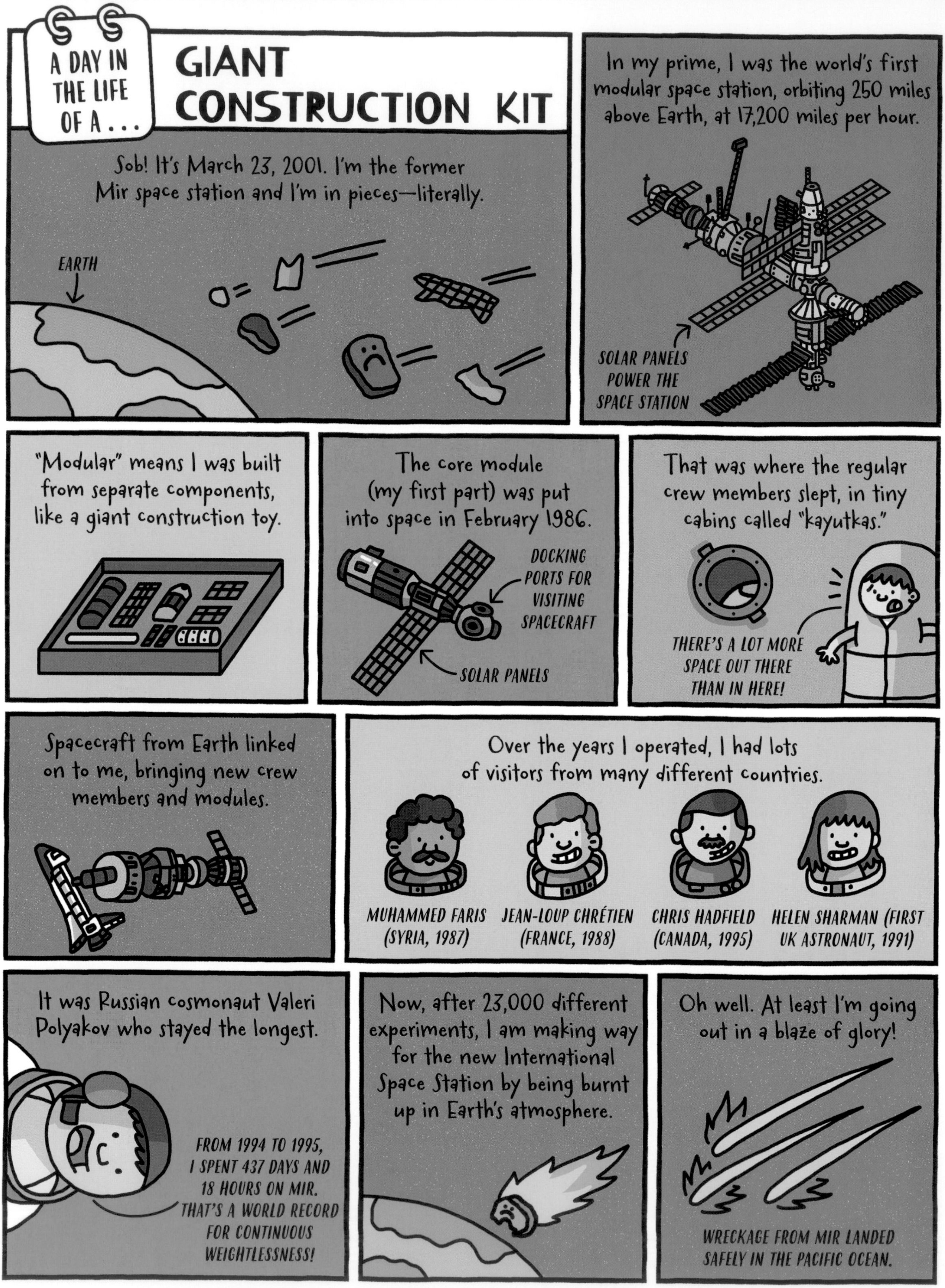
A DAY IN THE LIFE OF A . . .
GIANT CONSTRUCTION KIT
Sob! It's March 23, 2001. I'm the former Mir space station and I'm in pieces—literally.
EARTH
In my prime, I was the world's first modular space station, orbiting 250 miles above Earth, at 17,200 miles per hour.
SOLAR PANELS POWER THE SPACE STATION
"Modular" means I was built from separate components, like a giant construction toy.
The core module (my first part) was put into space in February 1986.
DOCKING PORTS FOR VISITING SPACECRAFT
SOLAR PANELS
That was where the regular crew members slept, in tiny cabins called "kayutkas."
THERE'S A LOT MORE SPACE OUT THERE THAN IN HERE!
Spacecraft from Earth linked on to me, bringing new crew members and modules.
Over the years I operated, I had lots of visitors from many different countries.
MUHAMMED FARIS (SYRIA, 1987)
JEAN-LOUP CHRÉTIEN (FRANCE, 1988)
CHRIS HADFIELD (CANADA, 1995)
HELEN SHARMAN (FIRST UK ASTRONAUT, 1991)
It was Russian cosmonaut Valeri Polyakov who stayed the longest.
FROM 1994 TO 1995, I SPENT 437 DAYS AND 18 HOURS ON MIR. THAT'S A WORLD RECORD FOR CONTINUOUS WEIGHTLESSNESS!
Now, after 23,000 different experiments, I am making way for the new International Space Station by being burnt up in Earth's atmosphere.
Oh well. At least I'm going out in a blaze of glory!
WRECKAGE FROM MIR LANDED SAFELY IN THE PACIFIC OCEAN.

THE BIGGER PICTURE

ACTION STATIONS!

Space stations are hi-tech laboratories that orbit Earth. The scientists inside them carry out many different experiments. One of the things they study is the effect that spending long periods in space has on living things, ahead of humans one day traveling to Mars. Here are some famous space stations of the past, present, and future:

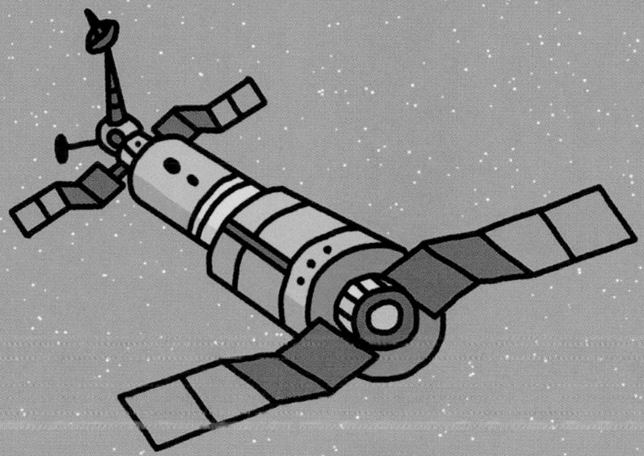

SALYUT 1

Salyut 1 ("Salute 1" in Russian) was the first space station. Launched by the Soviet Union in 1971, it was named in honor of Yuri Gagarin, the first human in space.

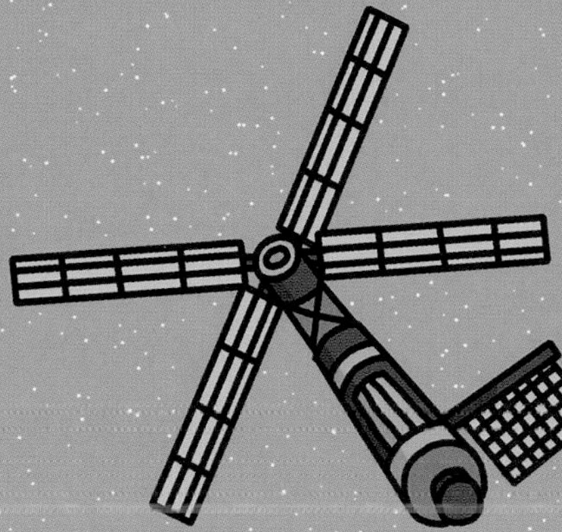

SKYLAB

Launched in 1973, Skylab was the first American space station. Hundreds of experiments were carried out on board, before it crashed to Earth over Western Australia in 1979.

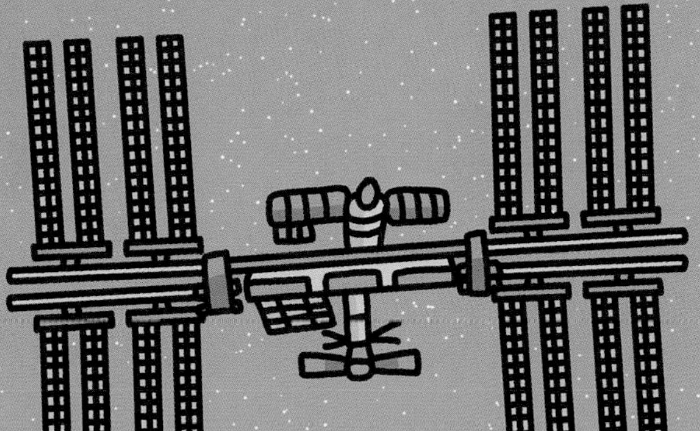

THE ISS

The International Space Station is the largest space lab built so far, and has been continuously crewed since 2000.

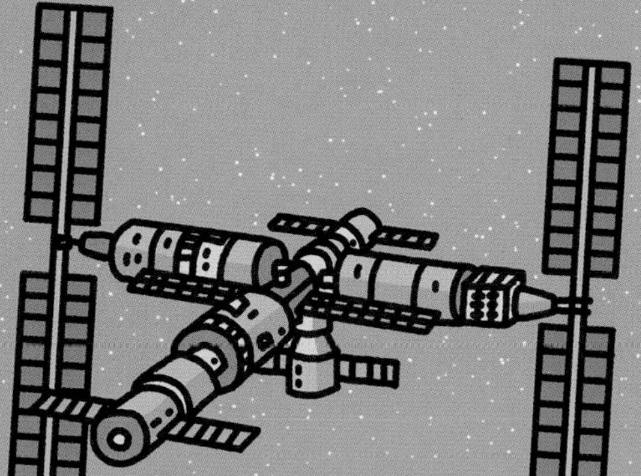

TIANGONG

China launched the first module of its Tiangong ("heavenly palace") station in 2021. The above picture shows what it may look like when completed.

The secret diary of an
ASTRO-MOUSE

An extract from the diary of ROD-3NT—also known as "Squeaky"—a mouse taken on board the International Space Station by scientists studying the effects of weightlessness

US FLOATING AROUND IN OUR CAGE

DAY 1

Talk about going up in the world! Only a few hours ago, our cage—containing me and nine other mice—was being stowed inside a big shiny rocket on Earth. Now we're floating around in our cage in a laboratory on board something the humans call "the ISS." I heard two of the humans (there are six in total) say they are going to begin observing us tomorrow. Well, two can play at that game—I'm going to study them while they study me!

THIS IS HOW THE HUMANS SLEEP

DAY 2

My human-watching has begun! I've anchored myself to the cage bars using my tail, and it turns out the humans do a similar thing to sleep. They use sleeping bags attached to the walls of their tiny cabins. One of them woke and washed up using a smear of water from a pouch. The water stuck to his skin and then he wiped it with a towel. I don't think they're allowed actual running water as it would float around—just like us mice!

DAY 4

Today I saw a human attach herself to a strange machine with a moving floor and run on it for over an hour. I think it's called a "treadmill." The humans do this every day to keep their bones and muscles strong. It reminded me of my exercise wheel back on Earth.

PUFF! PANT!

A HUMAN GOING NOWHERE FAST

DAY 5

Me and the other mice are really getting the hang of this floaty "weightlessness" thing. That has made the scientists really excited. They move around inside the space station using handrails, and us mice are now doing a similar thing with our feet. Everything up here seems slow and clumsy, but apparently the station moves so fast that it orbits the Earth every 90 minutes. That's 16 dawns every day!

FLOAT!

HOLD ON!
IT'S ANOTHER HUMAN!

DAY 6

Today was a Sunday, so most of the humans had the day off. Some emailed or called their families. Others just enjoyed the amazing view from the windows.

DAY 30

Hurrah! Our experiment is over and we're finally going home. I sure am looking forward to being heavy again. Bye!

WHAT A VIEW!

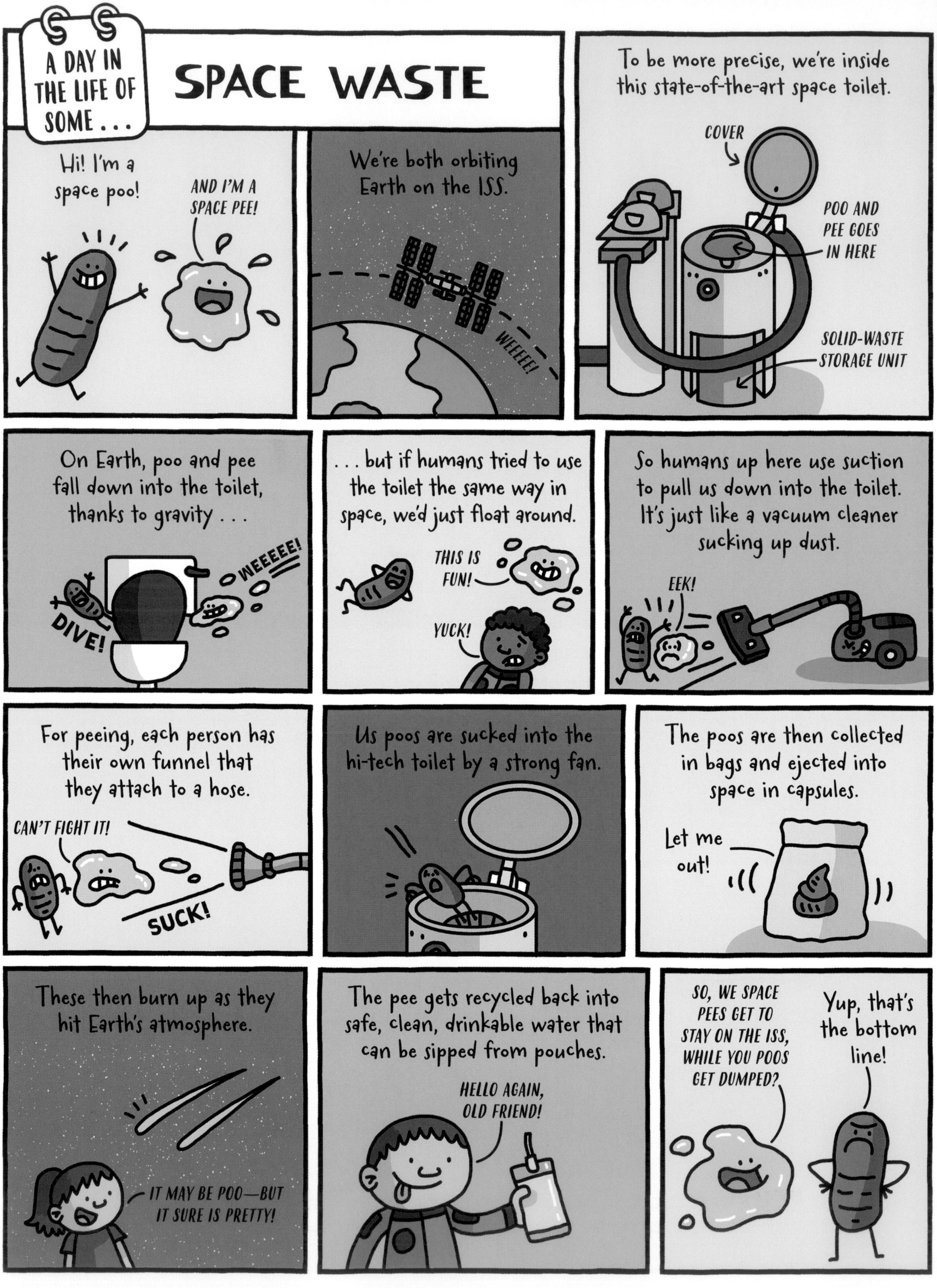
A DAY IN THE LIFE OF SOME . . .
SPACE WASTE
Hi! I'm a space poo!
AND I'M A SPACE PEE!
We're both orbiting Earth on the ISS.
WEEEEE!
To be more precise, we're inside this state-of-the-art space toilet.
COVER
POO AND PEE GOES IN HERE
SOLID-WASTE STORAGE UNIT
On Earth, poo and pee fall down into the toilet, thanks to gravity . . .
DIVE!
WEEEEE!
. . . but if humans tried to use the toilet the same way in space, we'd just float around.
THIS IS FUN!
YUCK!
So humans up here use suction to pull us down into the toilet. It's just like a vacuum cleaner sucking up dust.
EEK!
For peeing, each person has their own funnel that they attach to a hose.
CAN'T FIGHT IT!
SUCK!
Us poos are sucked into the hi-tech toilet by a strong fan.
The poos are then collected in bags and ejected into space in capsules.
Let me out!
These then burn up as they hit Earth's atmosphere.
IT MAY BE POO—BUT IT SURE IS PRETTY!
The pee gets recycled back into safe, clean, drinkable water that can be sipped from pouches.
HELLO AGAIN, OLD FRIEND!
SO, WE SPACE PEES GET TO STAY ON THE ISS, WHILE YOU POOS GET DUMPED?
Yup, that's the bottom line!

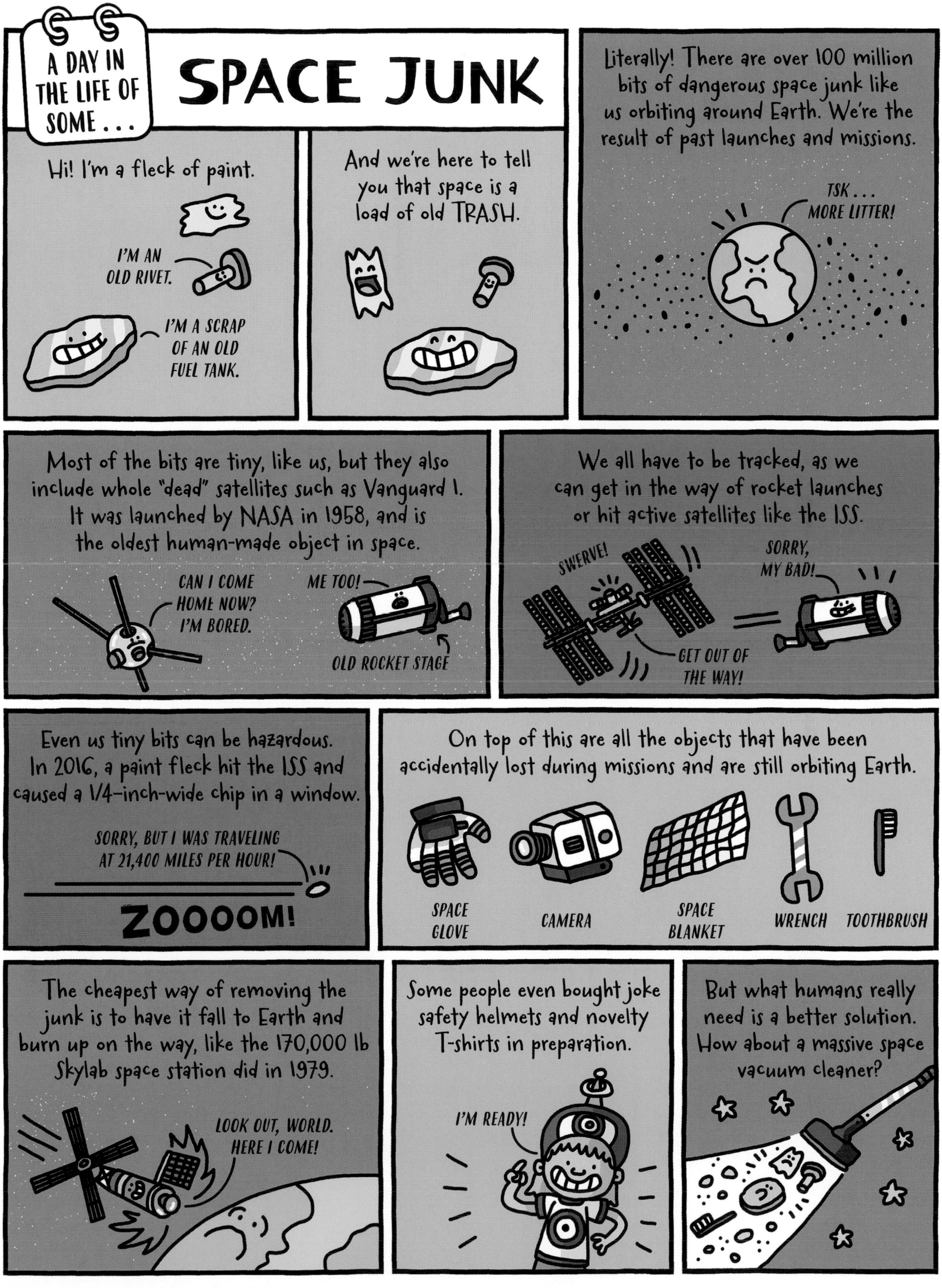
A DAY IN THE LIFE OF SOME . . .
SPACE JUNK
Hi! I'm a fleck of paint.
I'M AN OLD RIVET.
I'M A SCRAP OF AN OLD FUEL TANK.
And we're here to tell you that space is a load of old TRASH.
Literally! There are over 100 million bits of dangerous space junk like us orbiting around Earth. We're the result of past launches and missions.
TSK . . . MORE LITTER!
Most of the bits are tiny, like us, but they also include whole "dead" satellites such as Vanguard 1. It was launched by NASA in 1958, and is the oldest human-made object in space.
CAN I COME HOME NOW? I'M BORED.
ME TOO!
OLD ROCKET STAGE
We all have to be tracked, as we can get in the way of rocket launches or hit active satellites like the ISS.
SWERVE!
SORRY, MY BAD!
GET OUT OF THE WAY!
Even us tiny bits can be hazardous. In 2016, a paint fleck hit the ISS and caused a 1/4-inch-wide chip in a window.
SORRY, BUT I WAS TRAVELING AT 21,400 MILES PER HOUR!
ZOOOOM!
On top of this are all the objects that have been accidentally lost during missions and are still orbiting Earth.
SPACE GLOVE
CAMERA
SPACE BLANKET
WRENCH
TOOTHBRUSH
The cheapest way of removing the junk is to have it fall to Earth and burn up on the way, like the 170,000 lb Skylab space station did in 1979.
LOOK OUT, WORLD. HERE I COME!
Some people even bought joke safety helmets and novelty T-shirts in preparation.
I'M READY!
But what humans really need is a better solution. How about a massive space vacuum cleaner?

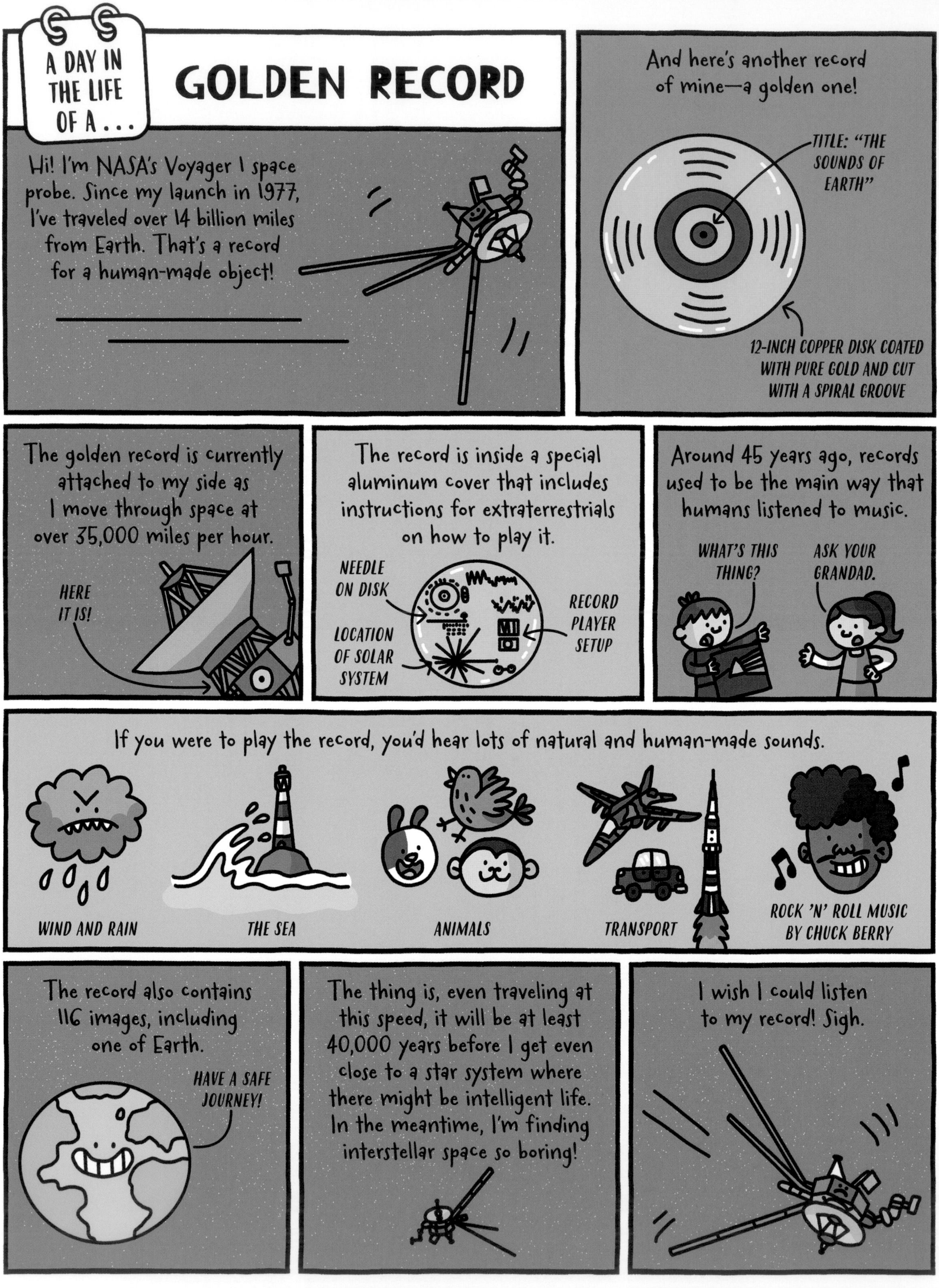
A DAY IN THE LIFE OF A . . .
GOLDEN RECORD
Hi! I'm NASA's Voyager 1 space probe. Since my launch in 1977, I've traveled over 14 billion miles from Earth. That's a record for a human-made object!
And here's another record of mine—a golden one!
TITLE: "THE SOUNDS OF EARTH"
12-INCH COPPER DISK COATED WITH PURE GOLD AND CUT WITH A SPIRAL GROOVE
The golden record is currently attached to my side as I move through space at over 35,000 miles per hour.
HERE IT IS!
The record is inside a special aluminum cover that includes instructions for extraterrestrials on how to play it.
NEEDLE ON DISK
LOCATION OF SOLAR SYSTEM
RECORD PLAYER SETUP
Around 45 years ago, records used to be the main way that humans listened to music.
WHAT'S THIS THING?
ASK YOUR GRANDAD.
If you were to play the record, you'd hear lots of natural and human-made sounds.
WIND AND RAIN
THE SEA
ANIMALS
TRANSPORT
ROCK 'N' ROLL MUSIC BY CHUCK BERRY
The record also contains 116 images, including one of Earth.
HAVE A SAFE JOURNEY!
The thing is, even traveling at this speed, it will be at least 40,000 years before I get even close to a star system where there might be intelligent life. In the meantime, I'm finding interstellar space so boring!
I wish I could listen to my record! Sigh.

SPACE INVADERS

Humans have been launching probes into space since Sputnik (see page 70). Most are radio-controlled from Earth, sending back valuable data until their power fails, they get too far away, or they crash-land (sometimes on purpose!). Here are some well-known probes:

LUNA 9 (USSR)

In 1966, Luna 9 became the first probe to land safely on the Moon. It sent back the first-ever TV pictures from the Moon's surface.

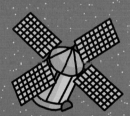

VENERA 9 (USSR)

When Venera 9 landed on Venus in 1975, it lasted just 53 minutes on the planet's super-hot surface.

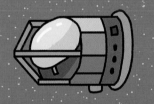

GIOTTO (EUROPEAN SPACE AGENCY)

Giotto studied Halley's Comet in 1986, getting to within 373 miles of its nucleus.*

NEAR SHOEMAKER (NASA)

In 2001, NEAR became the first probe to land on an asteroid. The probe is still there!

NEW HORIZONS (NASA)

In 2015, New Horizons became the first probe to fly by Pluto. It then headed off into even deeper space.

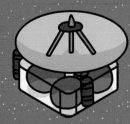

INTERSTELLAR EXPRESS (CHINA)

Interstellar Express is set to become the first non-NASA probe to travel to interstellar space.

*SEE PAGE 41 FOR MORE ON WHAT GIOTTO FOUND.

The secret diary of a
COMET CATCHER

An extract from the diary of "Rosetta," a probe sent to catch up with a comet

ME IN SPACE

JULY 2010

Well, since I was first shot into space by the European Space Agency in 2004, the time has just flown by—and so have I! I've flown by Earth (three times), Mars (once), and even a pair of big asteroids. I've sent lots of lovely info back home to Earth along the way. Frankly, I think I deserve a break!

SORRY I COULDN'T HANG OUT FOR LONGER.

APRIL 2014

Looks like I spoke too soon! Apologies for the lengthy silence, but I've been asleep for two and a half years. The agency shut me down in 2011, just after I passed beyond Jupiter, but I'm awake again now. I'm on the trail of the comet 67P/Churyumov-Gerasimenko (let's call it 67P/C-G for short).

SEPTEMBER 2014

Wow! I've become the first space probe to actually orbit a comet, and at just 18 miles out. I'm sending lots of photos back to Earth so the humans can pick a good landing site for the robotic lander I have inside me.

COMET 67P/C-G

NOVEMBER 12, 2014

Mixed news. My little lander "Philae" ("Phil" for short) landed on 67P/C-G today—three times! He bounced around and ended up in the wrong place. I hope he can still carry out his mission to study the comet.

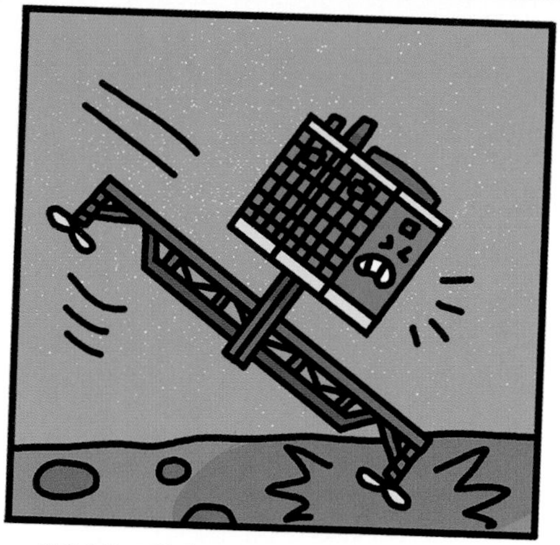

POOR PHIL HAD A ROUGH TIME

NOVEMBER 14, 2014

Hurrah! Little Phil has been in touch and sent me lots of info from the comet. The humans back on Earth were very excited, but now Phil has gone quiet again. Perhaps he's just having a nice long rest like I did. I hope so.

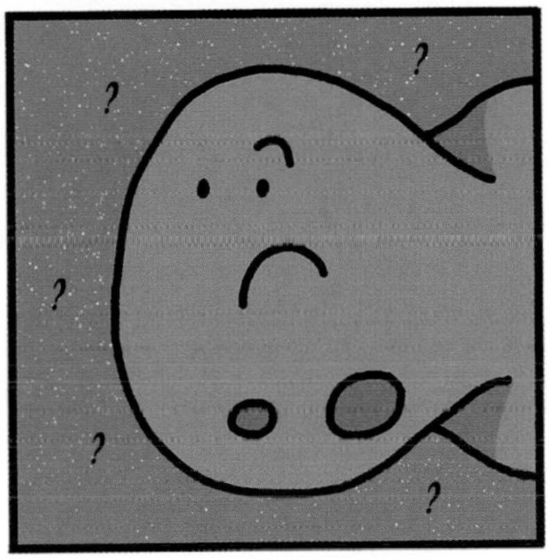
?
?
?
?
?

WHERE IS PHIL?

AUGUST 2015

That was exciting! I've just accompanied 67P/C-G on its closest approach around the Sun. Got some great pictures and data. Not heard from Phil since July—I hope he's okay.

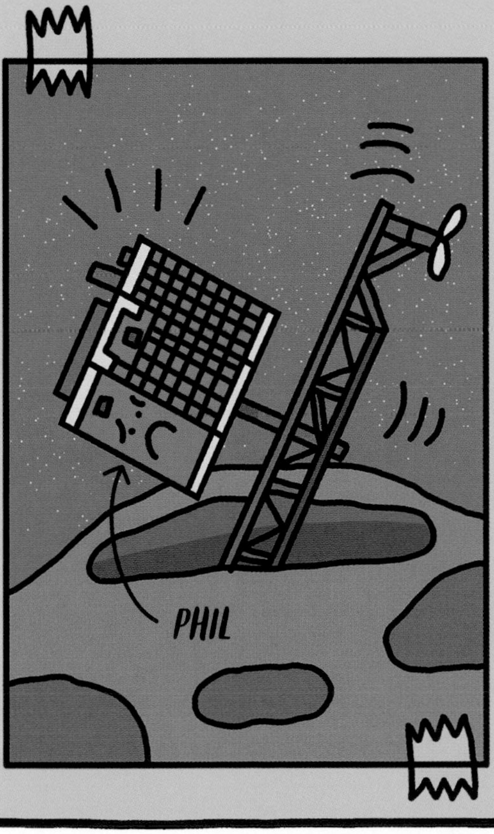
PHIL

SEPTEMBER 5, 2016

Hurrah (again)! My camera spotted Phil on 67P/C-G, stuck in a dark crevice where his solar batteries can't be recharged by the Sun's rays. I hope he's not lonely down there, all by himself.

SEPTEMBER 30, 2016

Well, Phil's got himself some company now. The agency has ended my mission by crashing me onto 67P/C-G. Now we'll both be on this lump of ice orbiting the Sun forever. I finally caught me a comet. Yay!

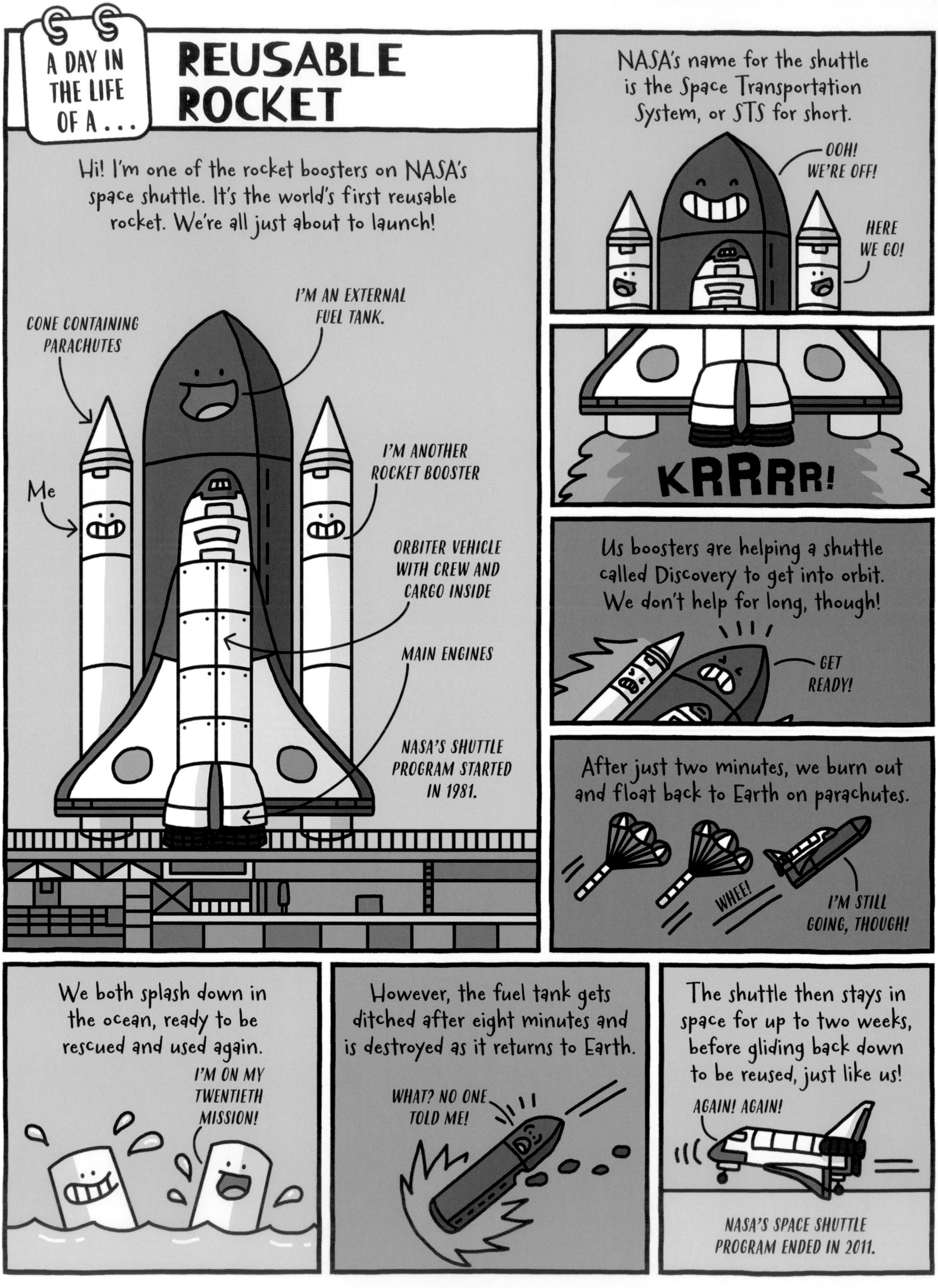
A DAY IN THE LIFE OF A . . .
REUSABLE ROCKET
Hi! I'm one of the rocket boosters on NASA's space shuttle. It's the world's first reusable rocket. We're all just about to launch!
CONE CONTAINING PARACHUTES
I'M AN EXTERNAL FUEL TANK.
Me
I'M ANOTHER ROCKET BOOSTER
ORBITER VEHICLE WITH CREW AND CARGO INSIDE
MAIN ENGINES
NASA'S SHUTTLE PROGRAM STARTED IN 1981.
NASA's name for the shuttle is the Space Transportation System, or STS for short.
OOH! WE'RE OFF!
HERE WE GO!
KRRRR!
Us boosters are helping a shuttle called Discovery to get into orbit. We don't help for long, though!
GET READY!
After just two minutes, we burn out and float back to Earth on parachutes.
WHEE!
I'M STILL GOING, THOUGH!
We both splash down in the ocean, ready to be rescued and used again.
I'M ON MY TWENTIETH MISSION!
However, the fuel tank gets ditched after eight minutes and is destroyed as it returns to Earth.
WHAT? NO ONE TOLD ME!
The shuttle then stays in space for up to two weeks, before gliding back down to be reused, just like us!
AGAIN! AGAIN!
NASA'S SPACE SHUTTLE PROGRAM ENDED IN 2011.

THE BIGGER PICTURE

VOYAGE OF DISCOVERY

NASA operated five shuttle spacecraft, all named after famous sailing ships: Columbia, Challenger, Discovery, Atlantis, and Endeavour. Starting in 1981, the shuttles carried many satellites into space, as well as 355 astronauts, the Hubble Space Telescope (see page 94), and parts of the International Space Station. The shuttle program ended in 2011, with Discovery—shown below—making a record 39 space flights.

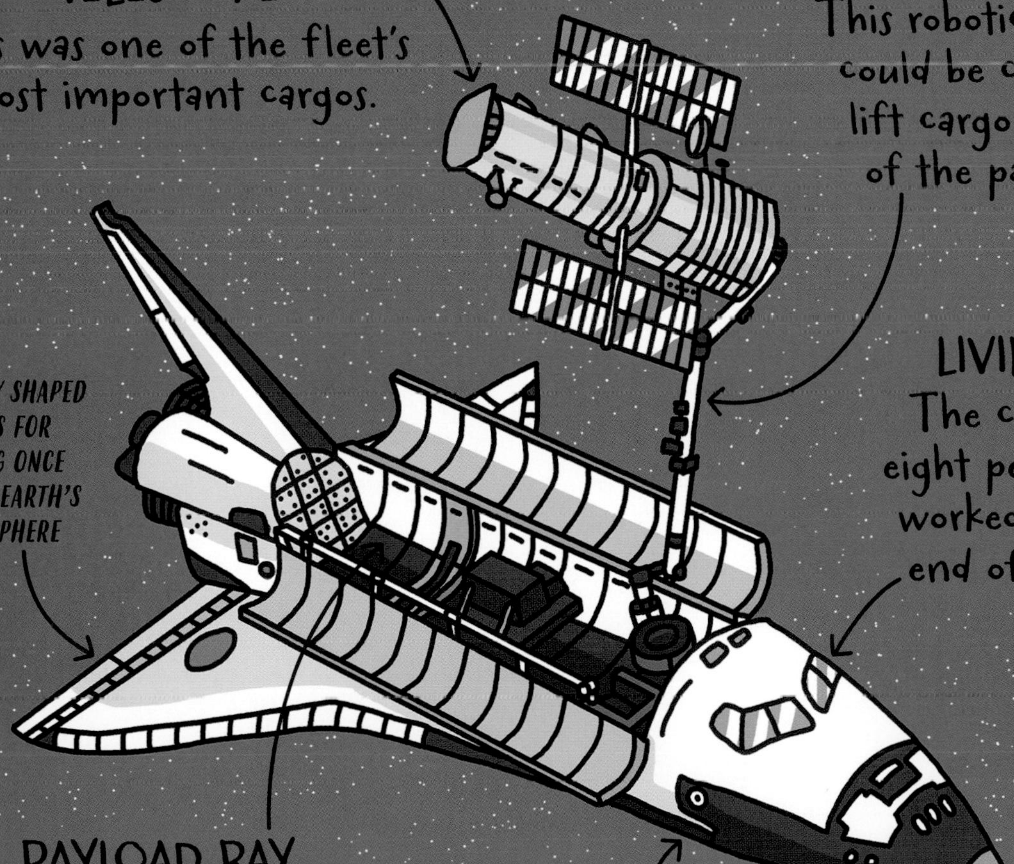

HUBBLE SPACE TELESCOPE
This was one of the fleet's most important cargos.
"CANADARM"
This robotic jointed arm could be controlled to lift cargo in and out of the payload bay.
SPECIALLY SHAPED WINGS FOR GLIDING ONCE BACK IN EARTH'S ATMOSPHERE
LIVING SPACE
The crew of up to eight people lived and worked in the front end of the shuttle.
THE SHUTTLE ORBITED EARTH AT 17,500 MILES PER HOUR.
PAYLOAD BAY
The cargo area, where items were stored to be taken into space.
PROTECTIVE TILES
These covered the shuttle to protect it from the massive heat caused by reentering Earth's atmosphere.

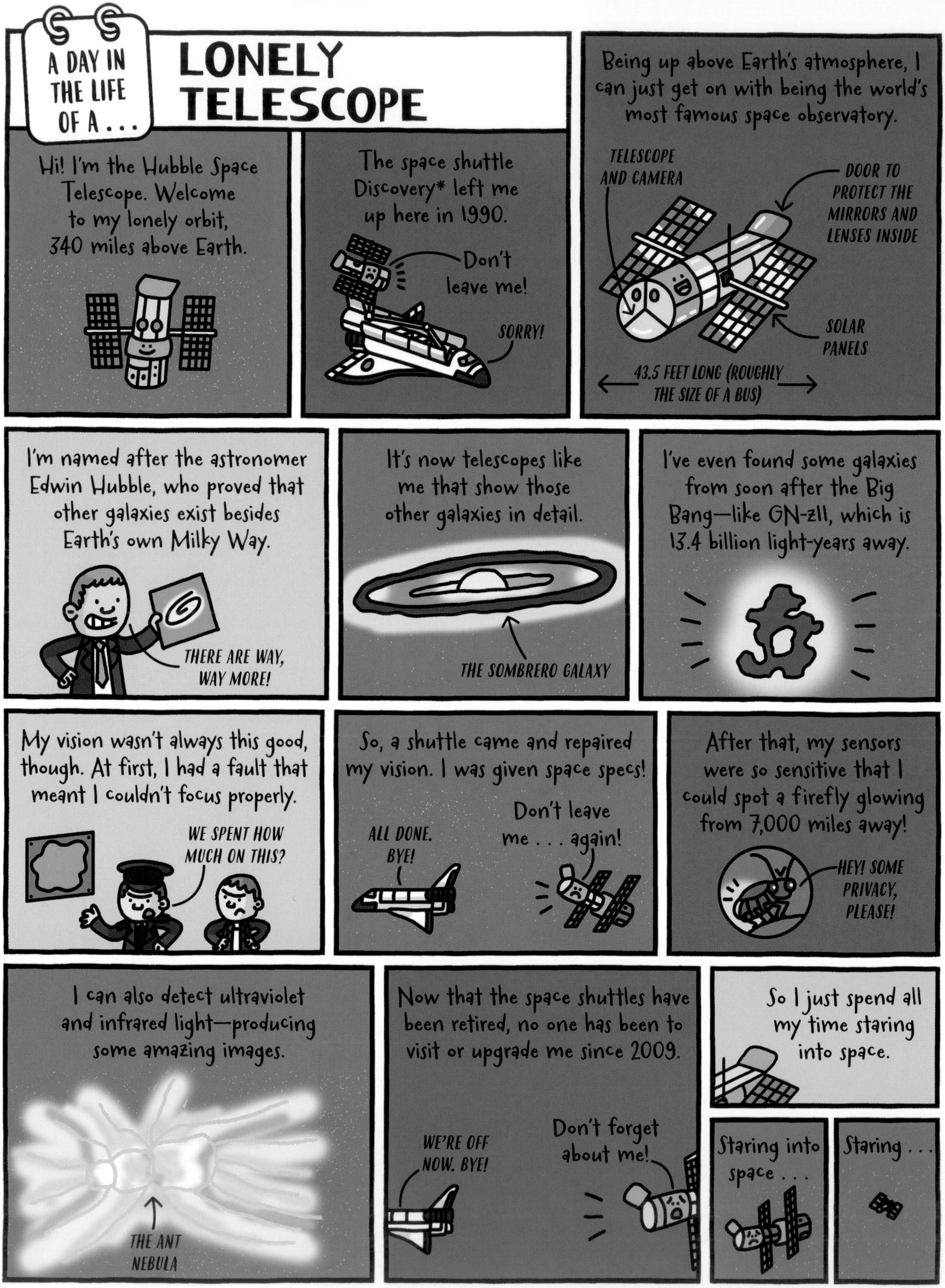
A DAY IN THE LIFE OF A . . .
LONELY TELESCOPE
Hi! I'm the Hubble Space Telescope. Welcome to my lonely orbit, 340 miles above Earth.
The space shuttle Discovery* left me up here in 1990.
Don't leave me!
SORRY!
Being up above Earth's atmosphere, I can just get on with being the world's most famous space observatory.
TELESCOPE AND CAMERA
DOOR TO PROTECT THE MIRRORS AND LENSES INSIDE
SOLAR PANELS
43.5 FEET LONG (ROUGHLY THE SIZE OF A BUS)
I'm named after the astronomer Edwin Hubble, who proved that other galaxies exist besides Earth's own Milky Way.
THERE ARE WAY, WAY MORE!
It's now telescopes like me that show those other galaxies in detail.
THE SOMBRERO GALAXY
I've even found some galaxies from soon after the Big Bang—like GN-z11, which is 13.4 billion light-years away.
My vision wasn't always this good, though. At first, I had a fault that meant I couldn't focus properly.
WE SPENT HOW MUCH ON THIS?
So, a shuttle came and repaired my vision. I was given space specs!
ALL DONE. BYE!
Don't leave me . . . again!
After that, my sensors were so sensitive that I could spot a firefly glowing from 7,000 miles away!
HEY! SOME PRIVACY, PLEASE!
I can also detect ultraviolet and infrared light—producing some amazing images.
THE ANT NEBULA
Now that the space shuttles have been retired, no one has been to visit or upgrade me since 2009.
WE'RE OFF NOW. BYE!
Don't forget about me!
So I just spend all my time staring into space.
Staring into space . . .
Staring . . .

*FIND OUT MORE ABOUT DISCOVERY ON PAGES 92 AND 93.

THE BIGGER PICTURE

SEEING STARS

The Hubble Space Telescope has proved to be a fantastic tool for observing the universe. However, there are many other space-based observatories currently in service, with more due to follow in the near future. Here are some of the best known:

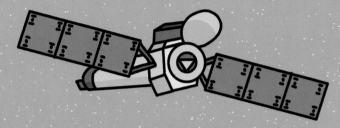

X-DETECTOR

NASA's Chandra Observatory detects X-rays coming from black holes—including the black hole at the center of Earth's Milky Way galaxy. Chandra also took the first X-ray images of Mars.

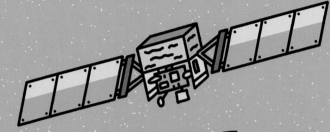

DARK SECRETS

Launched by NASA in 2008, the Fermi Gamma-ray Space Telescope has discovered many new pulsars (see page 49) and is also on the hunt for dark matter (see page 60).

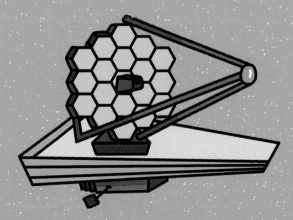

LEVEL UP

The James Webb Space Telescope, which launched in 2021, is named after a former NASA boss. The telescope is several times more powerful than Hubble and is probing even deeper into the universe, back to when the first stars were formed.

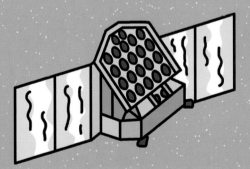

SIGNS OF LIFE

The European Space Agency's PLATO (PLAnetary Transits and Oscillations of stars) is due to launch in 2026. Its mission will be to look for Earth-like planets in the habitable zones of other stars, where life might exist.

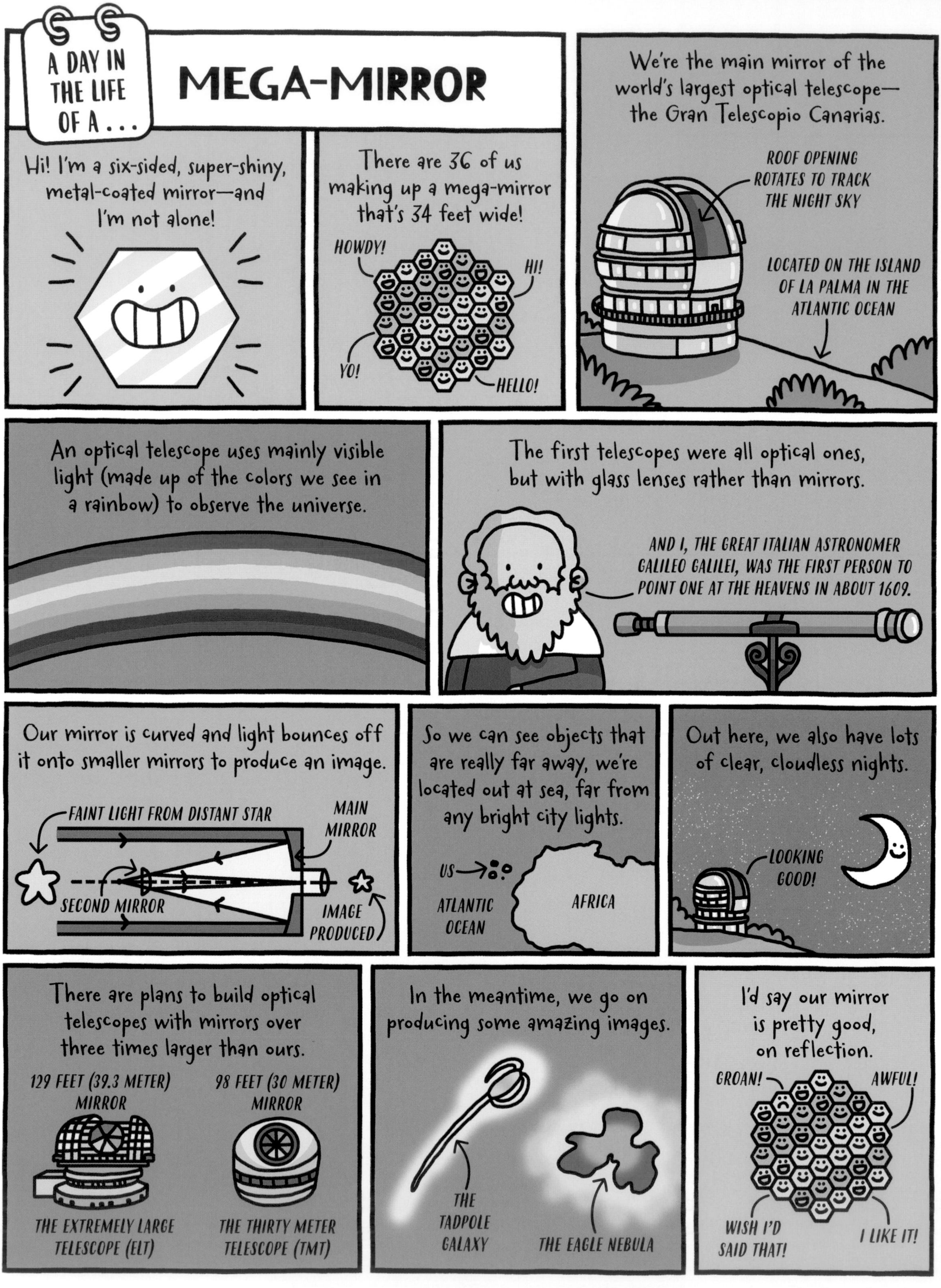
A DAY IN THE LIFE OF A . . .
MEGA-MIRROR
Hi! I'm a six-sided, super-shiny, metal-coated mirror—and I'm not alone!
There are 36 of us making up a mega-mirror that's 34 feet wide!
HOWDY!
HI!
YO!
HELLO!
We're the main mirror of the world's largest optical telescope—the Gran Telescopio Canarias.
ROOF OPENING ROTATES TO TRACK THE NIGHT SKY
LOCATED ON THE ISLAND OF LA PALMA IN THE ATLANTIC OCEAN
An optical telescope uses mainly visible light (made up of the colors we see in a rainbow) to observe the universe.
The first telescopes were all optical ones, but with glass lenses rather than mirrors.
AND I, THE GREAT ITALIAN ASTRONOMER GALILEO GALILEI, WAS THE FIRST PERSON TO POINT ONE AT THE HEAVENS IN ABOUT 1609.
Our mirror is curved and light bounces off it onto smaller mirrors to produce an image.
FAINT LIGHT FROM DISTANT STAR
MAIN MIRROR
SECOND MIRROR
IMAGE PRODUCED
So we can see objects that are really far away, we're located out at sea, far from any bright city lights.
US
ATLANTIC OCEAN
AFRICA
Out here, we also have lots of clear, cloudless nights.
LOOKING GOOD!
There are plans to build optical telescopes with mirrors over three times larger than ours.
129 FEET (39.3 METER) MIRROR
98 FEET (30 METER) MIRROR
THE EXTREMELY LARGE TELESCOPE (ELT)
THE THIRTY METER TELESCOPE (TMT)
In the meantime, we go on producing some amazing images.
THE TADPOLE GALAXY
THE EAGLE NEBULA
I'd say our mirror is pretty good, on reflection.
GROAN!
AWFUL!
WISH I'D SAID THAT!
I LIKE IT!

GET THE MESSAGE?

Radio telescopes listen out for radio signals generated by high-energy particles around stars and galaxies. Many of these telescopes are shaped like big, curved dishes, and can be joined together to form a mega-observatory called an "array." Radio telescopes are a key tool in the search for intelligent life elsewhere in space, and have even been used to try to make contact with aliens.

DISH OF THE DAY

The Green Bank Telescope in West Virginia, USA, has the world's biggest steerable dish. At 328 feet wide, it has an area larger than 30 tennis courts and has been searching for signals from alien life forms since 2000.

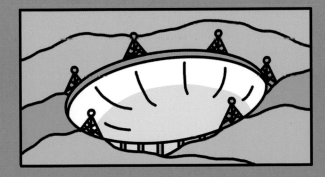

FAST WORKER

China's Five-hundred-meter Aperture Spherical radio Telescope (better known as "FAST") sits in a natural hole in the ground. FAST has an area larger than 30 football fields, making it the largest radio telescope in the world. It is surrounded by a 3-mile "radio silence" zone, where mobile phones and computers are banned.

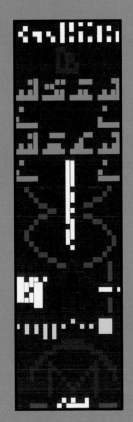

ARE YOU RECEIVING ME?

In 1974, the Arecibo Telescope sent coded signals into space that could be read as a picture showing a stick figure, the Sun and planets, a strand of DNA, and the telescope itself. Sadly, no aliens have replied yet.

THE EVEN BIGGER PICTURE

Men and women from many nations have spent time on the International Space Station, but training for space is a long, hard journey. Do you have what was once known as "the right stuff" to be an astronaut? Count down through the stages below to see if you can make it all the way to liftoff.

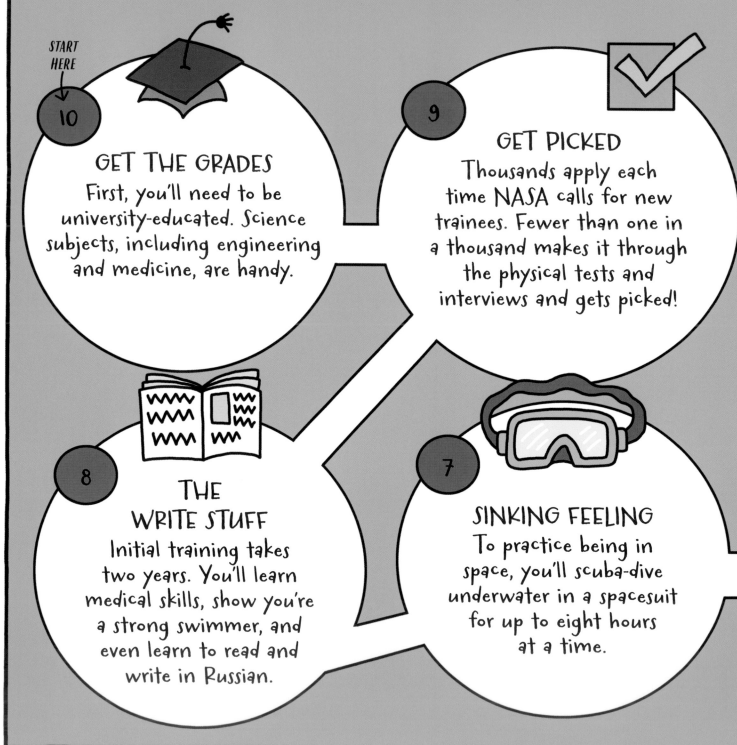

START HERE

10

GET THE GRADES
First, you'll need to be university-educated. Science subjects, including engineering and medicine, are handy.

9

GET PICKED
Thousands apply each time NASA calls for new trainees. Fewer than one in a thousand makes it through the physical tests and interviews and gets picked!

8

THE WRITE STUFF
Initial training takes two years. You'll learn medical skills, show you're a strong swimmer, and even learn to read and write in Russian.

7

SINKING FEELING
To practice being in space, you'll scuba-dive underwater in a spacesuit for up to eight hours at a time.

SO, YOU WANT TO BE AN ASTRONAUT?

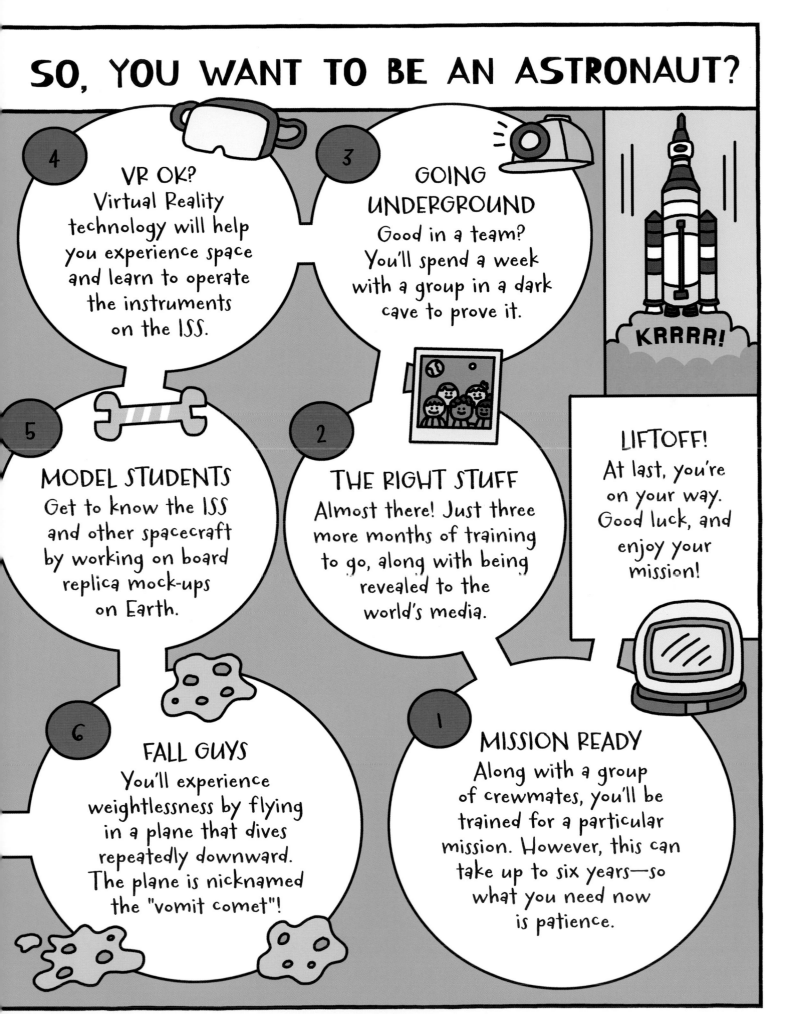

4 VR OK?
Virtual Reality technology will help you experience space and learn to operate the instruments on the ISS.

3 GOING UNDERGROUND
Good in a team? You'll spend a week with a group in a dark cave to prove it.

KRRRRR!

5 MODEL STUDENTS
Get to know the ISS and other spacecraft by working on board replica mock-ups on Earth.

2 THE RIGHT STUFF
Almost there! Just three more months of training to go, along with being revealed to the world's media.

LIFTOFF!
At last, you're on your way. Good luck, and enjoy your mission!

6 FALL GUYS
You'll experience weightlessness by flying in a plane that dives repeatedly downward. The plane is nicknamed the "vomit comet"!

1 MISSION READY
Along with a group of crewmates, you'll be trained for a particular mission. However, this can take up to six years—so what you need now is patience.

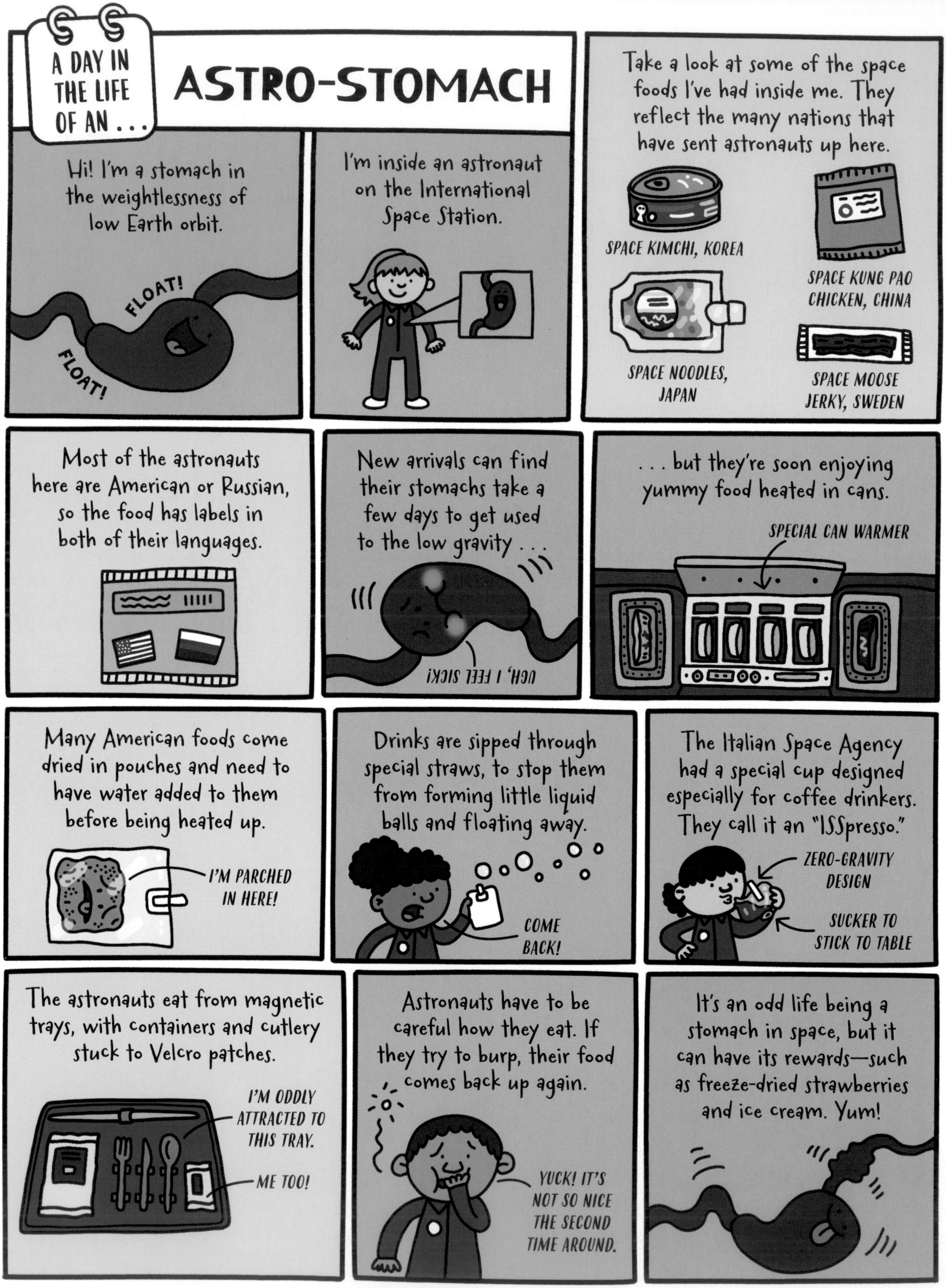
A DAY IN THE LIFE OF AN . . .
ASTRO-STOMACH
Hi! I'm a stomach in the weightlessness of low Earth orbit.
FLOAT!
FLOAT!
I'm inside an astronaut on the International Space Station.
Take a look at some of the space foods I've had inside me. They reflect the many nations that have sent astronauts up here.
SPACE KIMCHI, KOREA
SPACE KUNG PAO CHICKEN, CHINA
SPACE NOODLES, JAPAN
SPACE MOOSE JERKY, SWEDEN
Most of the astronauts here are American or Russian, so the food has labels in both of their languages.
New arrivals can find their stomachs take a few days to get used to the low gravity . . .
UGH, I FEEL SICK!
. . . but they're soon enjoying yummy food heated in cans.
SPECIAL CAN WARMER
Many American foods come dried in pouches and need to have water added to them before being heated up.
I'M PARCHED IN HERE!
Drinks are sipped through special straws, to stop them from forming little liquid balls and floating away.
COME BACK!
The Italian Space Agency had a special cup designed especially for coffee drinkers. They call it an "ISSpresso."
ZERO-GRAVITY DESIGN
SUCKER TO STICK TO TABLE
The astronauts eat from magnetic trays, with containers and cutlery stuck to Velcro patches.
I'M ODDLY ATTRACTED TO THIS TRAY.
ME TOO!
Astronauts have to be careful how they eat. If they try to burp, their food comes back up again.
YUCK! IT'S NOT SO NICE THE SECOND TIME AROUND.
It's an odd life being a stomach in space, but it can have its rewards—such as freeze-dried strawberries and ice cream. Yum!

THE BIGGER PICTURE

SPACED OUT

In space, humans are an alien species. People didn't evolve to spend time outside Earth's protective atmosphere and gravity. Here's how space can affect an astronaut's health, and some of the hazards a mission to Mars could pose:

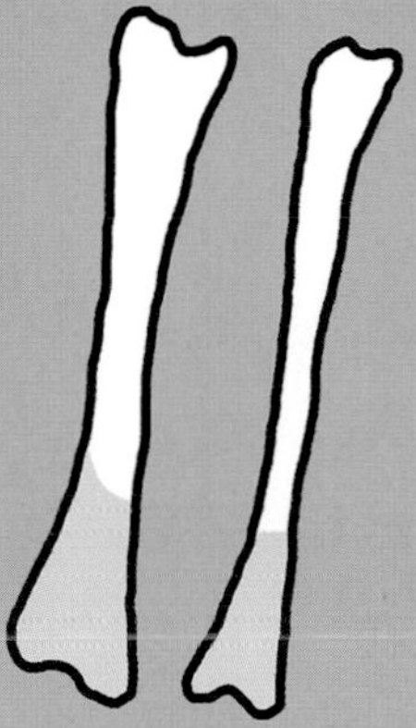

SHRINKING FEELING

Without Earth's gravity to give them a workout, bones and muscles soon begin to wither. This is why ISS crew members have to exercise every day.

LOOKING SWELL

On Earth, the heart works against gravity to pump blood up to the head. The heart carries on working this hard when there's no gravity, which makes astronauts' faces go puffy.

DON'T BUG ME

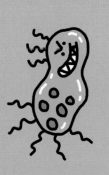

Bacteria and other microbes can become more infectious in space. Surfaces are coated in special chemicals to stop bugs from growing.

STARS IN THEIR EYES

Weightlessness can change the shape of the eyeball, causing blurred vision. Also, damaging particles called cosmic rays can affect the eye, causing a flashing sensation.

LACK OF TASTE

Due to fluids collecting in their heads (like when you have a bad cold), many astronauts find their favorite food tastes dull. To compensate, they eat spicier, hotter food instead.

YUCK!

CRYING SHAME

If all these risks get you down, here's more bad news. You can't have a proper cry in space because the tears don't roll away from your eyes. Boo hoo!

THE EVEN BIGGER PICTURE

Human exploration of space has produced some incredible stories. Here are a few of the odder moments:

LIQUID LUCK

Just before becoming the first person in space in 1961, Soviet cosmonaut Yuri Gagarin peed on the back wheel of the bus taking him to the launch pad. Other cosmonauts now do the same for luck, with some women cosmonauts preparing a cup of pee in advance.

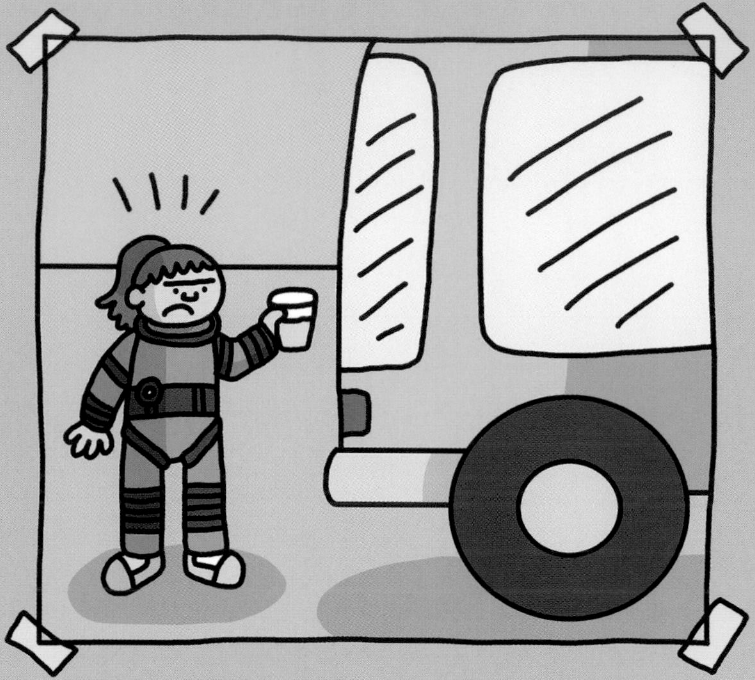

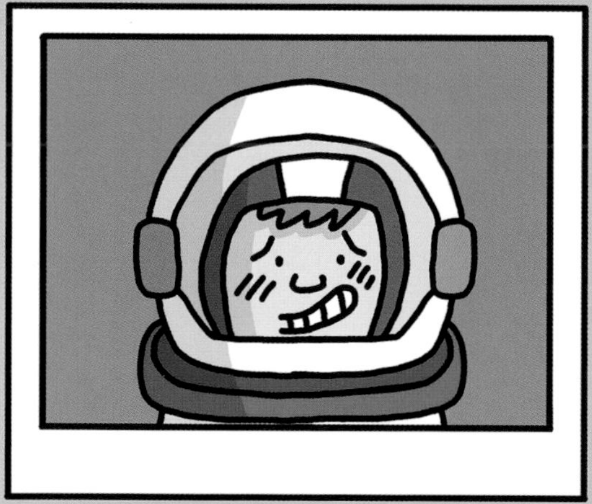

A GIANT LEAK FOR MANKIND

Apollo 11 astronaut Buzz Aldrin is best known as the second person to walk on the Moon in 1969, but he was also the first person to pee on the Moon. Because of a fault with his spacesuit, though, his pee ran down into one of his boots while he explored the Moon's surface.

MOON'S BEST DAD

Apollo 17 astronaut Eugene Cernan was the last person to walk on the Moon. In 1972, he wrote his daughter Tracy's initials ("TDC") in the lunar dust, and they're still there to this day.

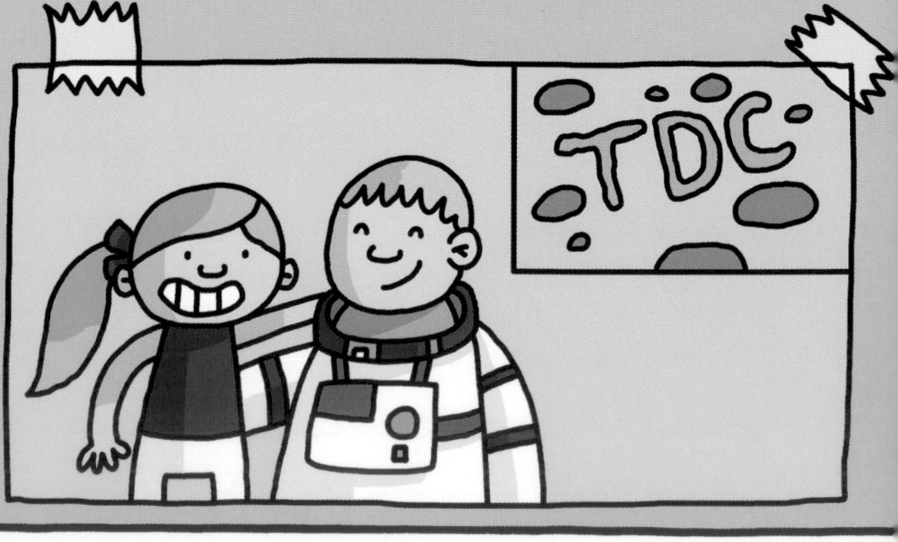
TDC

SPACE ODDITIES

KEEP ON RUNNING
In 2007, Indian-American astronaut Sunita Williams became the first person to run a marathon in space. She competed in that year's Boston Marathon from a treadmill on board the ISS.

SPACE JAM
Canadian astronaut Chris Hadfield sang the David Bowie song "Space Oddity" while on board the ISS in May 2013—and the video of his performance has over 50 million views on YouTube.

BOLDLY GONE
American actor William Shatner became the oldest person to journey into space at the age of 90. He spent ten minutes in orbit on board the Blue Origin space capsule on October 13, 2021. Shatner is famous for playing Captain James T. Kirk in the TV show Star Trek.

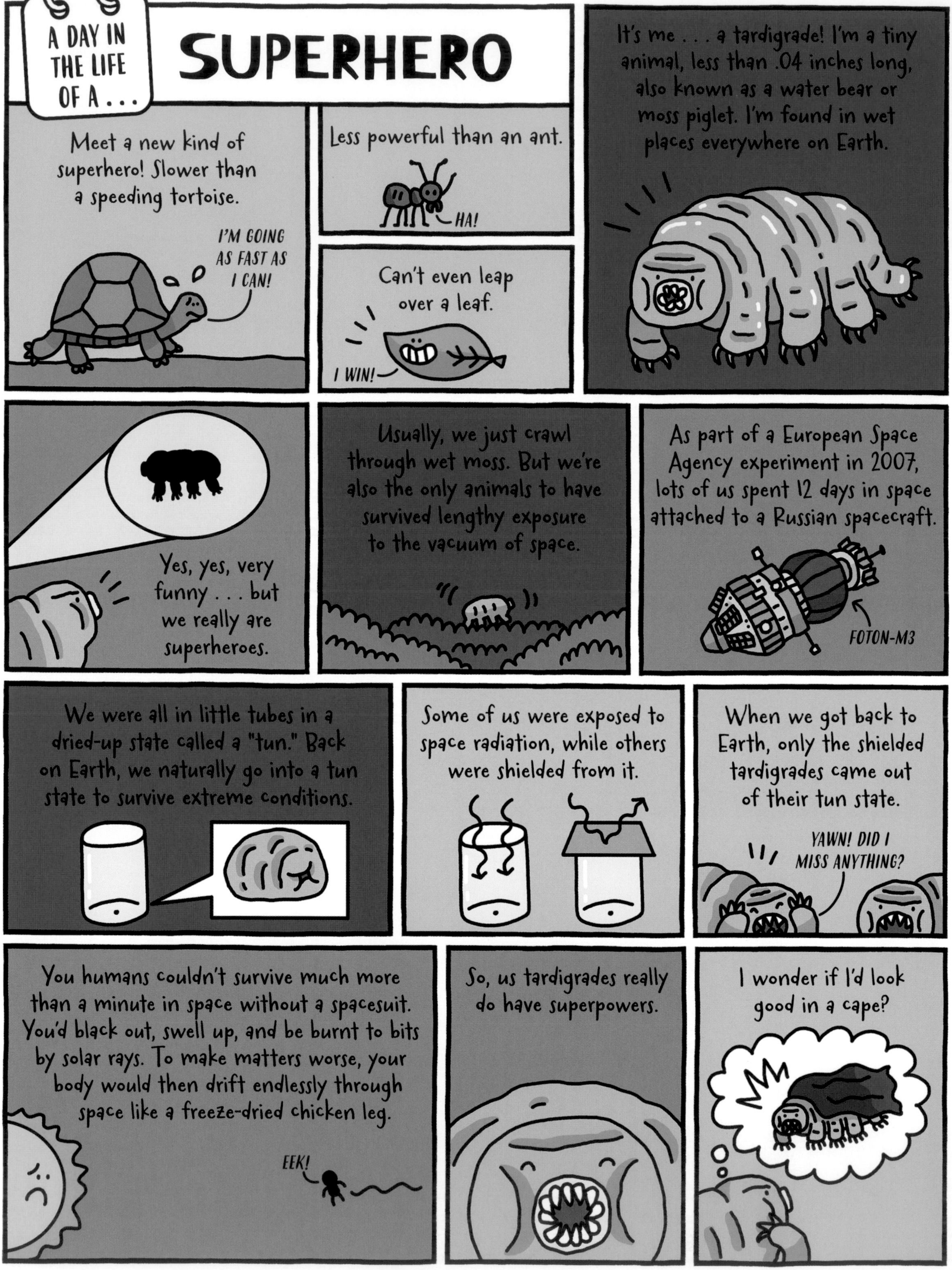

A DAY IN THE LIFE OF A . . .
SUPERHERO
Meet a new kind of superhero! Slower than a speeding tortoise.
I'M GOING AS FAST AS I CAN!
Less powerful than an ant.
HA!
Can't even leap over a leaf.
I WIN!
It's me . . . a tardigrade! I'm a tiny animal, less than .04 inches long, also known as a water bear or moss piglet. I'm found in wet places everywhere on Earth.
Yes, yes, very funny . . . but we really are superheroes.
Usually, we just crawl through wet moss. But we're also the only animals to have survived lengthy exposure to the vacuum of space.
As part of a European Space Agency experiment in 2007, lots of us spent 12 days in space attached to a Russian spacecraft.
FOTON-M3
We were all in little tubes in a dried-up state called a "tun." Back on Earth, we naturally go into a tun state to survive extreme conditions.
Some of us were exposed to space radiation, while others were shielded from it.
When we got back to Earth, only the shielded tardigrades came out of their tun state.
YAWN! DID I MISS ANYTHING?
You humans couldn't survive much more than a minute in space without a spacesuit. You'd black out, swell up, and be burnt to bits by solar rays. To make matters worse, your body would then drift endlessly through space like a freeze-dried chicken leg.
EEK!
So, us tardigrades really do have superpowers.
I wonder if I'd look good in a cape?

THE BIGGER PICTURE	SUITS YOU

Astronauts must wear special suits anytime they go outside their spacecrafts. The suits are heavy and awkward to move in, but provide them with oxygen and protect them from extreme temperatures and radiation. Known technically as an Extravehicular Mobility Unit (EMU), NASA's suit has remained much the same for over 40 years—and takes 45 minutes to put on!

LIFE SUPPORT SYSTEM
This provides oxygen and takes away carbon dioxide.

GLOVES
These have special tips for sensitivity when handling objects.

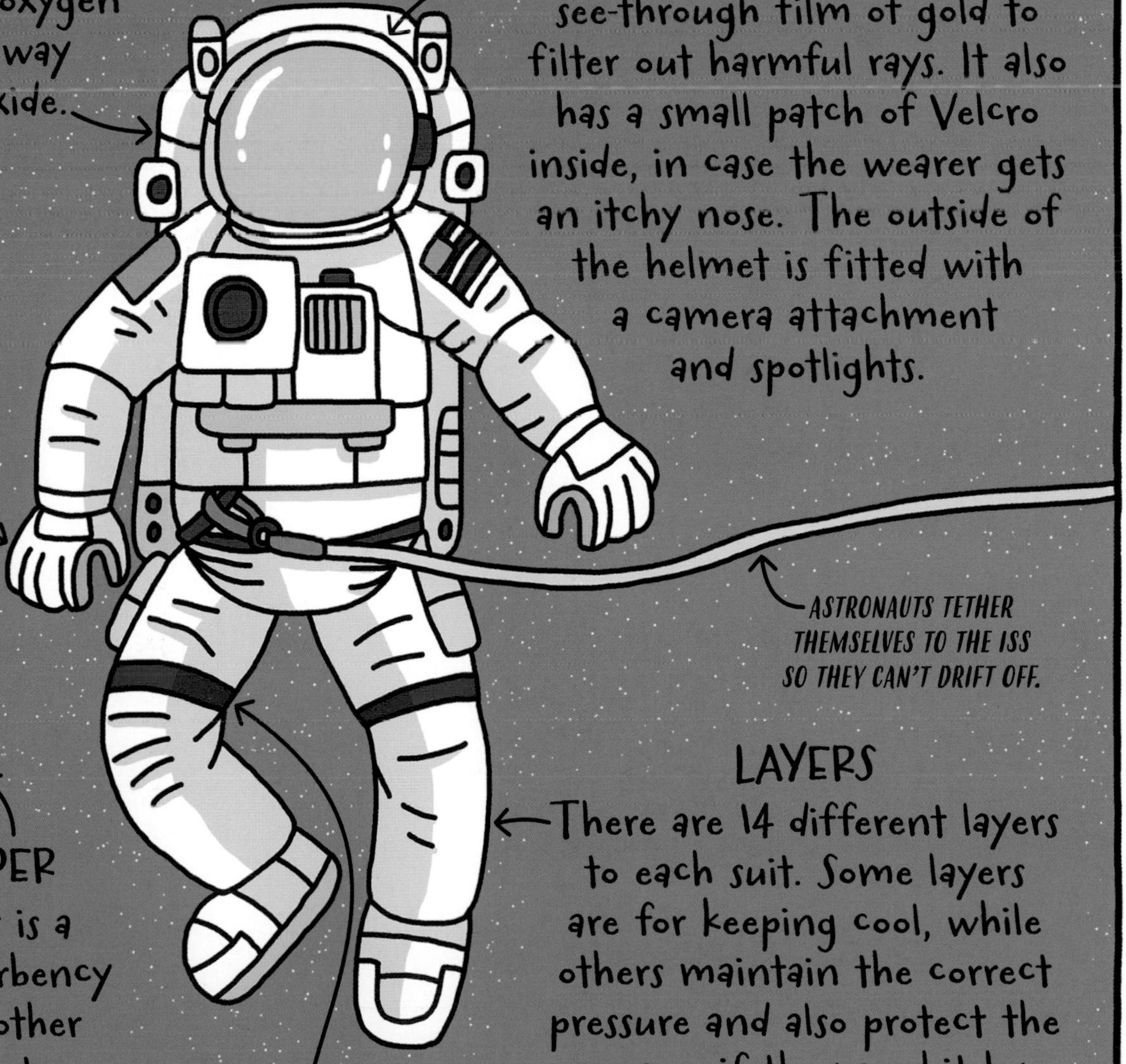

HELMET
The visor is coated with a see-through film of gold to filter out harmful rays. It also has a small patch of Velcro inside, in case the wearer gets an itchy nose. The outside of the helmet is fitted with a camera attachment and spotlights.

ASTRONAUTS TETHER THEMSELVES TO THE ISS SO THEY CAN'T DRIFT OFF.

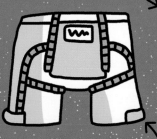

GIANT DIAPER
Inside the suit is a "maximum absorbency garment"—in other words, a giant disposable diaper.

COLOR-CODING ON EACH SUIT SHOWS WHICH ASTRONAUT IS INSIDE

LAYERS
There are 14 different layers to each suit. Some layers are for keeping cool, while others maintain the correct pressure and also protect the wearer if they are hit by speeding space dust.

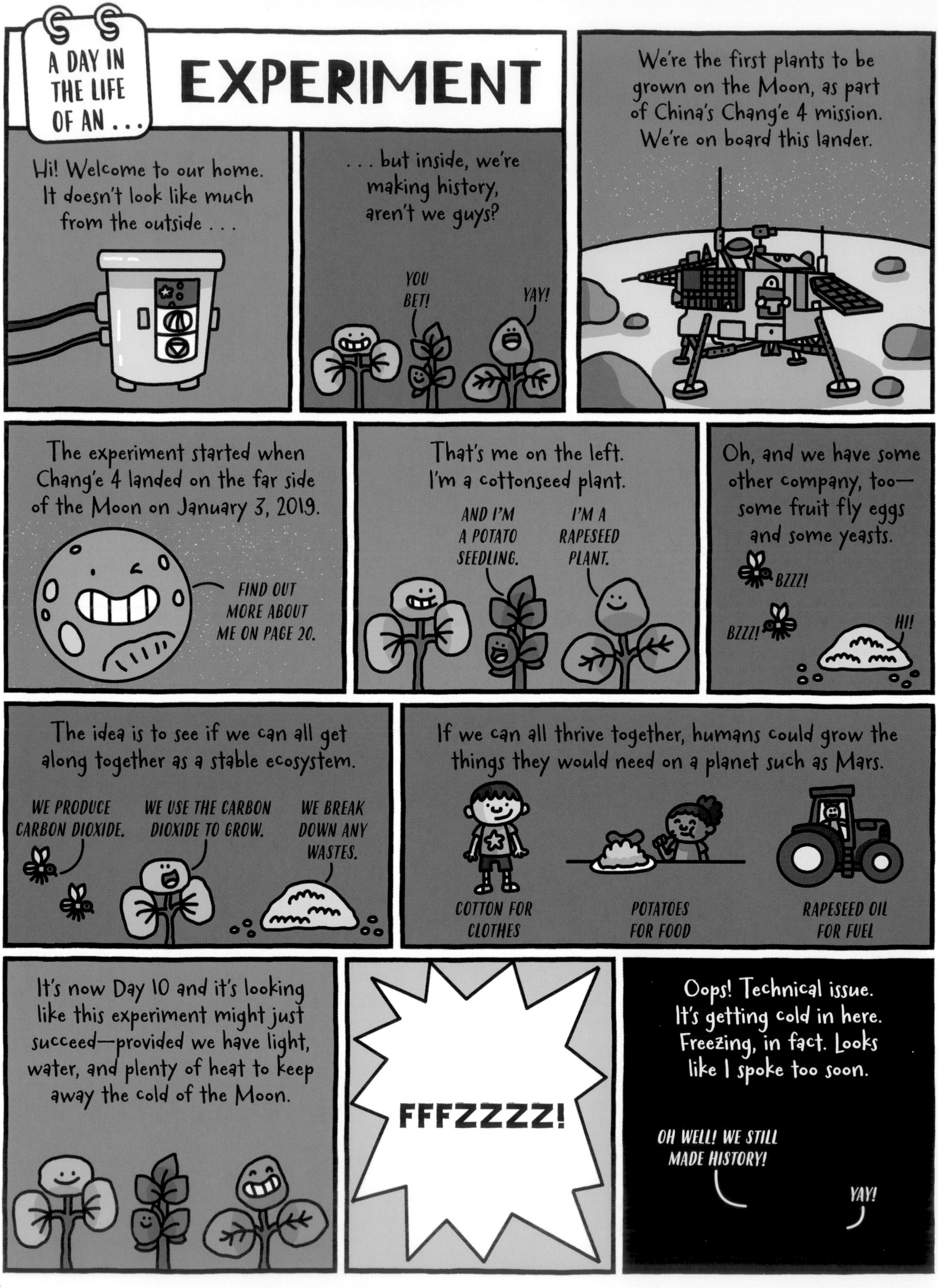

A DAY IN THE LIFE OF AN . . .
EXPERIMENT
We're the first plants to be grown on the Moon, as part of China's Chang'e 4 mission. We're on board this lander.
Hi! Welcome to our home. It doesn't look like much from the outside . . .
. . . but inside, we're making history, aren't we guys?
YOU BET!
YAY!
The experiment started when Chang'e 4 landed on the far side of the Moon on January 3, 2019.
FIND OUT MORE ABOUT ME ON PAGE 20.
That's me on the left. I'm a cottonseed plant.
AND I'M A POTATO SEEDLING.
I'M A RAPESEED PLANT.
Oh, and we have some other company, too—some fruit fly eggs and some yeasts.
BZZZ!
BZZZ!
HI!
The idea is to see if we can all get along together as a stable ecosystem.
WE PRODUCE CARBON DIOXIDE.
WE USE THE CARBON DIOXIDE TO GROW.
WE BREAK DOWN ANY WASTES.
If we can all thrive together, humans could grow the things they would need on a planet such as Mars.
COTTON FOR CLOTHES
POTATOES FOR FOOD
RAPESEED OIL FOR FUEL
It's now Day 10 and it's looking like this experiment might just succeed—provided we have light, water, and plenty of heat to keep away the cold of the Moon.
FFFZZZZ!
Oops! Technical issue. It's getting cold in here. Freezing, in fact. Looks like I spoke too soon.
OH WELL! WE STILL MADE HISTORY!
YAY!

THE BIGGER PICTURE

OUT TO LAUNCH

Today, there are space programs in countries all over the world. Their launch sites tend to be in remote areas or close to an ocean, as launching a large rocket full of fuel can be very dangerous. Here are some of the most important liftoff locations:

1. The Soviet Union launched Sputnik 1 from the Baikonur Cosmodrome in Kazakhstan in 1957, starting the space race with the USA.

2. Cape Canaveral, Florida, was the launch site for the first American astronaut, Alan Shepard, in 1961.

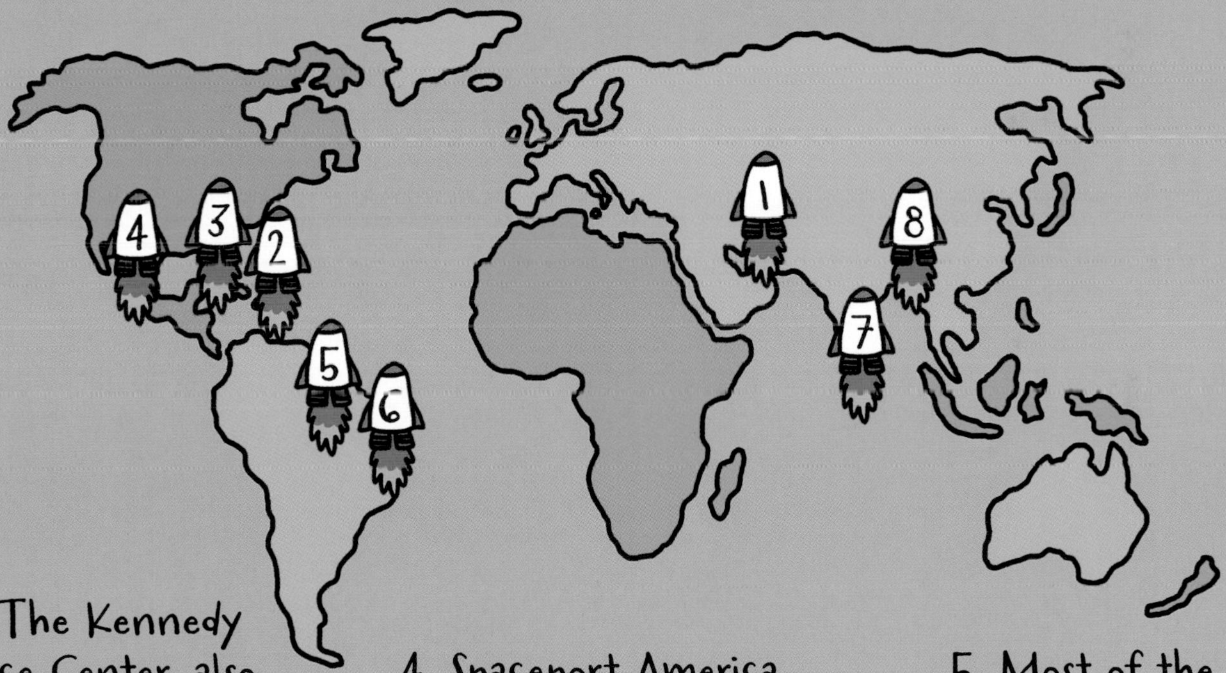

4
3
2
5
6
1
8
7

3. The Kennedy Space Center, also in Florida, was the launch site of the Apollo 11 mission that took the first humans to the Moon in 1969.

4. Spaceport America, in New Mexico, will be a hub for space tourists using the Virgin Galactic space service.

5. Most of the European Space Agency's missions launch from the Guiana Space Center in French Guiana.

6. Alcântara, Brazil, is the launch site used by the Brazilian Space Agency.

7. The Indian Space Research Organization launches satellites into space from the barrier island of Sriharikota in the Bay of Bengal.

8. China's main launch site is the Jiuquan Satellite Launch Center in the Gobi Desert, Inner Mongolia.

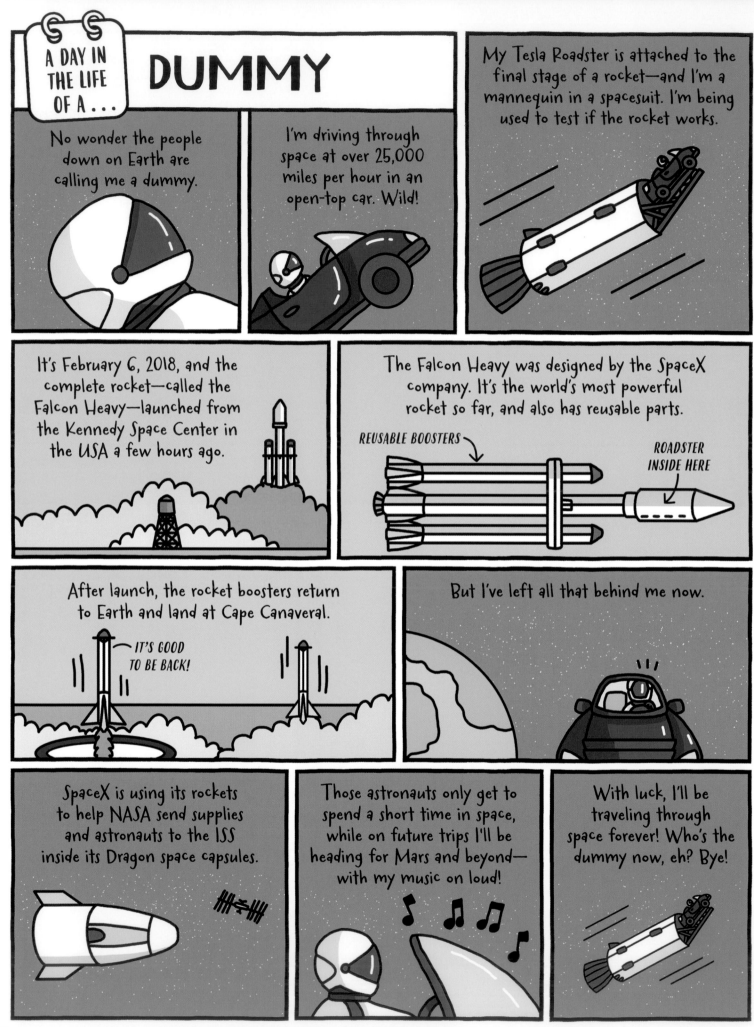

A DAY IN THE LIFE OF A...

DUMMY

No wonder the people down on Earth are calling me a dummy.

I'm driving through space at over 25,000 miles per hour in an open-top car. Wild!

My Tesla Roadster is attached to the final stage of a rocket—and I'm a mannequin in a spacesuit. I'm being used to test if the rocket works.

It's February 6, 2018, and the complete rocket—called the Falcon Heavy—launched from the Kennedy Space Center in the USA a few hours ago.

The Falcon Heavy was designed by the SpaceX company. It's the world's most powerful rocket so far, and also has reusable parts.

REUSABLE BOOSTERS

ROADSTER INSIDE HERE

After launch, the rocket boosters return to Earth and land at Cape Canaveral.

IT'S GOOD TO BE BACK!

But I've left all that behind me now.

SpaceX is using its rockets to help NASA send supplies and astronauts to the ISS inside its Dragon space capsules.

Those astronauts only get to spend a short time in space, while on future trips I'll be heading for Mars and beyond—with my music on loud!

With luck, I'll be traveling through space forever! Who's the dummy now, eh? Bye!

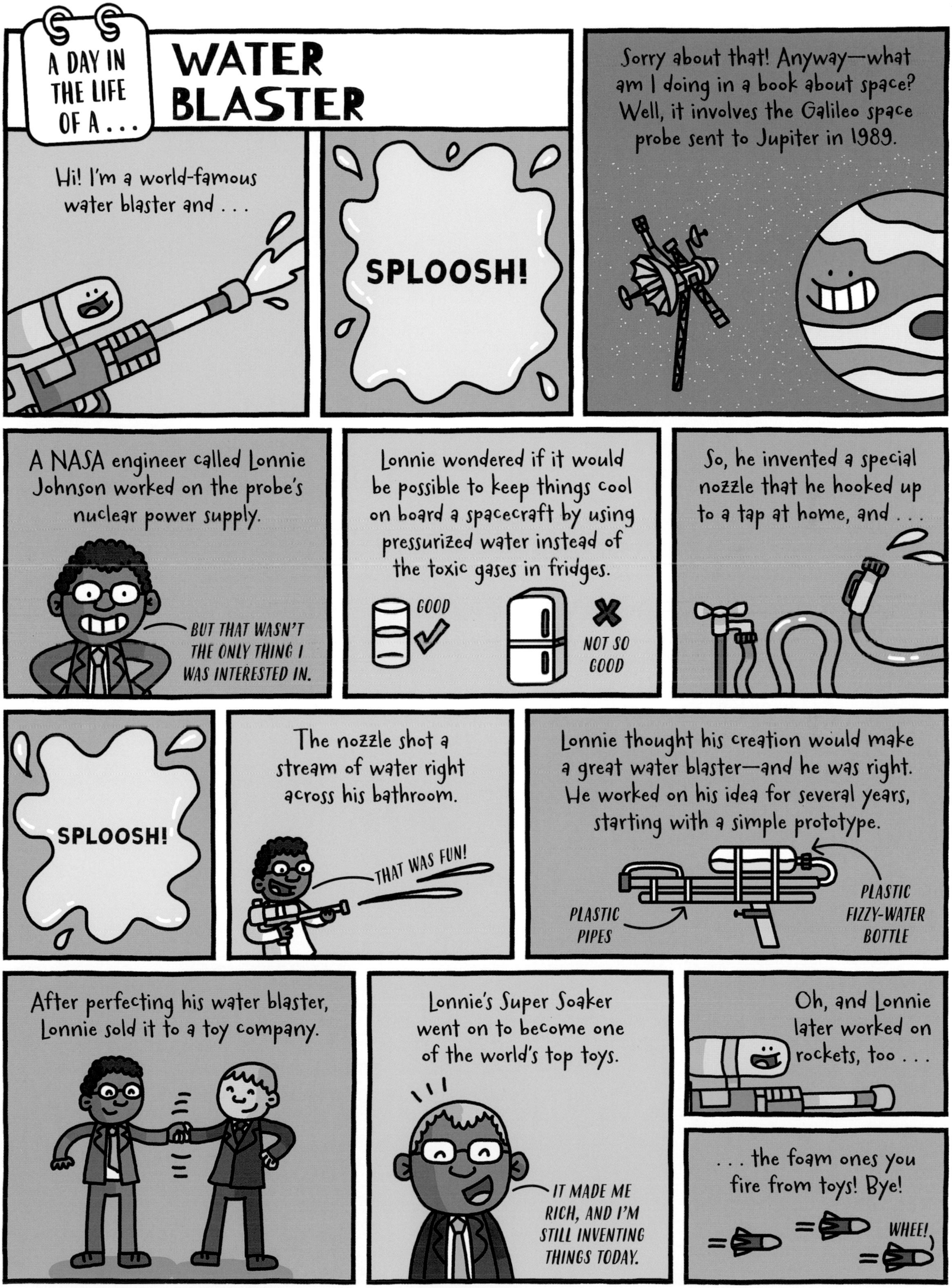
A DAY IN THE LIFE OF A . . .
WATER BLASTER
Hi! I'm a world-famous water blaster and . . .
SPLOOSH!
Sorry about that! Anyway—what am I doing in a book about space? Well, it involves the Galileo space probe sent to Jupiter in 1989.
A NASA engineer called Lonnie Johnson worked on the probe's nuclear power supply.
BUT THAT WASN'T THE ONLY THING I WAS INTERESTED IN.
Lonnie wondered if it would be possible to keep things cool on board a spacecraft by using pressurized water instead of the toxic gases in fridges.
GOOD
NOT SO GOOD
So, he invented a special nozzle that he hooked up to a tap at home, and . . .
SPLOOSH!
The nozzle shot a stream of water right across his bathroom.
THAT WAS FUN!
Lonnie thought his creation would make a great water blaster—and he was right. He worked on his idea for several years, starting with a simple prototype.
PLASTIC PIPES
PLASTIC FIZZY-WATER BOTTLE
After perfecting his water blaster, Lonnie sold it to a toy company.
Lonnie's Super Soaker went on to become one of the world's top toys.
IT MADE ME RICH, AND I'M STILL INVENTING THINGS TODAY.
Oh, and Lonnie later worked on rockets, too . . .
. . . the foam ones you fire from toys! Bye!
WHEE!

THE BIGGER PICTURE

SPACE SPIN-OFFS

The short history of human space exploration has already had many benefits for those back on Earth. You might be surprised to discover that some of these inventions have their roots in space technology.

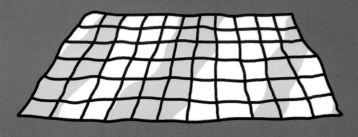

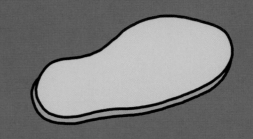

IT'S A WRAP

Carried by many hikers for keeping warm in emergencies, the thin, metal-coated, plastic sheet known as a "space blanket" was first made to protect spacecraft from the Sun's rays.

SWEET FEET

The special fabric used in footwear inserts to control the smell of sweaty feet is also used to protect astronauts from airborne odors on the ISS.

SNAP HAPPY

The tiny cameras found on mobile phones were originally developed in the 1990s for use in space.

WITHOUT WIRES

Wireless headphones were created as a clever way to free astronauts from trailing wires and cables.

FRESH AIR

The famous cushioning system used in Nike Air trainers originally came from research into spacesuit design.

HOT PANTS

Many race-car drivers wear hi-tech underwear made from a fabric developed to keep astronauts comfy and cozy in space.

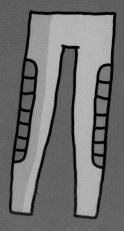

THE BIGGER PICTURE

MANY HAPPY RETURNS!

Humans last visited the Moon in 1972. Now NASA, along with space agencies from several other countries, has plans to put the first woman and first person of color on lunar soil before the 2020s are out. The Artemis program will use a huge new rocket called the Space Launch System (SLS) to take people to the Moon and—one day—to Mars!

SPACE LAUNCH SYSTEM

The first SLS will be 320 feet high. That's taller than the Statue of Liberty. Later versions will be even bigger.

STARSHIP HLS

SpaceX is developing a new lunar landing craft known as the Starship HLS (Human Landing System).

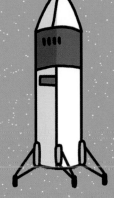

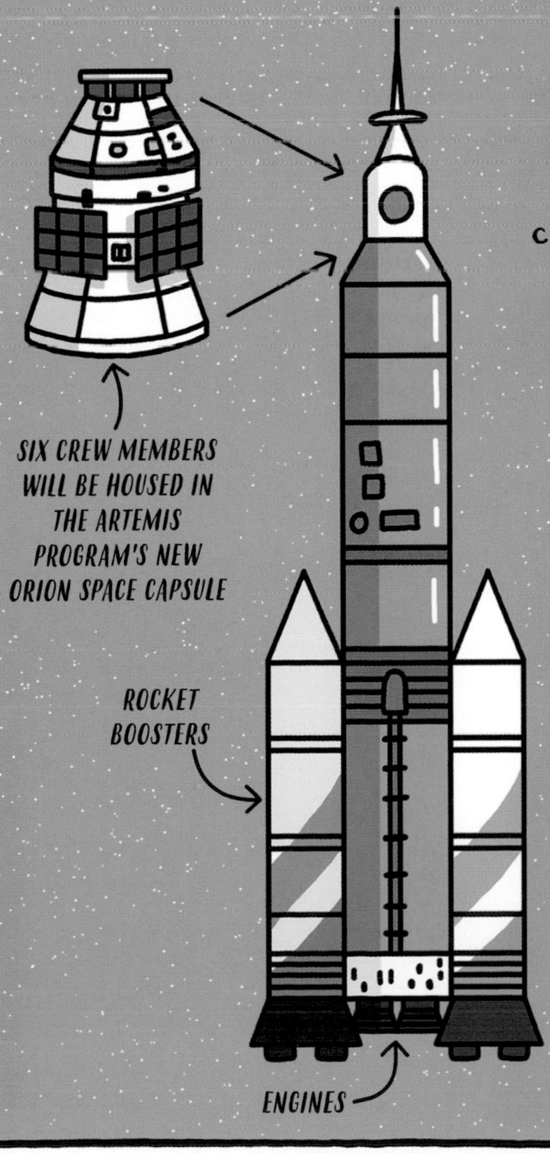

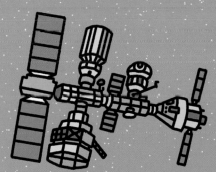

SIX CREW MEMBERS WILL BE HOUSED IN THE ARTEMIS PROGRAM'S NEW ORION SPACE CAPSULE
ROCKET BOOSTERS
ENGINES

LUNAR GATEWAY

The Lunar Gateway—a mini space station in constant orbit around the Moon—is also planned, to allow more visits to the lunar surface.

SUIT-ABILITY

New spacesuits are being developed for use inside (on the left) and outside (on the right) spacecraft. This time, they're being designed with both male and female astronauts in mind.

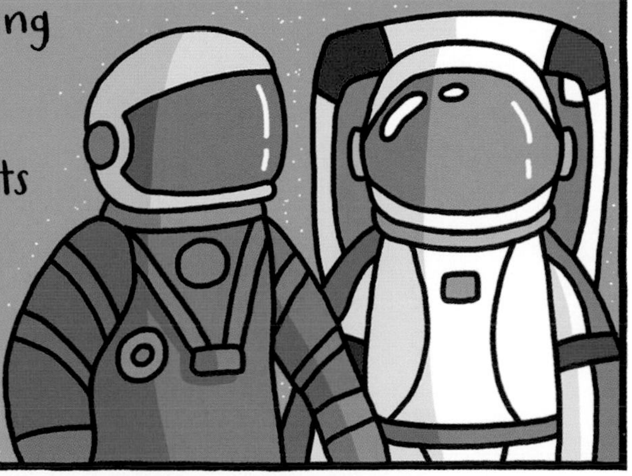

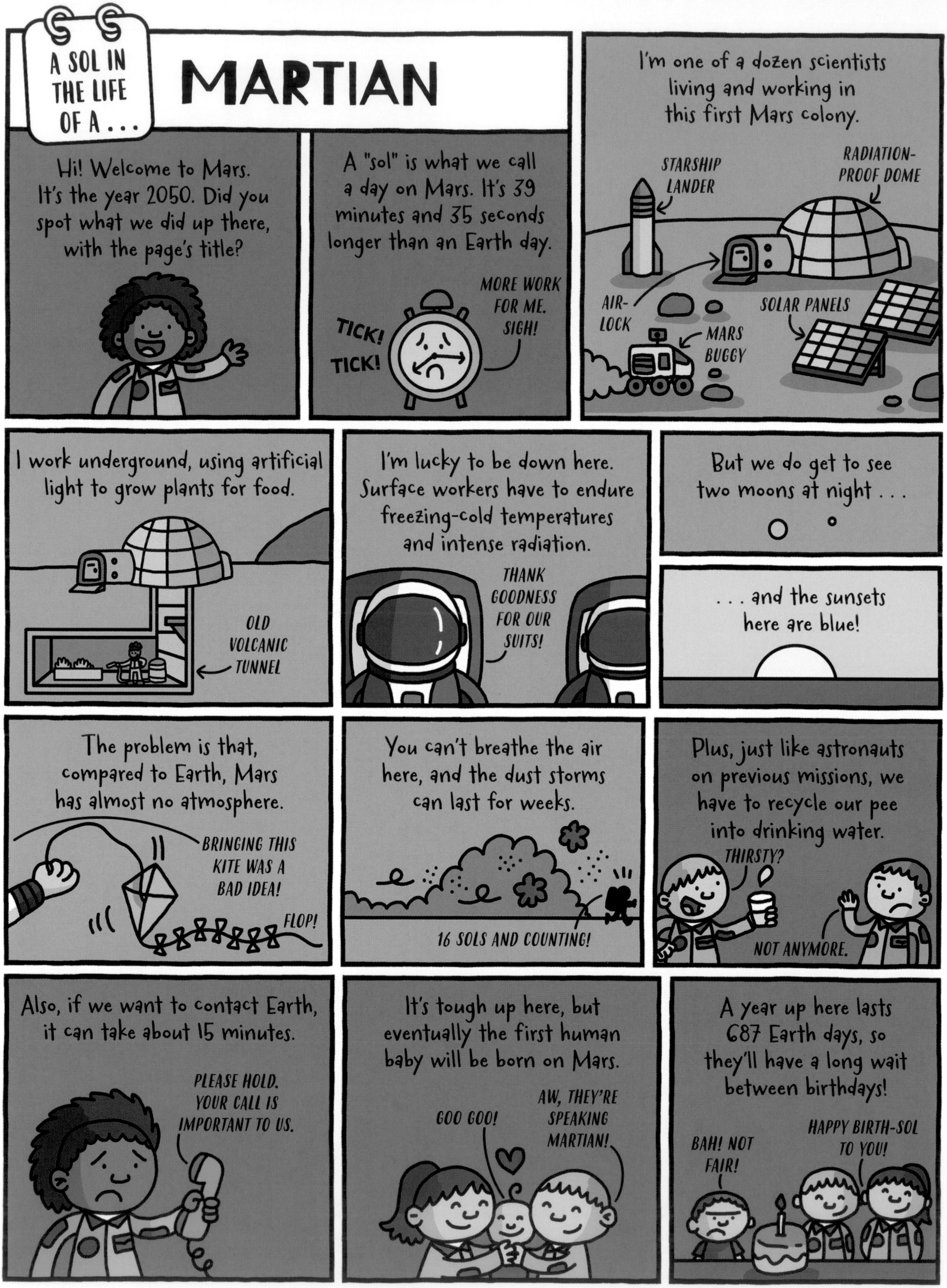
A SOL IN THE LIFE OF A . . .
MARTIAN
Hi! Welcome to Mars. It's the year 2050. Did you spot what we did up there, with the page's title?
A "sol" is what we call a day on Mars. It's 39 minutes and 35 seconds longer than an Earth day.
TICK! TICK!
MORE WORK FOR ME. SIGH!
I'm one of a dozen scientists living and working in this first Mars colony.
STARSHIP LANDER
RADIATION-PROOF DOME
AIR-LOCK
SOLAR PANELS
MARS BUGGY
I work underground, using artificial light to grow plants for food.
OLD VOLCANIC TUNNEL
I'm lucky to be down here. Surface workers have to endure freezing-cold temperatures and intense radiation.
THANK GOODNESS FOR OUR SUITS!
But we do get to see two moons at night . . .
. . . and the sunsets here are blue!
The problem is that, compared to Earth, Mars has almost no atmosphere.
BRINGING THIS KITE WAS A BAD IDEA!
FLOP!
You can't breathe the air here, and the dust storms can last for weeks.
16 SOLS AND COUNTING!
Plus, just like astronauts on previous missions, we have to recycle our pee into drinking water.
THIRSTY?
NOT ANYMORE.
Also, if we want to contact Earth, it can take about 15 minutes.
PLEASE HOLD. YOUR CALL IS IMPORTANT TO US.
It's tough up here, but eventually the first human baby will be born on Mars.
GOO GOO!
AW, THEY'RE SPEAKING MARTIAN!
A year up here lasts 687 Earth days, so they'll have a long wait between birthdays!
BAH! NOT FAIR!
HAPPY BIRTH-SOL TO YOU!

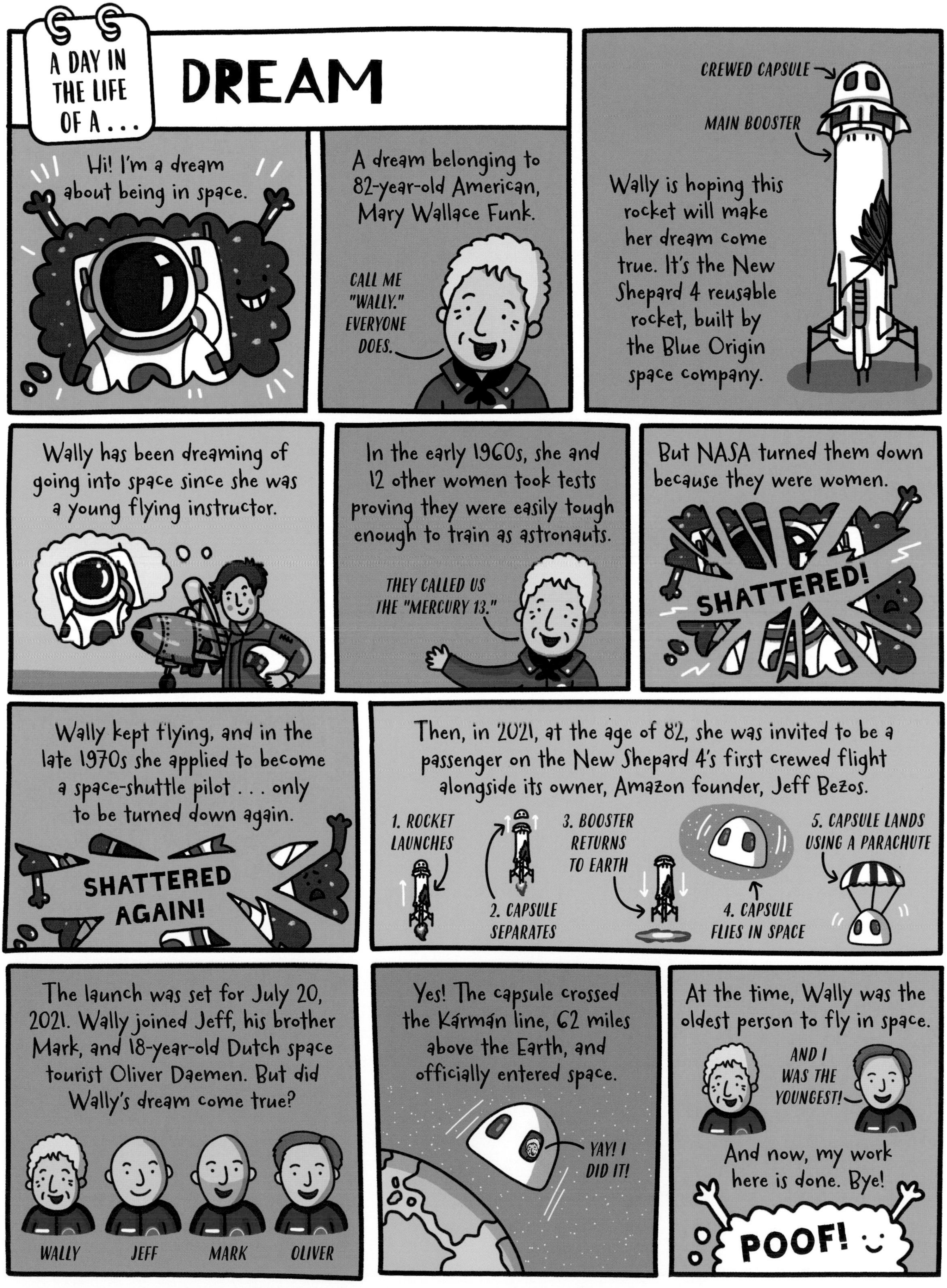

A DAY IN THE LIFE OF A . . .
DREAM
Hi! I'm a dream about being in space.
A dream belonging to 82-year-old American, Mary Wallace Funk.
CALL ME "WALLY." EVERYONE DOES.
CREWED CAPSULE
MAIN BOOSTER
Wally is hoping this rocket will make her dream come true. It's the New Shepard 4 reusable rocket, built by the Blue Origin space company.
Wally has been dreaming of going into space since she was a young flying instructor.
In the early 1960s, she and 12 other women took tests proving they were easily tough enough to train as astronauts.
THEY CALLED US THE "MERCURY 13."
But NASA turned them down because they were women.
SHATTERED!
Wally kept flying, and in the late 1970s she applied to become a space-shuttle pilot . . . only to be turned down again.
SHATTERED AGAIN!
Then, in 2021, at the age of 82, she was invited to be a passenger on the New Shepard 4's first crewed flight alongside its owner, Amazon founder, Jeff Bezos.
1. ROCKET LAUNCHES
2. CAPSULE SEPARATES
3. BOOSTER RETURNS TO EARTH
4. CAPSULE FLIES IN SPACE
5. CAPSULE LANDS USING A PARACHUTE
The launch was set for July 20, 2021. Wally joined Jeff, his brother Mark, and 18-year-old Dutch space tourist Oliver Daemen. But did Wally's dream come true?
WALLY
JEFF
MARK
OLIVER
Yes! The capsule crossed the Kármán line, 62 miles above the Earth, and officially entered space.
YAY! I DID IT!
At the time, Wally was the oldest person to fly in space.
AND I WAS THE YOUNGEST!
And now, my work here is done. Bye!
POOF!

THE BIGGER PICTURE

OUT OF THIS WORLD?

Earth remains the only place in space where life is known to exist. However, many people believe that extraterrestrial life is out there, and may even have visited Earth. Some sightings of UFOs (Unidentified Flying Objects) have been shown to be hoaxes, while others remain a mystery. Here are some notable "alien encounters":

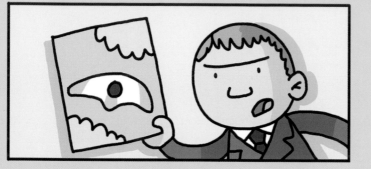

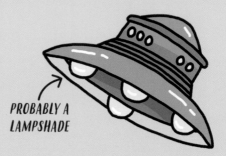

PROBABLY A LAMPSHADE

SAUCER-Y

Pilot Kenneth Arnold claimed to have seen nine silvery shapes flying over Washington State, USA, in 1947. Newspapers called them "flying saucers" and sparked a global interest in UFOs that continues today.

UFO HOAX

In the 1950s, Polish-American George Adamski took a now infamous photo of what seemed to be a UFO. Sadly, the photo was proven to be a fake.

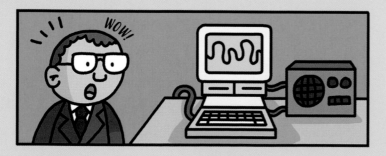

WOW!

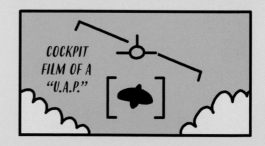

COCKPIT FILM OF A "U.A.P."

WOWSER

In 1977, a radio telescope at Ohio State University picked up a strong signal coming from the constellation Sagittarius. An amazed astronomer wrote "Wow!" next to the blip, which remains unexplained.

WATCH THE SKIES

In 2021, the United States Air Force admitted their pilots had reported over 140 sightings of UFOs, for which they had no explanation. However, they prefer to call them UAPs (Unexplained Aerial Phenomena).

GLOSSARY

It turns out that there is a lot going on in a single day, as well as lots of new terms to learn. This glossary gives you a brief explanation of some of the harder words or phrases you may have come across.

Airlock
A room used to move between two areas of different air pressure. In a spacecraft, astronauts enter the airlock and seal the door behind them, before leaving through another door to go outside the craft.

Asterism
A cluster of stars, often forming part of a constellation.

Asteroid
A rocky object that travels around a star. Asteroids are similar to planets, but are much smaller and vary in size.

Astrology
The non-scientific study of stars and planets, with the belief that their movements have an influence on people's lives.

Astronaut
A person who has trained to travel into space and gone beyond the Earth's atmosphere.

Astronomy
The scientific study of space.

Aurora
A display of colored light in the sky, caused by air molecules colliding with particles from a star (or the Sun, in Earth's case).

Binary star system
Two stars orbiting together.

Celestial pole
The point in the night sky around which all visible stars rotate. In the northern hemisphere, stars rotate around the north celestial pole. In the southern hemisphere, stars rotate around the south celestial pole.

Comet
A ball of ice, rock, and dust traveling around the Sun. Comets have long tails that can be millions of miles long.

Constellation
A group of stars that appear to form a pattern or picture in the night sky.

Corona
The outer atmosphere of the Sun, or any other star.

Cosmonaut
An astronaut from Russia or the former Soviet Union.

Cosmos
Another word for the universe.

Crater
A large hole in the surface of a planet or moon. Craters are often caused by collisions with asteroids or comets. The craters on the Moon are so big that they can be seen from Earth without a telescope.

Crescent
The narrow, curved shape of the Moon seen from Earth during its first or last phase.

Ecosystem
All the plants and animals living together in an area, and the relationships that exist between them.

European Space Agency (ESA)
The main European organization dedicated to space exploration. ESA is a joint project involving 22 different European nations.

Extraterrestrial
Anything occurring or existing outside Earth. Extraterrestrial is also another word for an alien.

Extravehicular Activity (EVA)
See Spacewalk.

Full Moon
The fully rounded shape of the Moon seen from Earth.

Galaxy
A system of stars and interstellar matter. Some galaxies stretch millions of light-years across and contain hundreds of billions of stars.

Gibbous
The slightly bulging shape of the Moon seen from Earth when it is more than half-visible, but not quite full.

International Space Station (ISS)
A structure that has been orbiting the Earth since 1998. The ISS is crewed by astronauts (and cosmonauts) from a number of different nations.

Interstellar space
The space between the stars in a galaxy.

Kuiper Belt
A ring of icy objects found beyond the orbit of Neptune.

Light-year
The name given to a distance of 6 trillion miles. It is called a light-year because it is the distance traveled when moving at the speed of light for one year.

Lunar
A word used to describe anything related to the Moon.

Mass
The amount of matter an object contains.

Matter
Any physical, material substance. All solids, liquids, and gases are made up of matter.

Meteor
A small, rocky body of matter (a meteoroid) burning through Earth's atmosphere. Meteors are also known as shooting stars.

Meteorite
When a meteoroid hits Earth's surface, it becomes known as a meteorite.

Meteoroid
A rock flying through space after breaking away from a comet or an asteroid.

Microbe
A very small living thing that can only be seen using a microscope.

Moon
A moon is an object that is similar to a planet, but orbits around another planet. "The Moon" refers specifically to Earth's moon.

NASA
The agency of the American government responsible for space travel and research. The letters NASA stand for National Aeronautics and Space Administration.

New Moon
The phase of the moon in which the side facing the Earth is dark, so it appears to be invisible or only slightly visible.

Nuclear reactor
A machine that is used to produce nuclear energy.

Observatory
A building or structure used as a base for observing and studying space, usually with a telescope. Telescopes that have been launched into space, such as the Hubble Space Telescope, are also considered to be observatories.

Orbit
The curved path taken by an object in space as it travels around and around a planet, moon, or star.

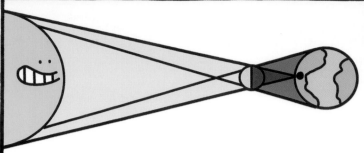

Ozone
A colorless and toxic form of oxygen. A layer of ozone above the Earth's surface protects the planet from the harmful rays of the Sun.

Photon
A particle of light.

Planet
A large, round space object that moves around the Sun.

Plasma
A state of matter that is classed as neither solid, liquid, nor gas. Hot plasma is found inside the Sun and most other stars.

Probe
An uncrewed craft sent into space to gather and send information back to Earth.

Radiation
Tiny particles of any radioactive substance. Exposure to radiation can be very dangerous to humans, animals, and other forms of life.

Russia
One of the nations that previously made up the Soviet Union.

Satellite
Satellites can be natural or human-made. A natural satellite is any object that orbits around a planet or star. A human-made satellite is a piece of equipment sent into space to gather, send, or exchange information.

Sextillion
A huge number. One sextillion is written as a one followed by 21 zeros.

Soviet Union
The Soviet Union, also known as the Union of Soviet Socialist Republics (USSR), was a state spanning the northeast of Europe and north of Asia. In 1991, the Soviet Union broke up into 15 separate nations, including Russia.

Space race
The period between 1957 and 1975, when the USA and the Soviet Union competed against each other to be the first explorers of space.

Spacewalk
Also known as an Extravehicular Activity or EVA, a spacewalk is when an astronaut leaves their spacecraft to work outside in space.

SpaceX
An American designer and manufacturer of spacecraft and rockets, founded by Elon Musk.

Trinary star system
Three stars orbiting together. Two of the stars normally orbit each other in a binary star system, while the third star orbits at a greater distance.

Universe
The whole of space, including galaxies, stars, planets, and everything else within it.

USSR
See Soviet Union.

Vacuum
An entirely empty space that contains no matter of any sort.

Visible light
The light that can be seen by the human eye. The human eye can see the range of light represented by the colors of the rainbow. However, there are other colors (such as ultraviolet) that humans cannot see.

Waning
The Moon in any phase between Full Moon and New Moon, where its illuminated area seen from Earth appears to be decreasing.

Waxing
The Moon in any phase between New Moon and Full Moon, where its illuminated area seen from Earth appears to be increasing.

Yeast
A fungus that is commonly used to make bread rise.

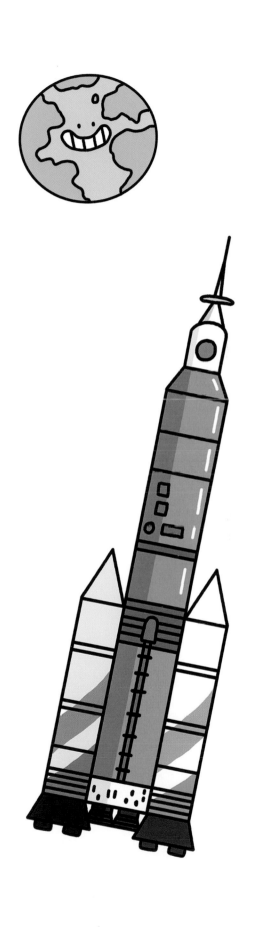

ABOUT MIKE AND JESS

What do Mike Barfield and Jess Bradley get up to all day, eh? Find out below!

Mike Barfield is an award-winning writer and cartoonist, living in a small village in North Yorkshire, England. He has been staring at the stars since he was a small boy, and still gets up in the middle of the night in the hope of spotting exciting events in space. Sadly, there are lots of clouds where he lives.

Jess Bradley is an illustrator and comic artist from Torquay, England. As well as writing and drawing for *The Phoenix*, she also writes for *The Beano* and illustrates a variety of children's books. During her day, she enjoys painting in her sketchbooks, watching scary films, and letting her son beat her at Mario Kart.